THE UNEQUAL OCEAN

MAXIMILIAN VIATORI

THE UNEQUAL OCEAN

*Living with Environmental Change
along the Peruvian Coast*

THE UNIVERSITY OF
ARIZONA PRESS

TUCSON

The University of Arizona Press
www.uapress.arizona.edu

We respectfully acknowledge the University of Arizona is on the land and territories of Indigenous peoples. Today, Arizona is home to twenty-two federally recognized tribes, with Tucson being home to the O'odham and the Yaqui. Committed to diversity and inclusion, the University strives to build sustainable relationships with sovereign Native Nations and Indigenous communities through education offerings, partnerships, and community service.

ISBN-13: 978-0-8165-4965-8 (hardcover)
ISBN-13: 978-0-8165-4966-5 (ebook)

Cover design by Leigh McDonald
Cover photo by Maximilian Viatori
Typeset by Leigh McDonald in Warnock Pro 10/14 and Good Headline Pro (display)

Publication of this book is made possible in part by funding from the Iowa State University Publication Endowment, Iowa State University Foundation, and the Department of World Languages and Cultures, ISU.

Library of Congress Cataloging-in-Publication Data are available at the Library of Congress.

Printed in the United States of America
♾ This paper meets the requirements of ANSI/NISO Z39.48-1992 (Permanence of Paper).

For Anneke, Elio, and Nico

In memory of my Uncle Rod

CONTENTS

List of Illustrations		*ix*
Introduction		5
1.	Making Waves	31
2.	Plastic Ocean	66
3.	Precarious Weather	100
4.	Squid Life	127
	Epilogue	167
Acknowledgments		*179*
Notes		*181*
References		*193*
Index		*213*

ILLUSTRATIONS

FIGURES

1. The view of the Pacific Ocean from Lima's coast. 6
2. The net in Enrique's boat. 7
3. The view from the artisanal fishing wharf of the bay in Chorrillos and Lima's skyline. 22
4. Erosion on Playa Makaha next to the sidewalk and third lane of the expressway. 23
5. A surfer watches the waves at La Pampilla before entering. 32
6. A surfer crosses the sidewalk at La Pampilla. 33
7. A surfer catches a wave at La Pampilla. 40
8. Plastic garbage, a Styrofoam cup, and seaweed that had washed onto the Playa Agua Dulce in Chorrillos. 68
9. Needlefish in the fish market on the Chorrillos wharf in March 2017. 101
10. Artisanal fishers unload jumbo squid on the dock in Chorrillos. 162

MAPS

1. The Pacific Ocean. 2
2. Lima's Coast. 3

THE UNEQUAL OCEAN

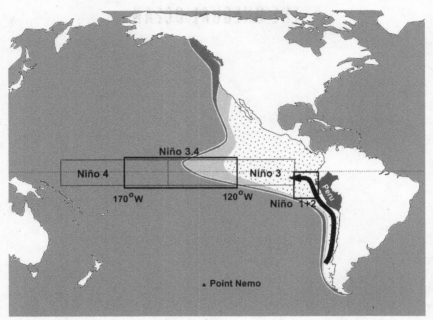

MAP 1 The Pacific Ocean. The black arrow represents the approximate flow of the Peru Current. The dotted and shaded zones off the west coast of the Americas represent the approximate historical and expanded ranges of the jumbo squid (following Staaf, Zeidberg, and Gilly 2011). The El Niño zones mark the areas used by meteorologists to track the development of warming, cooling, or neutral trends in the equatorial Pacific Ocean. Cartography by Yibo Fan.

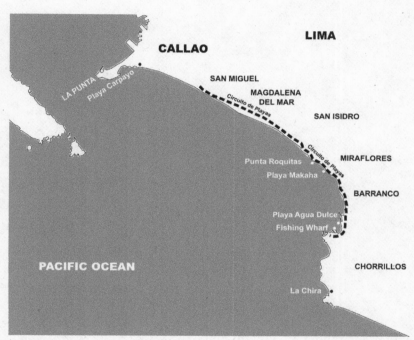

MAP 2 Lima's coast. Cartography by Yibo Fan.

INTRODUCTION

MARCH 2015

ENRIQUE shot me a wry smile as the small wooden boat we were in crested a wave and my stomach lurched into my throat. Moments before the old engine in the boat's hold had stalled as a set of waves came rolling in from the Pacific Ocean. The first wave made the boat bobble from side to side and the next rocked the boat with more vigor. Enrique worked quickly to get the motor running so that he could turn the boat's deep hull into the waves. He managed that move just before the third wave. As the bow went up and over it reproduced the feeling of weightlessness you get when you go over the top of a hill in a car. With the engine motor at full force, we headed toward the horizon, where an endless sky met the equally vast Pacific Ocean (see figure 1). Behind us was the dry, gray-tan coast of Lima, Peru.

Once we were a nautical mile or so from the coast, Enrique idled the engine and put on his rubber boots and a plastic poncho. He pulled out a green nylon net from the ship's hold and began unrolling it (see figure 2). The purpose of our trip was for Enrique to show me and several graduate students what the manual labor of setting a net and bringing it in was like. Enrique asked one of the students, who had been working with artisanal fishers on the dock, to help with the process and started the engine again so that the net, which was about fifty meters long, could be drawn out into the

FIGURE 1 The view of the Pacific Ocean from Lima's coast. Photo by Maximilian Viatori.

water. As they did that, I sat on the gunwales of the boat, which had been worn bare by years of work, and watched the oars cut through the water as the boat moved slowly forward. Over the previous three years, I had spent considerable time looking at the ocean from different points on Lima's coast, but especially from the fishing dock in Chorrillos. Fishers are constantly watching the water for signals that they can use to discern what temperature the water might be, how much sediment is in it, or whether it is safe to go out. Slowly, I had learned about how waves broke along certain stretches of Lima's coast and under what conditions, as well as how water moved in and around the bay. This was the first time I had experienced the power of one of those waves and the sheer energy that was stored in it.

Enrique is one of about two hundred artisanal fishers who operate out of a small wharf in Chorrillos, a coastal district of Lima (see figure 1). Fishers are defined by Peruvian law as "artisanal" if they use nonmechanized methods (such as hand-drawn nets) and small wooden-hulled boats mostly to catch table fish (as opposed larger metal boats used to catch fish that will be processed as meal). Since 2012, I have been traveling to Chorrillos to learn about the struggles that Enrique and other fishers face to make a precarious living through artisanal fishing. Not only do fishers deal with an increasingly altered ocean ecology but their manual labor is devalued in Lima's labor market, and within ever-shifting elite cultural oppositions they are racialized and classed as social and spatial Others. The intertwining of fishers' lives with ocean ecologies and urban political economies is critical for thinking about how different people experience ecological and climatic changes in the eastern Pacific Ocean in deeply unequal ways. And yet, dominant ways of knowing and representing social relationships, the ocean, and the climate crisis tend to erase this entwinement.

FIGURE 2 The net in Enrique's boat. Photo by Maximilian Viatori.

SEPTEMBER 2019

When not on the water with fishers like Enrique, I worked on the beaches of Lima's Costa Verde, an area that has been shaped by a long history of racialized and classed tensions over its development as a site for work, recreation, and transportation. Flooding along Lima's coast happens every year during high-wave events. Artisanal fishers are forced to stop working until conditions improve and it is safe for them to go out again. These events also lead to the closure of streets in low-lying neighborhoods of Callao and along Lima's central coastal zone, the Costa Verde, and sometimes lead to the closure of beaches and outside lanes of traffic. During a research trip to Lima in September 2019, I spent hours each day walking along the Costa Verde. The districts that comprise the Costa Verde are among the most affluent in Lima, although there are socioeconomic differences among them. The residential and commercial areas of these districts sit above the coast on a plateau. To access the lower coastal shelf, I usually walked down one of several sets of winding, concrete stairs. At the bottom there are covered pedestrian bridges, which cross the six-lane expressway that runs along the base of the Costa Verde's cliffs. The human-expanded beaches of the Costa Verde are popular sites for public recreation, and they are connected by a series of sidewalks, some of which are elevated in places so that they sit just above the normal high-water mark. On my long ambles I noticed many parts of the walkways and the beaches below that had been damaged by recent high-wave episodes. For example, along the locally famous Playa Makaha (named after Makaha beach in Hawai'i), sections of the paved walkway had collapsed and fallen onto the beach below or the edges of the concrete slabs were exposed as the sandy soil below had visibly eroded.

On September 24, the week after my trip to Lima, the United Nations Intergovernmental Panel on Climate Change (IPCC) published its first *Special Report on the Oceans and Cryosphere in a Changing Climate* (Pörtner et al. 2019). The extensive report underscored the dramatic changes that have been occurring in the world's oceans, such as increased acidification, rapid warming, profound alterations to ocean ecosystems and species distributions, and rapidly rising global mean sea levels. The report also revealed that shrinking glaciers and melting polar ice sheets have led to significant reductions in the world's cryosphere, which constitutes all the places where water exists as ice. The report's authors, 130 scientists from 37 countries, revealed that changes in the oceans and cryosphere were occurring at a much faster rate than previously understood, which led them to revise projections of how and when the earth's oceans and frozen spaces would experience unprecedented changes. The report's authors predicted that multimeter sea level rises could occur as soon as 2100 and would affect three times as many people as previously expected if dramatic measures were not taken to reduce worldwide carbon emissions. Such sea level rises would be compounded by an intensification of severe weather, such as more extreme El Niño warming events and tropical cyclones, and greater variation in waves and tides. These changes would have a profoundly negative impact on the millions of people who live in coastal cities around the world, such as Lima.

Numerous media outlets in Peru's capital covered the IPCC report and its primary findings and predictions. According to *El Comercio* (2019a), Lima's center-right newspaper of note, the IPCC report advised dramatic reductions in human produced CO_2 to slow the changes and buy time to adapt to the "rising waters that would favor storms and giant waves" that would "redefine the coastal zones of the world, where populations are concentrated." The *El Comercio* article underscored the cost of reducing CO_2 emissions and the relatively weak political will in more developed countries to act quickly, but it did not link the IPCC's findings to Peru or to Lima. This seemed odd to me, given that most of Peru's population lives on or near the coast. Approximately eleven million people (roughly one-third of the national population) live in greater metropolitan Lima, the only national capital in South America located on the Pacific coast.[1] The same was true of the other stories I read in Peru's media. A similar story appeared in *Gestión* (2019), the country's business daily. The lead of the article emphasized that, according to the IPCC, the world's oceans could rise over a meter by 2100, which would displace millions of people around the world. Furthermore, the article reported that "extreme phenomenon such as El Niño could become more frequent and severe," leading the IPCC authors to stress adaptation as "an effective response" for countries to consider how to reduce "factors of vulnerability, such as coastal urbanization." These are all important issues for Peru, where coastal cities experience regular climatic fluctuations and sometimes disastrous coastal flooding due to El Niño warming. However, the article did not explicitly link the IPCC's findings with Peru.[2]

This was a trend that I noticed in the months that followed as I watched for reports on rising sea levels in the Peruvian media or published by scientists in Peru. Most of the media coverage of sea level rise that I read focused on broader global or regional impacts.[3] I did find several discussions of how rising sea levels might affect Lima or the surrounding coastal areas. One, which was published in *El Comercio* (2019b), reported that a new global study had revealed that sea level rises would be greater than previously anticipated and would affect 300 million people around the world by 2050. The report noted that "in the coming decades, if the climate crisis is not slowed down or attenuated, the coasts of Callao, Ancón, Barranco, Chorrillos, Lurín, Chilca, etc., will flood at least one time per year." Included in the report were two maps of Lima's coast, which depicted two different scenarios—one showed the areas that would be affected if carbon emissions continued unabated and a second showed the areas that would be affected if carbon emissions were curbed dramatically. In both scenarios, the zones to the north and south of central Lima that would be impacted by projected flooding were areas of comparably low socioeconomic status. Vulnerability to increased flooding from rising sea levels mapped almost perfectly onto poverty in coastal Lima. For example, one area that would be impacted in both scenarios is the district of Villa El Salvador, which is located in Lima's southern cone and was founded in 1971 by 4,000 squatters who used government reforms in land occupation laws to claim the stretch of coastal desert that is now home to over 350,000 people.[4] Villa El Salvador is one of Lima's poorest districts, with almost half of its residents occupying the lowest income bracket in recent government censes (INEI 2016). What seemed to me to be a clear link among rising sea levels, socioeconomic variability, and poverty was left unacknowledged in the *El Comercio* article.

Recent scientific studies have analyzed basin-wide oceanic conditions as well as local atmospheric and geophysical variations to model how sea level rises might affect different parts of Lima's coast.[5] Upon reading these studies, I found that explicit analyses of the relationships among climatic conditions, social vulnerability, and political economy were mostly absent. One study of the coast south of Lima analyzed how projected sea level rises from global warming would impact different beaches (Tejada de la Cruz 2018, 61). The study incorporated aspects of human geography, such as population density and land use, to demonstrate that "social factors contribute to the increase of vulnerability of the coastal zone" (60). The author found that zones of high population density have higher levels of vulnerability—defined as the likelihood that coastal geographies and ecosystems would be able to adapt to sea level rises. The study did not incorporate the capacity of local populations to adjust in the face of such changes in its definition of vulnerability. Nor did it provide a sociohistorical context for understanding why such spatial variability exists or what has caused it, other than to comment that "common problems in the area include informal land invasions of the coastal strip" (63). This approach reinforced the idea that coastal nature was something that humans had put in danger, without considering how humans were part of nature or how social and economic inequalities were bound up with natural systems in ways that put specific groups of people and the places they live or work in greater vulnerability.[6]

LIFE, INEQUALITY, AND THE OCEAN

Discussions of rising sea levels and their projected impacts on Peru's coastal cities reveal how important aspects of the global climate crisis are experienced and represented in profoundly unequal ways. Rising sea levels are affecting millions of people around the world and, as the IPCC report makes clear, will affect far more in the coming decades. In this regard, sea level increases are a global and collective phenomenon. At the same time, how specific groups of people are impacted by rising seas varies depending on not only their geophysical location but also their position within global, regional, and local political ecologies. Sea level variability exists because of differences in prevailing winds and currents around the world as well as geomorphic differences, which means that some coastal areas have and will experience more rapid sea level increases than others. However, equally important for understanding why and how people experience the impacts of rising sea levels differently are systemic inequalities, disparities in political and economic influence, and histories of uneven development. In Lima, racialized social and economic disparities entwine with differences in the city's physical nature and material infrastructure to expose impoverished coastal residents, such as artisanal fishers, to greater vulnerability and potential harm from sea level increases.[7]

These disparities were absent from the representations of rising seas circulating in public discussions and reporting in Peru. The resulting erasures of the disparities in experiences of sea level changes and their accompanying environmental impacts occur as information about climatic and environmental phenomena is translated back and forth from one scale—such as local, regional, or global—to another. Scientific research relies on the constant decontextualization and recontextualization of facts so that they can be translated from one context or scale to another and retain meanings that will be recognizable in a range of social and political spaces and institutional settings (Jasanoff 2005; Latour 1999; Mathews 2014). The IPCC report is a synthesis of existing research that was conducted in specific social, political, and environmental contexts (Jasanoff 2013). When producing and scaling "up" this research, scientists stripped away local, context-specific meanings so that the relevant facts could be presented as evidence of global climatic phenomena. In the process, important social facts, such as how specific political economies shaped a particular research project or how historical inequalities impacted on-the-ground experiences or knowledge of such climatic phenomenon, were also stripped away.

These omissions are not unique to Peru but are emblematic of broader dynamics in how knowledge about the environment is produced and represented. Research in anthropology and related fields demonstrates the importance of analyzing the production of climate knowledge for understanding "our ability to think through problems and imagine solutions" (O'Reilly et al. 2020, 17). This research highlights multiplicities of climate knowledge and the kinds of world-making they enable (Cruikshank 2007; Hastrup 2013; Ingold 2002), as well as the politics and material practices by which certain forms of knowledge come to be authoritative accounts of the environment while other forms of knowledge are selectively included or completely excluded (Fortun 2014; Viatori 2019). Donna Haraway (1988) asserts that all knowledge is "situated"—it is produced and derives its meaning from its positioning within specific social contexts. However, certain forms of environmental knowledge circulate more widely than others and are represented as "universal" because they are enabled by and in turn bolster the authority of different governance projects at particular scales.

Marybeth Martello and Sheila Jasanoff (2004, 6) show that beginning in the 1970s environmental issues were framed as "politically borderless," "global" problems. This globalization of the environment enabled new governmental regimes that required the production of scientific knowledge on a "global" scale. In the process of taking on environmental management, "mega-institutions" such as the UN and the World Bank discovered that producing "shared cognitive foundations for global environmental regulation required further institutional innovation, and the new environmental regimes were fitted out with a panoply of scientific and expert bodies, such as the Intergovernmental Panel on Climate Change" (6). This move was met with the development of "counterexpertise" by NGOs such as Greenpeace, which produced their own (sometimes competing) scientific accounts of environmental issues (7). Martello and Jasanoff (2004, 7) argue that the globalization of environmental governance was also characterized by the "paradoxical rediscovery of the local" as it became evident "that other relevant actors, as well as their understandings of nature, could be integrated into environmental governance only at scales much more modest than the planet as a whole." In institutions such as the UN, scientific modelling became the authoritative means for knowing "global" climate change, while "local" knowledge was promoted for the study of the vulnerability of people in certain places as a key to improving people's lives "on the ground" (13).

This differential framing of "global" scientific research and "local" knowledge reinforces a clear hierarchy among forms of climate knowledge.[8] It also establishes what experiences and knowledge practices can be scaled up or down and still retain their relevance within prevailing discourses of environmental governance and what experiences are supposedly too particular or too bound to specific local contexts to circulate more widely. This dynamic is critical for understanding how the production of climate knowledge is entwined with the production of inequalities in what experiences "count" as emblems of broader climatic issues and therefore should be addressed by environmental governance.

Extensive semiotic work goes into creating dominant ways of knowing ocean natures by simplifying myriad complex relationships so that they become "legible" (Scott 1998) to powerful actors. For these representations to function and convey their intended meanings they must be "read" using socially or institutionally approved methods of interpretation and points of reference (Igoe 2017). In their groundbreaking work on the representation of linguistic difference, Susan Gal and Judith Irvine (2000, 37) argue that the production of dominant "interpretive structures" involves not only simplification but also the "erasure" of particular "persons or activities." This means that "facts that are inconsistent with the ideological scheme either go unnoticed or get explained away" (38). This is true not only of the ideologies of language that Gal and Irvine analyze but of semiotic systems that different actors create to organize, interpret, and act upon ecological, spatial, and social relationships. Even the scales that different actors deploy to represent spatial or temporal relationships are always cultural and political constructions that highlight certain relationships while hiding others (Strathern 2004; Swyngedouw 2004; Tsing 2000). Erasures are produced not only when powerful actors selectively translate certain facts from one scale to another (Gershon 2019) but also in how such actors establish the scale at which certain issues are viewed and define the semiotic boundaries of that scale (Carr and Lempert 2016).

In this book, I trace how powerful actors and analysts in Peru represent the ocean through semiotic processes of translation, decontextualization, and erasure. Recognizing the significance of these processes is important not only for understanding how critical aspects of climatological and ecological crises are erased in public discourse but also for revealing how racializing and classist discourses are inserted into discussions about climate change and environmental problems as they are translated, (re)contextualized, and scaled. I pursue questions such as, Who decides what scale is the most significant for conveying the potential impacts of rising seas and what fits within that scale? Is it the "global," the "national," or the "local"? And why does flooding along Lima's tourist beaches count as a potential "local" impact, while the negative effects on artisanal fishers do not? Questions such as these underscore the work that goes into establishing the facts of an oceanic issue, defining the ways in which it will be measured, how it should be represented, and from what perspective it should be understood.

For instance, many elite residents of Lima would read the list of districts most likely to be affected by rising sea levels through imagined maps of the city that situate districts and neighborhoods differently within imagined race-class hierarchies. In Lima, and throughout Peru, race is not articulated primarily through ideologies of biological purity or genetic inheritance (de la Cadena 2000). Rather, categories of whiteness, "mixedness," Blackness, and Indigeneity emerge and are contested through ever-shifting oppositions between assumptions about cultural practice, bodily comportment, language, class status, and spatial relationships (Greene 2016; Weismantel 2001). Within these relationships, imaginaries about place become proxies for racializing and classing residents of certain areas (Gandolfo 2009). Discussions about issues such as rising sea levels are thus racialized and classed without recourse to explicitly racist or classist language.

The scientific report I discuss above frames the problem of rising sea levels as the result of "informal land invasions of the coastal strip," which have been carried out mostly by darker-skinned, impoverished people whom the report implicitly blames for making coastal landscapes more vulnerable to flooding, erosion, and landslides. Such readings evacuate structural inequalities from discussions of the climate crisis by obscuring the significant ways in which enduring race-class disparities in Peru have forced historically marginalized people into greater precarity as they move from rural areas or smaller cities to Lima in search of better livelihoods. These readings are significant because they emanate from positions of power and considerable social capital and thus have tremendous influence in defining climatic and ecological problems in ways that enable elite gazes and forms of governance that perpetuate environmental inequalities through the production of racialized, classed, or spatialized Others.

This situation underscores the importance of critically analyzing widely circulating readings of the climate crisis and using such analyses to pose alternate readings that highlight the central role that ongoing racialized inequalities, relationships of capital accumulation and exploitation, and unjust political ecologies play in the production of contemporary climatological and environmental crises. This is particularly significant given the prominence of oceans in worldwide discussions about and representations of the climate crisis. Just as the Amazon rainforest was used to articulate an environmental movement around deforestation and the greenhouse effect beginning in the 1980s and the arctic and its megafauna served as rallying points for concerns about a warming world, oceans have emerged as new icons of global climate awareness and activism campaigns. There has never been a more important time for thinking about how we understand the ocean.

In an oft-cited essay on climate change, Bronislaw Szerszynski (2010) emphasizes that it is critical to think about how we "read" the present climate crisis. Scientific analysis demonstrates that humanity is changing the earth's climate, and technology offers solutions in policy and behavior changes and schemes to alter the earth's climate through engineering. Such schemes rely on a simple relation of causation that obscures "evolving human metabolism with nature" and the importance of semiotic relationships for understanding such changes (11). To counter this, Szerszynski (24) asserts that our "reading" of climate change must be historical and able to "discern in our unruly weather not just the future ruins of our past and present hubris, but also the global relations of power and inequality that have shaped our carbon metabolism." Scholars working across a wide range of disciplines have constructed these kinds of interpretations of the Anthropocene, the current era in which systems created by and for the unequal benefits of some humans over other humans (as well as nonhumans) have taken center stage in driving the earth's climate.[9] Works by Bret Gustafson (2020), Donna Haraway (2016), David McDermott Hughes (2021), Jason Moore (2015), Anna Tsing (2015), Paige West (2016), Kathryn Yusoff (2019) and others have centered systemic racism and genocide, multispecies displacements, and global networks of capital accumulation and dispossession in their analyses not only of the unfolding climate crisis but also of the ways in which we understand and define solutions to it.

These works, which offer critical alternatives to the dominant ways of representing climate change, have served as inspiration for the analyses that I produce in this book of four issues that have emerged as primary concerns within global environmental discourses about changing oceans: coastal development, plastic pollution, extreme weather events, and overfishing. Development booms have occurred in many coastal zones around the world, where roughly 40 percent of the world's population lives and where rising sea levels threatened such development. Whether they live close to the ocean or not, consumers around the world have become more aware of the explosion of plastic pollution in the world's oceans and its ubiquity in marine webs of life. Warming oceans also have begun to impact weather patterns, increasing the risk of severe and unpredictable weather events as ocean temperatures and water and air circulations change. Finally, fish, crustacean, and cephalopod populations have declined globally because of decades of overharvesting combined with the impacts of ecological degradation, pollution, and climate change–driven ocean acidification.

Global environmental campaigns and policy discussions about these issues have contributed to awareness about the critical role that oceans play in regulating the earth's climate and the myriad impacts of a warming world on oceans (and vice versa). In 2017 the UN declared a "Decade of Ocean Science for Sustainable Development," which runs from 2021 to 2030. According to the decade's website, "Much needs to be done to reverse the cycle of decline in ocean health, with changes and losses in the structure, function, and benefits obtained from marine systems."[10] Such prominent and influential ways of knowing and representing oceanic crises reduce complex phenomena to narrow sets of economic and technological considerations and solutions, obscuring the multispecies inequalities, extractive ecologies, and global supply chains that have both produced and imperiled the material, cultural, and environmental relationships that comprise ocean natures. This work of stripping environmental issues of their specific histories and multispecies contexts makes it possible to assign blame for climatic and ecological crises and their impacts to racialized and classed populations, while obscuring the systemic inequalities that have not only produced such crises but also disproportionately subject less powerful people and nonhuman species to their negative impacts.

In contrast, the readings I offer in this book of waves and coastal development, the circulation of ocean waste, El Niño warming events, and the extraction of jumbo squid draw on experiences and ways of knowing that have been submerged by widely circulating readings of the Anthropocene's oceans. Based on almost a decade of careful ethnographic and archival research in Peru, I bring together and keep in view the natural, political, and economic processes that have combined to produce historically specific ecologies in the eastern Pacific Ocean. My analysis reveals the historical agency of specific waves, currents, and nonhuman species in the creation and imperilment of these ecologies. Moreover, my research shows how artisanal fishers, such as Enrique, understand these ocean ecologies in ways that emphasize multispecies engagements and material relationships, as well as their unequal positions within them. These alternative ways of knowing and representing, which are often overlooked or marginalized by more powerful actors, provide critical departures for exploring how cultural systems are bound up with and made possible by humans' relationships with nonhuman species, physical environments, and ocean ecologies and how these phenomena have been shaped by race-class inequalities. Such alternative readings are essential for theorizing life in a time of oceanic upheavals in ways that are socially and environmentally just.

AT THE WATER'S EDGE

Oceans are constantly moving and changing in unpredictable ways. The ocean's fluidity and instability present unique challenges not only to artisanal fishers but also to industrial entanglements and long-standing attempts to "fix" the ocean. This tension between fluidity and fixity is at the very core of climate politics and is crucial for rethinking oceanic natures in the Anthropocene. The world's oceans made the development and expansion of modern capitalism possible by providing relatively unfettered movement across large distances, thus forging the flows and connections vital to global trade (Steinberg 2001). Capitalism in turn remade oceanic natures by territorializing the surface of the ocean and standardizing coasts through infrastructural interventions.

In his historical research on coasts, John Gillis (2012, 2014) demonstrates that shores are constantly shifting "ecotones"—zones of connection between land and sea where multiple ecosystems overlap to create a unique environment. He argues that the idea of a coastline was "a fiction inscribed on a fractal environment that bore no likeness to its smooth, continuous contours" that was "called into being by the rise of the continental nation state, which needed something that appeared to be a fact of nature to reinforce its fragile boundaries" (Gillis 2014, 163). Analyzing representations of climate change, Amitav Ghosh (2016, 33, 80) similarly asserts that the materiality of coasts is a product of the bourgeois modernist belief in (some) humans' ability to regulate nature and make it predictable. He asserts that older port cities rarely were built right on the coast so that they were protected from the uncertainties of the open ocean. In contrast, colonial ports often were built on the water's edge to facilitate the shipping trade that was the bulwark of colonial empires coupled with the confidence that humans could overcome the sea (52). Coastal urban centers such as New York and Mumbai were "linked to each other not only through the circumstances of their founding but also through patterns of trade that expanded and accelerated Western economies. These cities were thus the drivers of the very processes that now threaten them with destruction" (75–76).

These port cities initially were connected through wind-driven sailing ships. In the nineteenth century, coal-powered steam engines enabled dramatic increases in the sizes and cargo capacity of ships and the distances they covered, and led to the expansion of port facilities in urban coasts around the world and their connections via rail to coal mines or pipelines to oil. In the twentieth century, oil-powered steam engines and later internal combustion engines further expanded global shipping capacity. In the twenty-first century, 90 percent of the world's goods and more than 50 percent of the world's oil are transported on ships (George 2013; Levinson 2006). Powered by fossil fuels, the global economy literally flows on the surface of the ocean. Moreover, the world's oceans have functioned as free sinks for absorbing the carbon emitted not only by shipping traffic over the past two hundred years but for land-based emissions from around the world. For decades the ocean's work as a carbon sink enabled worldwide emissions to expand while mitigating the impacts of those emissions on the atmosphere. Without this work, "CO_2 levels in the atmosphere would jump by nearly 50 percent, amplifying the speed and severity of climate change" (Buesseler et al. 2022). In addition to carbon sinks, in recent decades oceans also have functioned as free disposal sites for petroleum-based plastics, which have become central to global production, shipping, and consumption, and have transformed oceanic life all the way down to the microscopic level.

Successive waves of colonialism, imperialism, and capitalism have been predicated on fixing the ocean and its coasts through various processes that have sought to replace the ocean's fluidity and unpredictability with stability, thus making the ocean a backdrop against which human progress presumably could unfold. While these attempts to fix the ocean momentarily produced the conditions for the expansion of carbon capitalism around the world, as Ghosh (2016) argues, they also created the conditions for their own undoing. Oceans have absorbed so much excess carbon that they have become increasingly acidic in recent decades, threatening entire webs of marine life. Carbon emissions have outstripped the ability of the oceans to absorb them, thus contributing to human-induced global warming. As oceans warm, they take up less atmospheric carbon, exacerbating the process. Moreover, as ocean water expands, it takes up more space thus contributing to sea level rises, which also are increasing due to melting glaciers. And expanding warm zones in the world's oceans negatively impact the flows of currents and global weather patterns, which have become more volatile. These increasingly unpredictable oceans meet purposefully fixed coastlines around the world that cannot withstand the growing instability of the seas. Gillis (2014, 164) argues that when "beaches are seawalled, dunes levelled, and shores built on, some of the most fertile margins of the world—wetlands, deltas, estuaries—disappear in an astonishingly short time. The result is not a shore that is a more stable and protected coast: but one that is significantly more vulnerable than ever before."

This reality underscores the need to think about the intertwining of oceans, inequality, and climate. Throughout this book, I emphasize the historically specific connections and zones of contact that exist between ocean-based and land-based ecologies and processes in ways that reveal the complexities, tensions, and contradictions that emerge from these connections. Peru's oceanic and coastal spaces are experiencing profound changes as commercial fishing, coastal development, shifting weather patterns, and ocean pollution alter existing ecologies. Moreover, Peru is one of the most vulnerable countries to climate change, despite being one of the world's smallest producers of greenhouse gases (Magrin et al. 2014). Approximately one-third of the country's population lives in the capital city of Lima, which is located on a thin strip of desert.[11] Two-thirds of Peruvians live on or near the coast, and as urban coastal populations grow, so too do the number of Peruvians living in areas vulnerable to climate hazards, such as the extensive El Niño flooding that besieged considerable portions of the coast in 2017.

The Spaniards established Lima's colonial center inland on the Rímac River to protect it from the ocean and maritime piracy. The centers of government, financial, and social power in Lima remain on the plateau above the ocean. However, critical infrastructure and a significant portion of the city's impoverished neighborhoods occupy low-lying coastal areas that are at high risk of rising seas and flooding in the coming decades. Lima's port city of Callao is located directly on the coast, providing it with ready access to the shipping traffic that was crucial to the colony's economy, but also exposing it to the uncertainties of the sea. Callao was wiped out by a tsunami from the 1746 earthquake that destroyed much of Lima, and the port city had to be rebuilt completely (C. F. Walker 2008). It is now the hub for the country's export economy, boasting Peru's largest port, international airport, and infrastructure for refining, processing, and shipping the country's mineral and agricultural and fishing exports. Most of Callao's population is also low income, and *pueblos jóvenes* ("young towns," or informal settlements) have emerged in and around the port infrastructure, where residents have been exposed to high levels of industrial contamination (Graeter 2020, 22). Greater Lima's population has boomed in recent decades as people move from the countryside and smaller provincial cities in search of better livelihoods. These migrants have expanded the city's geographical peripheries, especially the northern and southern "cones," into coastal zones that are prone to flooding and in danger of projected sea level rises in the coming decades (Takahashi et al. 2014). Recent studies forecast a range of impacts, from the submersion of Lima's beaches and coastal roads, to the regular flooding and damage of Callao's port infrastructures, to the contamination of freshwater supplies with saltwater (Bergmann et al. 2021). One study identified Lima as a critical area where a "'very high' portion (>50,000) of the local population will be exposed to rising sea levels by 2090" (Reguero et al. 2015). The percentage of the population exposed to coastal flooding increases significantly when El Niño events are factored in (Losada et al. 2013).[12]

A number of anthropologists have highlighted the impacts of ecological crises on Peru and Peruvians, and their work has underscored the importance of examining how such crises intersect with racialized, classed, and gendered inequalities in the country.[13] My analyses in this book are inspired by and seek to contribute to these discussions by drawing on research with socially marginalized and racialized fishers and coastal residents in Lima to highlight the limitations of dominant ways of knowing and representing the ocean and to propose alternatives. The experiences of these fishers and residents reveal the challenges that the ocean's fluidity and unpredictability present not only for their increasingly tenuous livelihoods at sea and on land but also for attempts to fix the ocean through the establishment of surf spots, coastal infrastructure, and extractive industries.

This book emerged from a long-term research project on the experiences of artisanal fishers in Lima with changing fisheries politics, regulatory regimes, and ecologies (Viatori and Bombiella 2019). From 2012 to 2017, I made annual trips to Peru to interview fishers, government regulators and officials, and fisheries biologists. The themes that I explore in this book were things that came up in interviews or that I saw or heard about as I spent time with fishers going about their daily lives on the dock in Chorrillos (see figure 3). I watched fishers unloading jumbo squid when other catches were slow. I noticed erosion along newly constructed sidewalks and expressway lanes along Lima's Costa Verde (see figure 4). I talked with fishers about the unusual heat as we sat in the shade of one of the dock's awnings during the 2017 coastal El Niño warming event. I watched as fishers untangled plastic trash from their nets or local officials posted red flags along nearby beaches warning people that the water was not safe for swimming. Initially, I made a quick note of these things and then moved on to other issues that fishers identified as pressing concerns or that I thought had a more direct bearing on my research. However, over time these issues continued to come up in my work, and I realized that I needed to bring them out of the background

FIGURE 3 The view from the artisanal fishing wharf of the bay in Chorrillos and Lima's skyline. Photo by Maximilian Viatori.

of my research and make them the focus of a new project. During trips in 2017, 2018, and 2019, I broadened my interviews to include architects and city planners working on coastal development and surfers dealing with ocean pollution and coastal erosion and had conversations with fishers about how they were dealing with recent El Niño warming events. I also delved into the Instituto del Mar del Perú's (Marine Institute of Peru) archives to learn about the history of scientific research and regulation on Peru's jumbo squid fishery. Finally, I built a personal archive of television broadcast video clips, social media posts, and newspaper articles on the 2017 El Niño event and its aftermath, public debates over coastal development in Lima, and ocean pollution.

FIGURE 4 Erosion on Playa Makaha next to the sidewalk and third lane of the express-way. Photo by Maximilian Viatori.

I drew together these different strands to create interpretations of oceanic and coastal ecologies in Peru that emphasize the ecological, political, and cultural relationships that are often obscured by dominant representations of the ocean. My goal in doing so is to highlight the need to examine how we come to know environmental and climatic problems and define solutions to them to further social and environmental justice. However, the readings I produce are one set of options that have been shaped and constrained by the limitations of my research. As a North American anthropologist employed at a research university, I have had the privilege and the resources to travel to Peru for a few weeks at a time, conduct interviews and observa-tions, and then leave when work or personal responsibilities demand. One result of this is that there are myriad daily interactions, relationships, and subtle exchanges that have not made it into my research. Moreover, over the years many, but certainly not all, of my research participants have been men, given that fields such as artisanal fishing tend to be male dominated in Peru. While I problematize and comment on this throughout the book, my final analyses undoubtedly bear the artifacts of this gender imbalance. Finally, as a North American anthropologist writing for a predominantly North American audience, I have highlighted aspects of my subject that make it clear that what is unfolding in the eastern Pacific Ocean is linked to broader hemispheric and global inequalities in commodity chains, political influence, and environmental responsibility. All of this is to make the necessary anthropological point that this book offers but one provisional reading of the ocean—other readings, which could highlight different connections and inequalities, are possible and needed for defining a more just social and environmental future.

Three important themes emerged from my research on disparities in how different people and species have experienced dramatic changes in the eastern Pacific's ecology because of coastal development, increased oceanic pollution, extreme weather events, and overfishing. These themes are: (1) the social nature of the ocean and the importance of how it is represented, (2) the tenuous and contingent nature of oceanic ecologies, and (3) the entwinement of ecological change and the history of capital accumulation and development. Throughout this book I trace and analyze these themes and their significance for understanding the production, imperilment, and precarity of contemporary ocean life. My analysis reveals a complex image of Peru's global seascapes as historical spaces comprised of precarious lifeworlds that are tenuously arranged in ways that expose different people, nonhuman species, and places to unequal levels of harm.

First, the social nature of the ocean has become utterly apparent as anthropogenic climate change warms and acidifies oceans, and waves become choked with plastic garbage (among other dramatic and clearly visible changes), making struggles over how to understand oceanic natures a critical aspect of climate politics. Recent work in the "blue humanities" (Mentz 2009; Gillis 2013), "critical blue studies" (Deloughrey 2017; Hessler 2018), and maritime anthropology (Claus 2020; Helmreich 2011; Helmreich and Jones 2018; McCall Howard 2017; Telesca 2020) has demonstrated how long-standing mythologies about the ocean as the ultimate wild space have submerged histories and practices of exploitation, violence, slavery, and inequality. Widely circulating narratives about environmental degradation and climate change in the world's oceans recognize human entanglements in the seas. However, they often do so in ways that perpetuate ideologies about pristine oceans (lamenting the loss of watery spaces "untouched" by human culture) or invoke overly simplified and dehistoricized concepts of "human" impacts on the ocean. The result is an ongoing submersion of political, economic, and social inequalities not only in how different groups of people experience such changes but also who bears responsibility for them or is able to articulate strategies for confronting them. Analyzing these inequalities is essential for articulating just strategies for dealing with a rapidly changing climate.

Second, ecologies and human-material engagements in the eastern Pacific Ocean are contingent and precarious. Historically particular oceanic natures are constantly shifting and contain the conditions of their own potential environmental change. For example, the industrial overfishing of certain species produces changes in trophic (food chain) and ecological relationships among other species, helping to hasten the decline of some while creating the conditions for others, such as jumbo squid, to expand their range. However, such expansion is tenuous as the level of squid extraction has increased dramatically in recent decades, creating the possibility for a decline or crash in squid populations and the economic flows that have emerged around their capture in Peru and across the Pacific Basin. Even seemingly fixed entities such as coastal infrastructures constantly morph as alterations in the seabed and coastal landscapes change the ways that waves break off the coast of Lima, altering circulations of water and sand and undermining built environments in new ways, which in turn leads to new deteriorations and alterations of coastal infrastructure.

Third, the climatic and environmental changes emanating from these Pacific Ocean ecologies cannot be understood without analyzing capitalist histories of organizing various natures. Nonetheless, they are not reducible to such histories. The material-cultural dynamics that comprise Pacific Ocean ecologies create unanticipated results and excesses that often threaten the very capitalist systems of organizing that helped to produce them in the first place. The historical agency of nonhuman entities and processes challenge the ability of political, scientific, and economic systems to not just control them but to name them, understand them, and know them. One consequence of this is that as state officials, corporate actors, environmental activists, scientists, and others attempt to govern and reign in such chal- lenges by scaling down oceanic processes to make them "manageable" within existing epistemological frameworks, they tend to reinscribe such processes with locally specific racializing and classed discourses. As I show throughout this book, this is a significant way in which seemingly "natural" phenomenon come to reinforce "social" inequalities.

THE CHAPTERS IN BRIEF

At this point, the need to critically examine predominant readings of the ocean and propose alternatives that emphasize the unequal political, eco- nomic, and environmental relationships that comprise oceanic ecologies should be clear. I have identified three key themes that emerge in this process and explore these themes in the chapters that follow. Each chapter focuses on a key issue facing contemporary ecologies in the eastern Pacific Ocean (and oceans in general): waves and coastal development, plastic contami- nation, extreme weather, and, finally, overfishing. I draw on ethnographic and archival research to trace how specific readings of these issues emerge through unequal exchanges, practices, and ways of knowing and how certain readings come to be privileged over others as well as the implications of such inequalities for addressing ecological and climatic crises.

In chapter 1, Lima's Costa Verde provides the subject for an exploration of the race-class politics of coastal development. This central stretch of the city's coast has been developed for often competing purposes: an expressway to ease vehicle traffic in Lima's center and a series of beaches for recreation. Prevailing discussions about the threat of rising seas and extreme weather to coastal cities often frame the issue in ways that reinforce a mythologized divide between the threatening nature of the ocean and the hubris of human, land-based development. This reading of the challenges that coastal cities face obscures the ways in which infrastructures and coastal natures, such as beaches and wave breaks, become infused with race-class meanings and inequalities. The history of infrastructural interventions in Lima's Costa Verde as well as public protests against them demonstrate the importance of studying the materiality and meaning of built networks for understanding how coastal infrastructure contributes to or challenges social and spatial inequalities. Surfers have been particularly active in protesting road expansion along the Costa Verde and have sought to defend a historically particular enactment of the Costa Verde's infrastructure that would "fix" existing material conditions, which are essential for producing rideable waves. However, this enactment of the Costa Verde's nature has been rooted in and has reproduced discursive constructions of race and class in Lima's elite social geographies. Surfers' efforts to save their waves reveal the subtle ways in which broader inequalities are remade, sometimes unintentionally, in coastal infrastructural struggles.

Plastic ocean waste, which has garnered considerable global attention in recent years, is the focus of chapter 2. Highly mediated images of beaches littered with all manner of disposable plastic products and turtles and fish trapped in plastic shopping bags have been key components of environmental campaigns to limit single-use plastics. Numerous corporations now advertise products that are made (at least in part) from plastics recovered from the ocean. Dominant readings tend to present plastic ocean waste as a crisis that has resulted from humans despoiling once-pristine seas and that can be addressed by consumers taking personal responsibility and making better choices about their plastic use—a reading that obscures inequalities in how and where waste accumulates in the world's oceans and who is made responsible for it. I provide an alternate view of this by situating the problem of ocean-borne plastic waste within ongoing elite concerns in Lima about the environmental and social contamination of the city's water and beaches. In Lima identifying substances as "waste" that is "out of place" in local seas is not as straightforward a process as it would seem. Rather, it involves different people invoking particular social relationships to establish the fact of ocean pollution and assign responsibility for its presence and clean up. I analyze this process as different actors—from environmental activists to government health regulators to media commentators to artisanal fishers—establish the facts of ocean waste in Lima's waters. These different actors interpret ocean waste in ways that sometimes overlap, but actors with greater social capital can produce knowledge frameworks that enable them to scale up and scale down ocean waste in ways that link it to broader discourses about ocean pollution or social contamination while also obscuring critical aspects of how less powerful actors are affected by and deal with waste. For example, state regulators or media commentators have blamed racialized "out of place" people for the presence of "out of place" waste along Lima's beaches, while also obscuring the unequal levels of environmental harm that socially marginalized residents, such as artisanal fishers or impoverished beachgoers, endure on a regular basis.

Extreme weather events are the subject of chapter 3. These events have become increasingly common and are one of the most significant ways in which people around the world have come to experience climate change. As the biggest ocean, the Pacific plays an outsized role in shaping the world's weather. Periodic shifts in winds and water temperatures in the equatorial Pacific cause regular warming (El Niño) and cooling (La Niña) cycles that affect weather around the world, producing droughts in some areas and rain and flooding in others. In 2017, a "coastal" El Niño led to warmer-than-usual sea surface temperatures in the eastern Pacific Ocean, producing torrential rains and flooding throughout significant portions of Peru. Different Peruvians read the coastal El Niño and discursively connected different scales of the climate phenomenon in ways that obscured, perpetuated, or highlighted social inequalities. State officials and opposition politicians discursively linked widely circulating images of local suffering with assertions about global warming, the failure of state services, and regional corruption in attempts to bolster their own political authority. As they scaled up and down from global to local levels of the climate phenomenon, they produced interpretations of the event that obscured critical and widespread aspects of the El Niño–caused suffering, which was overwhelmingly endured by impoverished Peruvians. In contrast, artisanal fishers framed the coastal El Niño not as a meteorological aberration or the result of key mistakes by state officials, but as part of ongoing climatic, ecological, and economic fluctuations that fishers saw as challenging their livelihoods and pushing them into increased precarity. Understanding this precarity is important for revealing how inequality is bound up with the production of knowledge about climate phenomena and who bears responsibility for dealing with and suffering through their impacts.

Chapter 4 explores Peru's jumbo squid fishery and how human and nonhuman lives are produced and imperiled in the Anthropocene. In the past decade, considerable attention has been given to the issue of overfishing, with hosts of news articles, books, and films circulating about why the world's oceans are "running out of fish" (Woody 2019) and what to do about it. Popular discourse on the subject largely echoes dominant economic and regulatory approaches to overfishing, which frame it as the result of poor fisheries management—too many boats pursuing too few fish. The story of jumbo squid provides a more complex analysis of overfishing and demonstrates that fisheries management is part of the problem. Peru's jumbo squid fishery emerged from attempts by fisheries managers and state scientists to identify uncommodified forms of sea life that could be turned into commodities at a time when overfishing had decimated traditional commercial stocks. Prior to 1991, jumbo squid was not targeted for commercial extraction. It now represents the country's second-most important fishery (behind Peruvian anchoveta). Jumbo squid stocks have proliferated as a result of climate change and ecological gaps left by the decimation of other species. The Peruvian state has legally reserved this fishery for artisanal fishers. However, the tenuous ecological assemblages that have made the jumbo squid fishery possible are threatened by pressure from industrial producers to remove legal protections on the fishery, multinational fleets targeting squid outside Peru's jurisdiction, and the squids' rapid adaptations to shifting ocean conditions that can cause dramatic fluctuations in their populations. The story of jumbo squid fishing reveals the importance of studying multispecies displacements for understanding how the extraction of certain species for the purpose of capital accumulation reorders entire ecological assemblages. Such reconfigurations imperil the precarious multispecies networks that make more-than-human life possible in the Anthropocene.

Taken together, the chapters of this book analyze ongoing challenges not only to Pacific Ocean ecologies but also regarding how we come to know and understand them. Given that the dynamics that I examine in this book continue to unfold, some of them at an alarmingly rapid pace, providing any semblance of a neat conclusion would be foolhardy. Instead, I offer an epilogue in which I examine a 2022 oil spill off the coast of Lima as a means of exploring the interpretations of the ocean I present in this book for environmental discussions in Peru and through the Pacific World.

NAMES AND MEASUREMENTS

Following standard ethnographic convention and the requirements of my institutional review board, I have protected the anonymity of my research participants by giving them pseudonyms. All place names are real as are the names of public figures who have been quoted in published print or audiovisual media, such as broadcast television interviews. In Peru, the metric system is used for land-based distance measurements, weights, and so on. However, in keeping with international maritime law and regulations, distances at sea are measured in nautical miles.

CHAPTER 1

MAKING WAVES

FTER a cup of coffee on September 8, 2019, I embarked on what has become a ritual that I conduct on the first morning of my trips to Lima. I walked from my small hotel to one of the green parks that line the top of the shoreline cliffs in the district of Miraflores. I followed the sidewalk through the park to a long set of concrete stairs that descend the steep, green hillside to the expressway below. Along the way there are several landings that serve as pivot points where the stairs twist and switch back, offering uninhibited views of the Pacific Ocean. At the base of the stairs there is a pedestrian bridge with yellow railings that spans six lanes of traffic. Once I crossed over, I walked down a flight of stairs and I was at the shore looking out at a surf break known locally as Punta Roquitas. It was late winter in Lima, and the sky was a featureless slate gray that was not too different in color from the ocean below. The waves were small, maybe only a meter high. At the parking lot below the pedestrian bridge, there were several surfers pulling on full-body wetsuits, a necessary piece of equipment for this part of the Pacific Ocean, where the water temperatures during September average a cool 16 degrees Celsius. Under normal conditions, the small but consistently breaking waves of Punta Roquitas offer an ideal medium for intermediate surfers who can carve a few good turns on their shortboards. I watched a few surfers catch rides before I continued along the coast, heading southeast along the sidewalk next to the expressway.

Once I left the Parque Ernesto Aramburú Menchaca, which overlooks the surf of Punta Roquitas, I walked onto a recently built elevated walkway that is squeezed between the outside lane of traffic and the small beach below. Along this part of the coast, the beaches are comprised mostly of medium-sized dark cobblestones. As the surf rushes in toward the shore and then quickly recedes, it makes a distinctive sound like gravel being dumped from a truck. The walkway has a metal guardrail to protect pedestrians from the traffic on one side and a fall onto the beach on the other. In a few hundred meters I arrived at La Pampilla, the next surfing spot on my route (see figure 5). There were new cars and trucks stacked together

FIGURE 5 A surfer watches the waves at La Pampilla before entering. The Club Waikiki sits at the base of the cliffs in the background. Photo by Maximilian Viatori.

FIGURE 6 A surfer crosses the sidewalk at La Pampilla. Cars are often parked right next to or on the sidewalk because there is only a narrow shoulder for parking. Photo by Maximilian Viatori.

along the narrow strip of parking next to the walkway. Out in the surf, there were a dozen or more people sitting on boards waiting to catch waves. La Pampilla is a favored spot for intermediate to more advanced surfers, given its proximity to the city and its reliability—there are rideable waves here almost every day of the year, morning and evening. A group of older men with dripping wetsuits were assembled next to some luxury SUVs with their longboards, discussing the conditions and reliving some of their morning rides through hand gestures and subtle twists of their torsos (see figure 6). There were even a couple of people with spotting scopes and binoculars watching the rides of some of the better surfers in the lineup.

I continued along the coastal walkway, slowly making my way to Playa Makaha. I walked along the shoulder of the expressway to avoid the portions of sidewalk that had collapsed, leaving a jagged edge of concrete in areas where strong winter waves have eroded the beach underneath the sidewalk. I passed a small parking lot and a rocky point where a few people were fishing and then saw the Club Waikiki across the road. Enclosed in the club's walled compound are a couple of swimming pools, exercise rooms, tennis courts, areas for sunbathing, and a bar and restaurant. Members, who until recently were all male, are from Lima's elite circles. Makaha is Lima's most popular surf spot for beginners with its choppy, gentle waves. Everyday there are a dozen or more surf schools with their tents set up along the beach where tourists can get a couple hours of instruction and all the gear they need to explore the local waves. In contrast to the rich members of the Club Waikiki, the instructors of these surf schools are mostly surfers who discovered surfing along the city's public beaches. The tourists who pay these instructors to get a Lima surf experience are predominantly foreign and are spending a day or two in the city before they go on to Cusco and Machu Picchu in the Andean highlands. The surf instructors' tents were nestled next to a small parking lot and another pedestrian bridge, which I ascended on my way back to Miraflores. If I had continued along the coast, I would not have been able to find another pedestrian bridge until I got to the next district, Barranco, which was almost three kilometers away. The bridge took me to a sidewalk that I followed up a steep incline that eventually led me back to the top of Miraflores's cliffs, where I followed the running paths through the parks on my way back to the hotel.

The beaches and surf breaks along my walk have been important sites for board surfing for almost a century. They have also played a significant role in the broader history of recreation in Lima. Recently, these areas have been at the center of conflicts among surfers, city officials, and planners over whether priority should be given to protecting surf breaks, pedestrian infrastructure, or car traffic in ongoing coastal development. At the end of April and the beginning of May 2015, surfers staged numerous protests against the expansion of the expressway that runs along the Costa Verde, a stretch of beaches and sand cliffs that provides the residents of Lima, Peru, with access to the Pacific Ocean. One of the largest of these demonstrations occurred on April 27, when approximately two hundred surfers blocked the expressway to protest the paving of a third lane, which led to the city dumping rocks off La Pampilla beach. The demonstration drew attention to the rocks and led the navy to fine the city and order that the rocks be removed immediately, citing a new law that protected wave breaks in historically significant surfing areas. Surfers were unsuccessful in contesting road expansion, which reduced public parking and the size of beaches in La Pampilla and other areas. However, surfers were able to halt modifications to the coast that would potentially affect the waves in what they claimed were important surfing zones.

Around the world urban coasts have become sites of contention as a growing portion of the global population moves toward coastal cities. Most of the world's largest cities—such as Dar es Salaam, Manila, Tokyo, New York, Rio de Janeiro, and Shanghai (to name a few)—are located on ocean coasts. In recent decades, coasts have become sites of rapid development and urban renewal as industrial harbors and ports have been rebranded as tourist destinations and gated communities increasingly have enclosed large stretches of popular beaches. The growing importance of the global tourist economy and the desirability of coastal spaces as sites for residential development also have driven this trend and have contributed to urban coasts as prime locations for real estate speculation and investment. Coastal development has led to real estate prices that exclude all but the wealthy from many coastal communities and place constraints on once-public beaches and oceans amid coastal privatization. In the surfing hot spot of Southern California, surfers and beachgoers have fought with wealthy homeowners in communities such as Malibu, where private landowners have relied on padlocked gates, no trespassing signs, and lawsuits to illegally restrict access to public beaches. In addition to fights over access, surfers around the world have sought to preserve surf conditions at their favorite spots. Global NGOs, such as Save the Waves Coalition (savethewaves.org), which is based in California, have monitored coastal development projects and coordinated with local activists to advocate against port expansion projects or coastal construction that would affect local surf dynamics.

Surfers in Lima framed their opposition to road expansion along the Costa Verde as a defense of coastal nature against runaway urbanization. However, the Costa Verde is an infrastructure that has emerged over the past century through various (and sometimes competing) efforts to transform Lima's coast into a system of beaches, roads, piers, breakwaters, and pedestrian walkways. What surfers defended was a particular version of the Costa Verde's infrastructure in an attempt to fix the physical conditions that were necessary for the continued production of the specific waves that they liked to surf. Surf breaks off popular beaches such as La Pampilla are produced when wind-driven ocean waves enter shallow water and crash into variations along the coastal floor, such as sand ridges. Under the right conditions, these interactions produce crests that surfers can ride. Waves are three-dimensional entities that can vary significantly in the same place because of changing weather conditions and storm surges (Steinberg and Peters 2015; Helmreich 2011). Winter storm waves have flooded expanded car lanes along the Costa Verde, and newly built pedestrian walkways have been eroded by the constant thumping of waves against concrete pilings. And yet, waves also are characterized by repetition and predictability, in terms of where and under what conditions they form. Surfers have feared that dumping rocks into coastal waters or expanding beaches to accommodate new car lanes would alter the physical nature of Lima's popular surf breaks, rendering them unable to produce consistently rideable waves when the right ocean conditions emerge.

To maintain the physical conditions necessary for good waves in Lima, surfers defended a "prior enactment" (Carse and Lewis 2017, 21) of the coastal environment, one that would preserve Lima's coastal infrastructure and underwater geography while also maintaining existing parking for ease of access. This enactment of the Costa Verde's nature is one that also has been rooted in and reproduced by elite imaginations of race-class geographies in Lima. A rich body of anthropological research demonstrates the importance of analyzing infrastructures as organizational systems or technologies through which political ideologies and inequalities take shape through material connections and exclusions (Appel, Anand, and Gupta 2018, 5).[1] An equally rich body of work has examined the politics of urban development in Lima, focusing on the ways in which migration from the Andes has changed the material infrastructures and imagined landscapes of the city.[2] Exploring how changing perceptions of the city's center and the vast shantytowns that ring the city, such works have highlighted the ways in which elites have deployed discourses about race, class, and space to reinforce existing inequalities (and create new ones). In contrast, less attention has been paid to the city's coast as a space for thinking about how elite discourses of race and class have been inscribed and read in the city's recreational spaces.

Beginning in the 1950s, municipal governments implemented a series of infrastructure projects to make the Costa Verde by constructing a roadway that linked Lima's coastal districts to a series of human-augmented beaches. The Costa Verde was to provide Lima's wealthy citizens with a naturally beautiful beachfront that would function as a sanctuary from rapid urbanization in the city's center, which was fueled by an influx of poor, mostly Indigenous migrants from the Andes. Within this elite coastal landscape, surfing held pride of place as a foreign-oriented sport that was socially and economically exclusive. Amid subsequent population booms, Lima's elite residents have had to alter urban landscapes to maintain coastal circuits of exclusion (Gandolfo 2009; Greene 2016). Surfers and other local recreational users pointed to recently built car lanes that were being eroded or flooded because they were too close to the ocean as clear evidence of government officials' unwillingness to protect the Costa Verde's natural beauty. These assertions drew upon, albeit in subtle and often unintended ways, long-standing discourses that equated recreational nature with white-elite coastal spaces.

Through a historical and an ethnographic analysis of the Costa Verde's infrastructures, I demonstrate how prevailing discourses about race and class distinctions have taken form and evolved in the materiality and meaning of the zone's system of surf breaks, beaches, paths, roadways, and parks. I begin by analyzing the historical materiality of the Costa Verde's infrastructure in conjunction with elite discourses about the zone and its relationship to imagined social landscapes. This analysis reveals how the physical space and transportation networks that linked the city to the sea were shaped by and in turn produced circuits of exclusion. I then turn to a discussion of surfing's place within elite ideologies and circuits of exclusion to demonstrate how the history of surfing in Lima relied on and reinforced elite spatial imaginations. This historical context is critical for examining recent surfers' protests against road expansion in the Costa Verde. Drawing on ethnographic interviews and media analysis, I explore recent tensions among government officials, planners, and surfers over whether priority for the development of the Costa Verde's infrastructure should be given to the expressway, private construction, or the preservation of the area's waves and surfers' access to them. Surfers' pitting of coastal nature against urbanization has obscured the reality that the Costa Verde's surfing infrastructure, and its broader infrastructural systems in general, have been shaped by and continue to provide unequal benefits to Lima's differently racialized and classed residents.

THE NATURE OF WAVES

What exactly is a wave, and what would it mean to protect one? The waves that surfers ride are unstable, ephemeral things that develop only when the conditions are just right and last for just a few seconds. As Tony Butt, Paul Russell, and Rick Grigg (2004, 10) write in their introduction to the science of surfing waves, no two waves are exactly alike because a variety of factors influence their shape, speed, and quality. Waves can result from tides (tidal waves), seismic force (tsunami waves), and wind (wind waves). The latter are the most important for surfers. According to the U.S. National Oceanic and Atmospheric Administration's "Ocean Facts" website, "Waves are created by energy passing through water, causing it to move in a circular motion" (NOAA 2021). Wind-driven waves are the result of friction between "wind and surface water" because as wind blows across the ocean's surface "the continual disturbance creates a wave crest" (NOAA 2021). The faster the wind, the longer it blows, and the greater the distance it can blow without being blocked, the bigger the resulting waves will be (Butt, Russell, and Grigg 2004, 35). Waves can travel across an entire ocean basin. As Gonzalo Barandiarán (2004, 31–32) points out in his work on Peruvian surfing, some of the best surfing waves along Peru's shores begin as storms off the coast of New Zealand.

The waves that surfers enjoy in Peru and other coasts around the world are the final products of global weather systems. "The most important source of waves for surfing," note Butt, Russell, and Grigg (2004, 30), is the "mid-latitude depression." These low-pressure systems form in the earth's middle-latitudes—the areas rough between 30 and 60 degrees latitude in the northern and southern hemispheres. This band is where warm air from the tropics meets cold air from the poles. In the southern hemisphere, the meeting of these air masses generates what is known as the "roaring forties"—strong, continuous winds that move from west to east around the world. Because of the absence of large landmasses in the southern Pacific Ocean and the less pronounced difference between tropic and polar temperatures in the southern hemisphere, there is less seasonal variation, which means that "the waves tend to be more consistent all year round" (20). Under the right conditions, temperature differences in the mid-latitudes also produce storms that help to disperse heat toward the poles. These storms form into vortices that rotate (clockwise in the southern hemisphere, counterclockwise in the north) and move from west to east, imparting much of their energy "to the sea's surface, generating a mixed up and seemingly random series of waves of all shapes and sizes, which will eventually organize themselves into clean lines of swell propagating towards [the] coast" (31). As the waves move farther from the storm, they begin to disperse and group into "sets" of "free-travelling" waves (40–41).

When these sets of waves get close to shore, the subsurface part of the wave meets the ocean floor or "bathymetry, which bends and warps [waves] into different shapes and sizes" (12). This buffeting slows down the bottom of the wave while the top of it, the surface water, continues to move quickly. The result (ideally) is a wave break that surfers can ride. Waves are a dynamic and ever-changing medium that surfers have to learn to read if they want to catch a ride. While each wave is a little different, surfers who frequent the same spots learn under what conditions and where good waves are likely to break. In an interview for *El Comercio*, world champion surfer Analí Gómez describes the process of reading incoming sets of waves and deciding when the conditions are right to paddle out and catch a good wave.

> You have to look at the sea before entering, you have to see the waves, the tumbles and begin calculating how often a set comes in, which is usually every ten minutes. So, you already have an idea. You have twenty minutes to enter and catch the wave. You go in, you paddle to where the set is coming from, because you don't want it to fall on you, you have to move. Your set is only twenty minutes (from when you enter the water), twenty-five minutes at the most. Within this time, you can catch ten or twenty waves, but only two good waves are worth the score before you move on to the next set. (Villalba 2015)

Gómez describes the feeling of catching a wave as one of "adrenaline" and "control" and says that while riding a wave "you forget all of your problems, it is very relaxing."

Surfers categorize different waves by the kind of obstructions that create the breaks in a particular area. The most common breaks are beach brakes, which are produced when waves break on a sand bar; reef brakes, which result when waves hit a coral reef (or artificial reef-like obstruction); and point breaks, where waves hit a point of submerged land, such as an underwater rocky point. Surfers often treasure point breaks because they tend to produce consistent waves that provide some of the longest rides. Perú is known around the world for its left-handed point breaks. The most famous of these is in Chicama, which is thought to have the longest left-handed break in the world. This means that surfers catching this wave have to turn to their left (when paddling toward shore) to get on the wave and catch a ride. There are good point breaks among Lima's surfing areas. For example, La Pampilla and Pico Alto (a wave south of Lima, which claims the highest surfable waves in Peru) produce good right-handed point breaks at low tide or when the waves are bigger. Point breaks in the city's waves are the result of rocky points that are found throughout the Costa Verde, many of which were constructed or augmented by the construction of breakwaters to help protect human-made or human-expanded beaches from the force of strong waves that break close to shore (see figure 7). There are also some

FIGURE 7 A surfer catches a wave at La Pampilla. Photo by Maximilian Viatori.

beach breaks in Lima, the best known of which is Makaha, which is also the best wave for beginners. As Barandiarán (2004, 52) notes, the waves of the Costa Verde tend to be small and manageable because the floor of the bay does not have any dramatic changes in depth—it becomes shallow gradually.

Surfers are able to predict where and when good waves will break by combining their knowledge of where the breaks are (the physical geography of the coast) and developing atmospheric conditions. It is often possible to predict at least four days in advance with relative certainty when good waves will hit the Peruvian coast by watching the weather in the South Pacific and looking for low-pressure systems that will provide the energy necessary for surfable waves (71). Surfers' ability to predict incoming waves has improved considerably over the past two decades. Since 1999, the navy has provided online wave forecasts through the Dirección de Hidrografía y Navegación (DHN, Directorate of Hydrography and Navigation). This project was funded initially by the government and the World Bank as a safety measure for port captains and others working in and around the water (74). This information has also been crucial for surfers trying to figure out when their favorite breaks will generate the best waves.

Surfers' engagements with the waves in specific surf areas have been shaped by historical practice, the development of expertise, and the state's provision of scientific knowledge. Yet surfers often obscure this context in their depiction of waves as natural phenomena in need of protection from coastal development, pollution, and other human-induced alterations of oceanic and coastal environments (Hough-Snee and Eastman 2017; Lawler 2011). In his Pulitzer Prize–winning surfing memoir, William Finnegan (2016, 608) describes waves as "the transformation of ordinary seawater into beautifully muscled swell, into feathering urgency, into pure energy, impossibly sculpted, ecstatically edged, and finally into violent foam." Finnegan recounts how he and other foreign surfers traveled the world in search of waves in places such as Samoa and Madeira and that they often named and claimed an informal ownership over them based on their belief that they possessed a unique appreciation for the beauty of these waves and the ocean in general. He also repeatedly decries the "discovery" of these areas for surf tourism and the negative impacts on his waves of "local" development such as the construction of roads and promenades that destroy the beauty of coasts and surf breaks (725–30).[3]

In their book on surfing and social theory, Nick Ford and David Brown (2006, 17–18) point out that more so than other sports, surfers tend to place more importance on the aesthetics of their experience ("beautiful" beaches, the glide of a good ride, and the "perfect" wave). A big part of this experience is what surfers perceive as the raw power and cleansing nature of the ocean's waves. Ford and Brown argue that such perceptions are linked to and informed by broader images of the ocean as a wild, natural space in which surfers embody themselves and escape from the drudgery of urbanization and land-based social norms and politics. This "surfer's gaze" is rooted in the "Romantic tendency in Western cultural development," which they argue is important for understanding how the sport is "embedded within [a] broader network of cultural meanings and history" (17). However, this analysis overlooks the specific historical, social, and political conditions under which surfing is practiced and has developed in certain places. As such, it largely reinforces a generic "Western" assumption that there is a clear separation between urban culture and ocean nature. In contrast, Karin Amimoto Ingersoll (2016, 41, 44; see also I. H. Walker 2008) argues that for Native Hawai'ian surfers "ocean literacy" frames the ocean not as a space opposed to land and outside of human culture but centers it as another site through which identity is embodied and created. In the broader context of Western colonialism in Hawai'i (and, as an extension of it, surf tourism), this literacy exists as an anticolonial practice that fosters an alternative vision of the relationships among people, seascapes, and landscapes.

Unlike Hawai'i, there is not an Indigenous history of modern board surfing in Peru. Rather, the sport was introduced by white-elites to Lima in the mid-twentieth century. Lima's waves are part of a broader coastal infrastructural system that was created to meet the recreational needs of Lima's elite residents. How and where surfers encounter waves along Lima's Costa Verde are products of specific infrastructures and the historical natures that they enact. Kregg Hetherington (2019, 6) points out that nature and the environment commonly have been viewed as antecedents to infrastructure, as the "infrastructure of infrastructure." However, he argues that anthropogenic climate change has upset this formula, as nature and infrastructure have folded in on each other and blurred easy distinctions and assumed temporalities. Ashley Carse (2012) explores these complex relationships of nature and infrastructure in his work on the Panama Canal zone. Carse (2012, 540, 556) explores how nature—in the form of systems of "dams, locks, and forests" that provide water for the canal—can become an infrastructure that delivers "critical services" while inscribing "politics and values . . . on the landscape." When examining such "natural" infrastructures, Carse (2012, 543) argues that it is crucial to ask: "How [do] historically contingent socio-technical systems shape which environmental services become valuable and who benefits from their delivery"?

The Costa Verde's waves are an "environmental service" that the city's coastal infrastructure provides to surfers and, during the summer, beachgoers. Within Lima's coastal infrastructure, waves are but one component along with human-augmented beaches and walkways, an expressway, and pedestrian bridges and parks. Furthermore, surf breaks along Lima's coast were created and influenced by coastal dredging and the construction of breakwaters and jetties as well as movements of seawater, sand, and rocks. In what follows, I explore the historical and social conditions under which these waves have acquired value for Lima's surfers and the role that the development of the city's coastal infrastructure has played in this process. During the twentieth century, the city's central beaches came to be spaces associated with ideas about white-elite space and cultural practices, such as surfing. The history of surfing in Lima has been shaped by ideologies of upper-class masculinity, and elite male surfers benefited unequally from the historical development of the city's coastal infrastructure. This sociohistorical context is critical for understanding how contemporary protests to protect the Costa Verde's waves and defend a particular enactment of coastal nature are entwined with elite ideologies of race, class, and space.

BEACHES FOR ALL

Since its inception, the Costa Verde has been framed by shifting elite ideologies of exclusion as an important space for reproducing perceived boundaries of sociocultural difference. For architect Ernesto Aramburú Menchaca, the transformation of the Costa Verde was a lifelong project to integrate Lima with its coast to beautify the city. Aramburú Menchaca sought to create a new nucleus for Lima that faced the ocean rather than hide from its threats. He hoped this center would rival the fabled Copacabana beach in Rio de Janeiro, which the architect took as his inspiration. In 1957, as the inspector of public works for the municipality of Lima, he proposed and oversaw the construction of a new expressway to link the city center with the coast. The construction of the road required a significant extension of the lower coastal shelf.

Fill from the upper shelf was used to extend the lower coastal shelf to create a platform for the road and create wide, sandy beaches that extended farther into the bay. As the mayor of the district of Miraflores (1970–76), he also oversaw the expansion of the expressway and construction of new boardwalks and walkways from which residents could enjoy the district's views of the ocean. According to Aramburú Menchaca, the development would benefit Lima's "asphyxiated population" by providing it with "oxygen" (*El Comercio* 1980).

Who needed this oxygen and why? Answering these questions requires an understanding of Peru's racial-spatial politics and Lima's history of urbanization. In Peru, elite discourses of race-class have been articulated through culture (a set of dispositions, bodily markers, comportment, and language) and as geography (a set of assumptions about what kinds of culture belong in and are symbolized by certain regions) (de la Cadena 2000; Weismantel 2001). Through such cultural and spatial relationships, Peruvian elites long have imagined Lima as the center of white, urban, modern culture in opposition to the Indigenous, rural, tradition-bound nature of the Andean countryside. In nineteenth-century Lima, the former colonial center was the seat of state, religious, and social power and status—all of which were assumed to decrease in intensity the farther one moved away from it (Panfichi 1995; Poole 1997). Elite residents built summer homes along the Pacific coast and made annual migrations to the seaside, where a series of paths and stairways directed them down to narrow cobble beaches where Indigenous attendants would help them into the water (Higgins 2005). Annual trips to the coast to bathe became an important practice through which Lima's elites sought to reproduce what they perceived to be their bodily and social differences from other inhabitants of the city.

The status of Lima's coastal districts as elite vacation spots transformed in the early twentieth century amid significant changes in Peruvian society. As Daniella Gandolfo (2009, 8) notes, during the 1930s and 1940s, Lima experienced "a demographic explosion" as Indigenous peasants left the rural highlands and settled in Lima's city center. The city's wealthy experienced this influx as an "invasion" and "fled" from the city center, converting summer retreats, such as Miraflores, into residential districts (8–9). As wealthy residents of Lima moved southeast, they relocated their summer homes to more secluded beaches outside of the city in fishing villages, such as Ancón and Pucusana, while fortifying the exclusivity of social clubs along the city's coast, such as the walled compounds of the Club Waikiki and the Lima Yacht Club. While elite ideologies of race-class framed society as composed of elites and poor masses, D. S. Parker (1998) traces the emergence at this time of an "idea" of Lima's middle classes among skilled workers who saw themselves as existing above manual laborers but below elites. Through the first half of the twentieth century a recurring demand among white-collar workers was the right to special summer hours that would enable them to take a long lunch and bathe in the ocean—a right that was denied manual laborers (Parker 1998, 147–50). This example underscores not only the ongoing discursive work necessary to maintain and rework the boundaries of social difference within perceived social hierarchies but also the role that recreational space and the coast played in the projection of shifting race-class ideologies in Lima. As more migrants arrived in the city, the colonial center became "saturated," and the newly arrived first moved to the "arid slopes of adjacent hills" and the banks of the Rímac River and later to the north and south of the city (Gandolfo 2009, 8). As the city's social landscape changed, Gandolfo (2009, 11) argues that elites engaged in the reconstruction of racial boundaries by erecting new circuits that maintained the "basic rule of avoidance."

Aramburú Menchaca's project to make the Costa Verde into a site for recreation easily accessed with a road to and from Miraflores occurred at a moment in which elite residents of Lima had converted the city's coastal districts into enclaves. It was they who had turned their faces to the ocean and craved its "oxygen" amid feelings that they were being "suffocated" by waves of new migrants. Making the Costa Verde was, as Aramburú Menchaca conceived it, a project of beautification and modernization, concepts that elite residents defined in contrast to the (mis)perceived "filth" and disarray of Indigenous migrants and the urban spaces they inhabited. By the end of the 1970s, the Costa Verde provided the residents of Lima's coastal districts with paths, stairs, beaches, and breakwaters (to protect newly created beaches from erosion). The imported surfboards that wealthy residents procured were an extension of this infrastructure—fiberglass boards that created new exclusive circuits into the Pacific Ocean that were accessible only to a small portion of the city's population or visiting tourists.

During the 1980s and 1990s, Lima experienced another dramatic shift that further challenged elite geographies. Economic crisis and a civil war between Shining Path guerrillas and the state army, which claimed more than sixty-nine thousand lives and drove thousands of highlanders to the city (CVR 2003). Between 1981 and 1999, Lima's population almost doubled. In his study of Lima's underground punk scene, Shane Greene (2016, 57) notes that these "massive demographic changes that converted Peru from a rural country into an urban one, completely redefined Lima's social and spatial dimensions in the process." In response, elite residents reworked racial-spatial discourses to fortify relationships of exclusion by racializing Lima's migrants "as urban cholos instead of rural Indians" (76; Weismantel 2001, 20). The concept of *cholo/a* became associated with the poor of the city's center and periphery and defined in contrast to the *pituco/a*, the white snob who prized foreign culture and was familiar only with the exclusive residential districts of the city (Greene 2016, 56–58). Within this ever-fluid set of oppositions, much of the Costa Verde represented a space in which pitucos/as from Miraflores and Barranco could practice recreational activities, such as surfing.

And yet, during the 1980s and 1990s, urbanization threatened the perceived natural beauty of this space as well. One consequence of Lima's population explosion was a boom in sewage, which was (and continues to be) dumped into the ocean. The largest collector in La Chira, just south of the Costa Verde, spewed a steady stream of (mostly) untreated human waste into the ocean, which the prevailing currents picked up and pushed along the beaches of the Costa Verde, leading to regular beach closures because of sanitation concerns. Amid a widescale cholera outbreak in 1991, Lima's news media ran regular stories highlighting the filthy state of the area's water and beaches (Viatori and Bombiella 2019, 80–84). Furthermore, as Lima expanded, traffic congestion throughout the city, including along the Costa Verde, became an increasingly pervasive problem. In 1995, state officials created the Autoridad del Proyecto Costa Verde (APCV, Costa Verde Project Authority) to coordinate the development of the zone by issuing regulatory norms for the coastal corridor that linked the district municipalities of Chorrillos, Barranco, Miraflores, San Isidro, Magdalena del Mar, and San Miguel. In its fifteen-year plan, the APCV's board provided drawings of a glistening Costa Verde with sailboats in the bay and waterfront resorts that would enhance its "touristic-recreational-cultural potential" (APCV 1995: 6). Invoking Aramburú Menchaca's vision for the coast, the APCV's plan emphasized the beautification of the Costa Verde as an important social goal, one that would contribute to the well-being of the city's residents.

This project of beautification was one that dovetailed with, and should be seen as part of, a massive urban regeneration project in Lima to counteract what elites perceived as the negative impacts of the city's Indigenization. Alberto Andrade, the mayor of Miraflores (1990–96) and, later, Metropolitan Lima (1996–2003) sought to restore Lima's city center by commercializing it and ridding it of its purported "filth," "decay," and social undesirables (Gandolfo 2009, 11). He also advocated for the development of the upper shelf to include new parks, walkways, malls, apartment buildings, hotels, and restaurants (x–xi), which contributed to a boom in real estate speculation and construction on the back of Peru's economic recovery in the late 1990s.

The APCV's decentralized structure and lack of enforcement capabilities facilitated such construction atop the Costa Verde's sandy cliffs. The mayor of Lima appoints the president of the Costa Verde, and the board is comprised of the mayor of each member district as well as a representative of the Greater Municipality of Lima and one at-large appointee, both of whom are also appointed by the mayor of Lima. The state regulatory norm that created the APCV also divided the management of the Costa Verde's spaces among Metropolitan Lima and the district municipalities that are present along the coast. Metropolitan Lima is responsible for financing the construction, expansion, and maintenance of the expressway of the Costa Verde and any nonvehicular infrastructure along or over it (such as pedestrian bridges or cycling lanes), a task that is executed by the Empresa Municipal Administradora de Peaje de Lima (EMAPE, Lima Municipal Administrative Company of Tolls). Each individual municipality is responsible for managing the beaches and cliff tops of its portion of the Costa Verde, including pedestrian infrastructure in those areas, such as stairs descending the cliffs to provide pedestrian access to the beaches. However, the district municipalities are supposed to obtain prior approval from the APCV for any proposed development on the beaches or cliff tops. In practice, the development of the Costa Verde has proceeded in a patchy and often uncoordinated manner in which individual district municipalities have pursued projects that best fit their own short-term desires for the development of their portions of the Costa Verde. The APCV has no authority to enforce the district's adherence to its plan, and there have been numerous instances in which district municipal governments have proceeded with the construction of buildings atop the coastal cliffs that did not follow the APCV's regulations.

The administrative structure of the APCV has enabled the prioritization of car traffic and automobile infrastructure. Because the municipal government of metropolitan Lima is solely responsible for the road, it has near-total oversight of its development, and since it can provide its own direct funding (in coordination with the state Ministry of Transportation), it has been able to move forward in a relatively direct manner with expansions to the expressway. In contrast, the cliff tops and the beaches (in theory down to the high-tide mark) are the responsibility of individual district municipal governments, each of which has proceeded with the development of its district in different ways. While such development is supposed to adhere to the regulations and falls under the oversight of the APCV, this is not always the case in practice. For example, in Barranco, the municipal government has issued permits for building almost to the cliff edge, despite APCV prohibitions of such construction. While Metropolitan Lima can move forward with the construction of boardwalks and bridges for pedestrians and cyclists, it must rely on the municipal governments of the individual districts to provide funding to complete these projects.

This patchy development has drawn criticism from residents, surfers, and urban planners. For example, architect and urban planner Wiley Ludeña told *La República*, Lima's center-left newspaper of note, that individual district municipalities see their portions of the Costa Verde only as spaces "from which they can extract rents," contributing to a lack of clear planning for integrating the coast into the city (Mendoza 2015). The result, Ludeña and others have complained, has been "unsightly" variation in how and to what degree each municipality has developed its coastal space. Furthermore, urban planners have argued that the new construction is not safe. The sandy cliffs of the Costa Verde are steep and unstable and Lima is seismically active because the Nazca and South American tectonic plates meet just off the Peruvian coast. The cliffs constantly shed sand and rock down onto the highway, a process that has buried old structures located at the base of the cliffs. Rockfalls have regularly closed one or more lanes of the expressway and have killed or injured numerous automobile drivers over the past twenty years (*El Comercio* 2016b).[4]

For many architects and urban planners in Lima, the Costa Verde's supposedly hodge-podge nature has been offered as clear evidence that rational development of the region to accommodate new building as well as recreation and transportation has been hamstrung by the byzantine nature of the APCV's decentralized bureaucracy and the corruption that has enabled politicians and developers to circumvent this red tape. In a similar vein, surfers have consistently lamented the impact that roadway expansion has had on local beaches and how cliff-top development has made the whole area uglier because it is more urban. Recently, such critiques have been framed as a struggle to ensure that the Costa Verde is "for everyone." Here it is critical to consider what this imagined "everyone" might mean within the spatial history of Lima and the Costa Verde in particular. In this context, languages of coastal beautification and protection draw upon elite discursive oppositions that position the Costa Verde and its bodily and culturally cleansing properties as an antidote to what elites perceive as the suffocating threat of informal urbanization that has come to dominate the city.

SAVING WAVES

Reading nature as a proxy discourse for race-class ideologies is essential for understanding recent tensions among surfers, planners, and politicians over the expansion of the Costa Verde's transportation infrastructure. Surfers have protested and complained that Metropolitan Lima has prioritized the expansion of the expressway at the expense of pedestrian bridges and staircases that connect the cliff tops with the beaches below, which are critical for promoting the Costa Verde as a recreational area. Upon entering office, mayor Susana Villarán (2011–15) promised to expand the pedestrian infrastructure in the Costa Verde by creating new "boardwalks, staircases, pedestrian bridges, bike lanes and jogging paths" (Vidal 2014). A center-left politician, Villarán sought to move beyond the city's infrastructural politics by instituting new urban planning initiatives, and so appeared ideologically in line with surfers' interests. However, surfers came to see her as an adversary because none of her proposed measures for new pedestrian infrastructure were implemented. Instead, in 2014 Villarán authorized a project to add a third lane in both directions to the expressway. Construction was delayed for several months by ongoing protests. The expansion of the expressway drew ire from surfers, who argued that the addition of an extra lane was impacting recreation along the Costa Verde's best beaches because parking areas were being destroyed to make room. The surfers also expressed concern that the lane expansion would require that more land be added to portions of the Costa Verde, resulting in altered wave dynamics.

Surfing has a long history in the Costa Verde as a sport practiced by the wealthiest of the city's men and boys. Carlos Dogny, a member of Lima's elite social circles, is credited with introducing board surfing to the Costa Verde during the 1940s. He learned to surf on a visit to Hawai'i, where he was gifted a board by the famed Duke Kahanamoku.[5] Upon his return to Lima, he named several beaches after popular Hawai'ian surf spots and founded the Club Waikiki in 1942 at the base of Miraflores's coastal cliffs. Matt Warshaw (2010, 133) emphasizes in his global history of surfing that the sport took on a distinctly elite character in Peru, in contrast to the "surf bum" image that came to be celebrated as the defining core of surf culture in other places, such as California. Scott Laderman (2014, 46) writes,

> The club was invitation only and restricted to two hundred members, each of whom paid a substantial entrance free (approximately $1,200 in 1964) followed by monthly fees. The beachfront grounds were extravagant. They contained a squash court, two pelota courts, a shuffleboard court, workout facilities, a heated pool, dining facilities with jacket- and bow-tie-clad waiters serving four-course meals, a bar, a marble dance floor, and staff to wax and carry one's surfboard to and from the water.

Membership continues to be invitation only, and it was not until 2010 that women were allowed to join.

In the 1950s and 1960s, Lima emerged not just as the center of Peruvian surfing, but also as a global center for the development of competitive surfing. Wealthy surfers from Lima used their holiday time to explore beaches outside of the city, "discovering" now-famous breaks in places such as Chicama (de la Rosa 2010). They also played a central role in organizing and hosting world surfing championships in collaboration with surfers from California, Australia, and South Africa. From 1956 to 1974, Lima held the Peru International Surfing Championships, considered at the time one of the two biggest and most important surf competitions in the world. Peruvian surfers quickly established themselves as the preeminent practitioners of their sport in Latin America, and their world championships helped to cement surfing's pride of place within the Peruvian sporting landscape. As Dexter Zavalza

Hough-Snee (2015) argues, surfing was not exported from California to Peru and did not follow a preestablished trajectory of colonial export. Rather, surfing was something that was brought to Peru by the country's elites, who learned the sport from Hawai'ian practitioners. From the 1960s onward, Peruvians increasingly viewed surfing as a sign of their country's modernity, a sport that had evolved on its own in Peru and in which Peruvians were able to compete on level ground with global powers, such as the United States.

Despite the growing popularity of surfing as an icon of Peruvianess, the sport has remained a predominantly upper-middle-class venture riven with socioeconomic and cultural exclusions. Laderman describes the experience of Gerardo Alberto Bejarano Ybarra to show how even at these international surf competitions, the social exclusions of Lima's surf scene were clearly apparent. Despite being Peru's strongest entrant at the 1969 competition, Bejarano had to borrow surf boards for his heats because he could not afford one of his own. Bejarano told a visiting surfer that he was "the only one without money" who surfed in Peru and noted that in return for using their equipment, rich local surfers forced him to retrieve and wax their boards (Laderman 2017, 58).

During the military governments of the 1970s and the economic crisis and civil war of the 1980s, the visibility and importance of Peruvian surfing diminished on the global stage. Wealthy surfers continued to ply Lima's waters, but international surf tourism to Peru dropped (de la Rosa 2010). This changed during the latter part of the 1990s and 2000s with a decline in political violence and an economic rebound. The country began hosting international competitions again and boasted several world champions, making surfers some of the most internationally decorated athletes in the country (Hough-Snee 2015; Wood 2009). Warshaw (2010, 460) argues that this visibility led to growth in its popularity, and by "the late 2000s, roughly half of Peru's surfers were from the expanding middle class."

This simple statistic is somewhat misleading. As Hough-Snee (2015, 204–5) notes, the number of surfers who are not from Peru's white, upper classes has increased in recent years. In addition to surfing's growing visibility within the Peruvian sporting landscape, the increased quality and decreased price of imported surfboards and wetsuits (mandatory in the cold waters of this part of the eastern Pacific) have enabled more Peruvians to get into surfing. However, in the past decade the cost of a second-hand surfboard still hovered around 450 soles—a sum that represented a significant portion of most Peruvians' monthly incomes. Surfing remains a pursuit that still is not accessible to the majority of Peru's coastal populations. Moreover, surfing's expansion has reinforced and developed within existing elite social geographies that preserve Lima's status as the urban, national center. Among Peru's surfing demographic there is a general bifurcation between surfers from Lima, who are mostly upper class, and those from the provinces who are of "significantly lesser socioeconomic status" (205; see also Wood 2009, 227).

In recent decades, the internationally recognized epicenter of Peruvian surfing has moved outside Lima to celebrated surf breaks in Punta Hermosa, Chicama, and Lobitos. Lima's surf breaks remain important sites within daily recreational geographies for local surfers who cannot get outside the city on a regular basis to surf. Most mornings, while many of the city's residents hustle to make a living, there is a line of luxury automobiles parked at La Pampilla, where mostly middle-aged men pay a local attendant to safeguard their keys and wallets while they play on their longboards in the waves. In the afternoons at Punta Roquitas, parents sit in their cars and watch their children surf waves and sometimes set up tripods and video cameras to record their best rides. Members of Club Waikiki occasionally wander out of their club's walls to Playa Makaha to catch a few gentle waves, while just down the road foreign tourists pay 120 to 180 soles per hour for board rentals and surf lessons.

Wealthy surfers from Lima also can travel on holidays to bigger or better waves in other parts of Peru. This mobility stands in stark contrast to many surfers outside of Lima, who stick to their local surf breaks and do not have the resources to travel for surf tourism (Hough-Snee 2015, 205). This disparity is evident in competitive surfing, in which "most of Peru's 200-something professional surfers pertain to the upper-middle class" (206). As evidence of the broadening base of surfing in Peru, Warshaw (2010, 460) points to the world champion Sofia Mulanovich. Mulanovich is the daughter of Croatian immigrants and is emblematic of Peru's new surfing elite who are well traveled, sponsored by global surf brands, and who have honed their craft at internationally celebrated surf breaks outside of Lima and around the world.

Warshaw does not comment on Analí Gómez, one of Peru's most successful surfers of recent years. Gómez is the Afro-Peruvian daughter of a fisher from Punta Hermosa, a small town just south of Lima, and who is known in Peruvian surfing circles as "la negra" (literally, "the black woman")

(Hough-Snee 2015, 205). Gómez learned to surf from her older brother, who lent her his board. She received her first board as a gift from Mulanovich, a friend who was born in and lived in Punta Hermosa as a child (Mauro 2005). In contrast to surfers from wealthy backgrounds, Gómez did not have the personal finances necessary to compete on the international circuit at events outside Peru and has required sponsorships to be able to travel to compete. Despite winning a world championship in 2014, Gómez publicly announced in 2016 that she would not be able to compete at international events outside of Peru because of a lack of sponsorships. "Unfortunately, I do not have any sponsors, so I have not been able to leave. Right now, it's like that, they are a bit racist. In surfing, the brands are supporting the blondes for the covers" (*El Comercio* 2016c). Contrast Gómez's situation with that of Mulanovich, known in Peru's surf circles as "la gringa" (a term used to denote not only whiteness but also foreignness) and who said in an interview for *Surfer* (Mauro 2005), "I was sponsored by Billabong when I was younger, which was great because I got a few wildcards. Then Roxy came along and took it to a whole new level for me. Now in Peru, surfing is getting so big the big corporate companies are getting involved. I just did a commercial for Telefonica, which is one of the biggest companies in Peru." In 2018, Gómez said in an interview that thankfully some brands had "opened their doors" and she was receiving enough sponsorships to travel and compete (Haddad 2018). Gómez's national and international wins represent historically significant breakthroughs in a sport dominated by white-elite men (Wood 2012, 424–26). Gómez consistently has named and commented on the racialized and gendered biases in Peruvian and global surfing (Salazar Albarca 2019). However, her experiences also underscore the ongoing and substantial challenges that surfers who are not from Lima's elite circles face in trying to make a living on the competitive circuit.

Surfing remains a recreational pursuit that is too costly (both in terms of time and money) for most of Lima's residents to practice. It also remains a predominantly male pursuit, despite the national visibility of women such as Mulanovich and Gómez. It is unusual to see women surfers in the lineups at Lima's popular surf breaks, which remain spaces for the reproduction of upper- and middle-class masculinities that are linked to and reproduced through the privilege of recreational surfing. For some surfers, their defense of the sanctity of Lima's surf breaks was, at least implicitly and in part, a defense of this privilege.

For other surfers, the defense of the Costa Verde's waves was less about their personal recreation and more about their ongoing ability to earn a living. There are surf instructors and surfers who are not from upper-class, white backgrounds and who use Lima's waves for work. These surfers sometimes make fun of the members of the Club Waikiki and trace their surf lineages not to elite Peruvian origins, but to globalized images of surf bum culture in California. For example, in 2018 I spoke with Roberto, a surfer in his fifties who placed his patched and well-worn surf boards out on the sidewalk at Makaha each day along with advertisements for his small surf school. He got into the sport when he was fourteen, body surfing for several years before he could buy a fiberglass board. After studying chemistry, he lived and worked abroad in Los Angeles, surfing famous breaks along Southern California's coast. Roberto claimed that the sport was invented in Peru thousands of years ago by fishers who used their *caballitos de totora* (a small reed canoe that is straddled) to explore the ocean and to have fun riding waves back into shore. Peruvian surfer Felipe Pomar (1988) has spent decades popularizing this nationalist history of the Peruvian Indigenous origins of surfing. Initially this represented a claim by Peru's surfing elites to assert an alternative narrative of surfing's origins, arguing that the sport originated in their country and then spread to Polynesia, where it was then reimported to Peru in its modern form. Hough-Snee (2015) argues that in recent years the narrative has gained traction among nonelite surfers, and he asserts that this Peruvian history of surfing unites all of the country's surfers across race-class boundaries. Roberto offered this narrative of Indigenous surfing not as a means to find common ground with elites from the Waikiki club but to offer an alternative to the claim that they were the ones who introduced surfing to Lima.[6]

While surfers such as Roberto distanced themselves from elite representations of the sport, they also engaged in the shared goal of protecting an enactment of the Costa Verde's infrastructure to fix the conditions for local wave production. Surfers' identities and their participation in the sport were shaped by their different and unequal positioning within dominant political ecologies and ideologies of race, class, and gender. However, these identities also emerged from individuals' engagement with waves and a widespread feeling among surfers that they had a special relationship to the ocean because of their intimate, often daily interactions with the subtle changes of its movements and the joy they derived from them. Analí Gómez touched on this shared sense of appreciation for the ocean when she commented in an interview, "I think that no matter how much of a surfer you are, everyone has respect for the sea, you never know what could happen there" (Villalba 2015). She added that Peruvian surfers were fortunate to have access to "waves that are practically perfect. All countries have good waves, but only for periods, during certain seasons. In Peru you can surf every day" (Villalba 2015). Protests to protect the city's breaks drew on this sense of respect for the ocean and the beauty of the city's waves, despite pronounced differences among the city's wave riders and their participation in the sport. Whether they surfed the waves in front of Club Waikiki or took multiple buses and walked through city streets with their boards to surf Punta Roquitas, Lima's surfers would all suffer if construction impacted the publicly accessible waves that they shared. At their protests, surfers often shouted for city officials to "give me back my beach!"

Surfers engaged in solidarity to argue that Lima's waves required state protection so that they would not be affected by poorly executed urbanization. In 2003, the Federación Deportiva Nacional de Tabla (FENTA, National Sports Federation of [Surf]Boarding), successfully pressured the Peruvian national congress to create Law 2780, which provides environmental protection for the best surf breaks along Peru's coast. The law stipulates that FENTA, in coordination with the Instituto Peruano de Deporte (IPD, Peruvian Institute of Sports), determines areas that should be registered as protected areas. In 2013, the law was made effective by presidential Supreme Decree No. 015–2013-DE. In 2015, Peru's National Surfing Federation joined with the Peruvian NGO Conservamos por Naturaleza to create the "HAZla por tu ola" (Do it for your wave) campaign to generate funding to conduct the necessary surveys of threatened waves and submit them to the navy so that they would receive protection under the new law. The campaign maintains a website where one can go and see the waves that have been protected, such as Rompientes de Miraflores in Lima.[7] A quick click on that wave directs you to an information page about where the wave is located, what threats exist to the proper functioning of the wave, and the history of the wave's protection status. In the case of Rompientes, a specialist was hired to conduct a study of the wave's historical significance, which was then presented to the navy, and, ultimately, approved. The wave now has protected status. The website also lists other waves that are threatened but not protected. Visitors can click on a particular wave and donate to help fund the process of obtaining protected status.

Raúl, an avid surfer who has enjoyed Miraflores's beaches since he was a kid and is a PhD ecologist, participated in environmental assessments for compliance with the surf law. As a surfer, Raúl saw the beaches of the Costa Verde change because of ongoing development, and so he began working with Peru's surfing federation to petition for the law that would prohibit "changing the topography of the coastline and the underwater substrate." In areas with protected waves, new structures cannot be built that would negatively affect local wave dynamics. To establish protected surf spots, Raúl said that topographic surveys were conducted along with assessments to demonstrate that certain areas were historically significant and influential surfing spots that deserved to be registered for legal protections.

Among the first waves to be protected were those off the following beaches in Miraflores: Punta Roquitas, Makaha, Redondo, and La Pampilla. The latter two beaches have been the primary sites of concern and protest for area surfers against the expansion of the expressway. Quique Labarthe, a fixture of the local surfing scene and owner of the Soul Surfer School, was asked to comment on the expressway for an article in *La República* (Vidal 2014). He said that "it is not conceivable that we would lose this public space in order to prioritize cars." He continued by pointing out that "here in Redondo and in La Pampilla, heavy machinery [for construction] has burst into a familiar recreational space and we have no information about what condition our beaches will be left in." Another surfer quoted in the article, Luis Boyle, expressed concern that the "iconic" beach of La Pampilla could end up like the beach at La Herradura.

Located in Chorrillos just south of the current boundaries of the Costa Verde, La Herradura was one of the most fashionable resort beaches for residents of Lima to surf and sunbathe during the mid-twentieth century, with a hotel and restaurant and a parking area next to the beach. One of a few naturally sanded beaches in the area, La Herradura sits in a small inlet with steep cliffs on two sides. The beach was largely destroyed in 1981, when Chorrillos's mayor, Pablo Gutiérrez Weselby, attempted to build a highway around the southern cliffs of Chorrillos to link the popular Pescadores beach with the beaches in La Herradura and La Chira to the south. Construction required blasting into the surrounding cliffs to clear a shelf for the road. The rubble from the demolition was dumped into the sea and changed the way the surf breaks on its way into the inlet. Rather than breaking farther out and exhausting their intensity by the time they reach the beach, the waves maintain their energy all the way to the beach. While La Herradura has become a challenging spot for expert surfers, the area is no longer safe for swimmers, and waves have destroyed the sanded beach.

As Barandiarán laments (2004, 90), La Herradura "was a dream beach before the construction of the road. . . . Now the [road]work has been eaten away by the waves and the shore is just a small strip of sand and stones." He argues that this precedent—a clear example of how badly coastal infrastructure construction could go wrong and ruin a great beach or wave— provided the impetus for later protests to save waves throughout Peru. In the 1990s, surfers opposed the construction of a fishing dock in Cabo Blanco, a popular beach and surf break in northern Peru in the city of Piura. Surf guides caution beginners against trying to surf the wave in Cabo Blanco, but for experts it is an almost perfect reef break that offers beautiful pipelines with heights of three meters on its best days. Surfers feared that the proposed dock would ruin the wave break and profoundly alter the surrounding beaches; hence, they formed, along with other local beach enthusiasts, the Asociación para la Conservación de las Playas y Olas del Perú (Association for the Conservation of Beaches and Waves in Peru) (90). The surfers and their allies were successful in saving the wave and the beach in Cabo Blanco, as the government agreed to move the pier to a different locale. Surfers and local NGOs concerned with the status of Peru's waves and beaches often repeat the cautionary tale of La Herradura and the success of Cabo Blanco in their admonitions for greater protections for the country's coast in the face of urban, coastal development. Most recently, this story has been told in a feature-length documentary called *A la Mar, un documental sobre la protección de olas del Perú*, which has been shown at adventure film festivals throughout the Americas.[8]

Surfers in Lima drew on these ideas about the need to protect Peru's threatened waves, asserting that road construction represented an urban alteration of their natural recreational area. Some also protested construction on the grounds that it would impact tourists' access to local surf spots. Along Playa Makaha, there are sixteen surf companies that have permits from the municipal government of Miraflores to set up small tents and charge tourists for surf lessons and board rentals. José and Luis, who agreed to interviews in 2015 and again in 2016, were instructors who worked on Playa Makaha.

Both were from impoverished backgrounds and had discovered surfing as kids visiting the city's public beaches. José's family was from a small Andean village and his parents had moved to Lima a few years before he was born. Luis and his family migrated from the Andes during the 1980s. José was concerned that road expansion would consume existing parking, making it difficult for tourists to access the beaches. Furthermore, he worried that increased traffic would make it harder and more dangerous for pedestrian tourists to access the Costa Verde's beaches. "It could hurt our business," Luis said, "and make it more difficult for surfers and tourists to come and go as they please." According to Luis, going to the beach and surfing were some of the most popular things for tourists to do when they visited Lima. He asserted that the Costa Verde made Lima unique—it was one of the few Latin American capitals with direct and easy access to the ocean and it was the distinctiveness of this feature that made it so important to protect from overdevelopment.[9]

Jose's and Luis's interests aligned with local elite surfers and residents of the city's coastal districts who sought to defend a prior enactment of the Costa Verde's environment from road expansion and thus fix the conditions for not only the production of the city's waves but also limited automobile access to them. Both elite surfers and surf instructors relied on some vehicular access to and parking near the beaches they surfed and worked, but they argued that too much traffic would alter the waves they or their clients enjoyed. These overlapping interests led to the first wave of protests that occurred in 2014, when Villarán approved the third lane expansion.

In December 2014, a group of surfers camped for two weeks on the Punta Roquitas beach in Miraflores and opposed the paving of a third lane between Punta Roquitas and La Pampilla. The surfers argued that the lane expansion broke state regulations (*La República* 2014). By law, the state controls Peru's coastal waters, including the first fifty meters of the coast inland from the high tide line. These first fifty meters are reserved for public use and state law bans construction within this zone (although this is often disregarded in practice). Surfers noted that if the asphalt for the road was poured, there would only be fifteen meters between the road and the maximum high-tide point (*La República* 2014). City officials responded that they were in the process of attempting to resolve the situation and come to a compromise that would not affect the beaches frequented by surfers. Ultimately, Villarán, who was close to the end of her term as mayor, decided not to move forward with construction and left the issue for her successor to decide.

Upon taking office, the new mayor, Luis Castañeda, quietly moved forward with paving the third lane. Castañeda was a right-wing, populist mayor who subsequently was blamed by many in Lima for unchecked, corrupt development. His move to expand the road led to the resumption of protests. Surfers were upset by the fact that half of the beach in Redondo was lost to lane expansion, and in La Pampilla the lane was built close to the water, limiting parking for the beach and exposing the road to destruction from high waves. EMAPE officials asserted that their construction projects would not in any way impinge upon local wave dynamics because they were only working on the already-existing road. In some places, such as La Pampilla, they argued that the road was close to the water not because they were taking up more beach space, but because erosion from the ocean had eaten up a growing portion of the beaches that had previously existed. However, shortly after its construction, the third lane in La Pampilla was already threatened by erosion because it was built so close to the ocean that, especially during high winter waves, the road's foundation was being washed away and undermined. To deal with this, the administration of Castañeda ordered that EMAPE deposit several tons of large rocks in the water just off the beach to shelter the road from large waves. This act sparked a renewed wave of protests in April 2015 led by surfers who argued that the rocks would make surfing more dangerous and affect how the waves broke along a beach whose surf break was protected by state law. The navy forced the city to remove the rocks, providing a win for local surfers concerned about how the beaches along fabled surf breaks were being impacted by what they saw as uncontrolled urbanization.

Tensions between surfers and Castañeda continued over his treatment of La Pampilla. In October 2015, he ordered the construction of an elevated sidewalk along the beach so that pedestrians and cyclists did not have to interact with automobile traffic while traveling up and down the expressway. Commenting on the sidewalk project, a municipal official said that it would "protect the lives of thousands of pedestrians who risk walking and moving along this coastal stretch" (*La República* 2015). The sidewalk was under one kilometer long. Less than one year after its construction, parts of its pilings were already falling apart because they had been built too close to the waves. Surfers and residents from Miraflores complained that the elevated walkway was an example of corrupt city politics and represented little more than an attempt on the mayor's part to bolster the public image of his administration by showing his ability to get something built on behalf of local pedestrians and cyclists. As evidence of this, public criticisms of the walkway focused on Castañeda's choice to have its guardrails painted yellow, the color of his political party.

DIFFERENT PUBLICS

In March 2016, I visited the offices of the Authority of the Costa Verde Project, the government agency responsible for drafting regulations for the development of Lima's coast, with two of my graduate students. We sat down at a small table in the main office to look over a folder of regulations and designs with Marta, one of the APCV's team of architects and planners. Over the course of an hour, we discussed the future of the Costa Verde and the challenges of creating parameters for developing the coast when the authority must rely on individual municipal governments to adopt and adhere to them. Marta showed us numerous proposed projects, including a gondola system for Miraflores that would connect tourists atop the sand cliffs with the beaches below. Such proposed projects, she noted, would contribute to the APCV's primary goal of developing the Costa Verde as a "public recreational space."

In her extended discussion of this goal, Marta made a point of explaining to us that the Costa Verde was a complex space that had been modified extensively to create opportunities for recreation. "It is often said that the Costa Verde is a natural space," she told us,

> but it is not natural in the sense that is used colloquially because the beaches have been created. When they did construction for the expressway, the earth that was moved was deposited in Miraflores in the beaches to gain land [from the ocean]. Therefore, we can't say that all of the Costa Verde is a natural zone.

Furthermore, Marta made it clear that surfing did not warrant special consideration in the APCV's plans. "There are different publics," she said, who use the area. "Surfers are one public," she noted, "they have a right to the beach, the same as all residents of Lima." "The priority is public space" in the APCV's development plan, she said, adding that "the idea is to cater to all audiences, and we must offer the same services without preferences." During a follow-up interview several months later, Marta reported that in all likelihood Metropolitan Lima would have to add sand and rock to the Costa Verde's beaches to extend them farther into the ocean to expand transportation infrastructure even more and still ensure there would be sufficient beach and parking. "Sacrifices will have to be made," she said, to ensure the best outcome for all users of the Costa Verde.

While surfers defended a prior enactment of the Costa Verde's environment that sought to fix the conditions for wave production, city officials and planners advocated for a different enactment that sought to balance the recreation and transportation needs of a growing city. Officials defended this enactment by countering surfers' claims that they had a special historical and aesthetic relationship to the city's coast and asserting, as Marta did, that the Costa Verde was created to serve all of Lima. However, the enactment that city officials promoted was one that was also entwined with prevailing racialized and classed inequalities that were evident in the material connections it enabled and blocked. Instead of fully countering the privileged status of surfing in the city's coastal infrastructure, this APCV enactment of the Costa Verde overlaid and at times emphasized inequalities among surfers who were racialized and classed differently. For example, disjunctures in the transportation infrastructure impacted surfers' access to public breaks, albeit in different ways for individual surfers, thus reinforcing social distinctions and exclusions.

On a typical day in May 2018, the sun was beginning to break through the morning fog as fifteen or more surfers bobbed in the waves off Punta Roquitas. The waves that morning were small and not breaking cleanly but were still ridable. Mario put on his wetsuit and waxed his board in preparation for a quick surf session as we talked. Mario was a student in his early twenties and said that he had been surfing for two years. He tried to surf almost every day by finding a little bit of time between work and classes to get in the water, usually at Punta Roquitas. Mario did not have a car and did not live within walking distance of the beach in one of the more expensive neighborhoods of coastal Miraflores, so he took a bus that stopped near one of the main thoroughfares in the district and walked a few blocks to the top of the cliffs where a set of stairs led down to a pedestrian bridge over the expressway and down to the shore. When he was done, he gathered his board and backpack and climbed back up the stairs to catch another bus to work. Despite the expanded car traffic along the Costa Verde, there was no public transportation on the expressway until 2018, when buses ran only during the peak months (and hours) of the summer beach season. This meant that surfers like Mario relied upon existing pedestrian infrastructure to access waves.

While the expressway's expansion and lack of accompanying work on pedestrian bridges has hampered access for surfers on foot who rely on public transportation, the same has not been true for wealthier surfers. While the parking space at La Pampilla was reduced by the road expansion, the thin strip of pavement is packed on an almost daily basis with luxury cars and SUVs that well-off surfers use to directly access the beach and avoid having to walk about a kilometer from the nearest pedestrian bridges while carrying their boards. In a more pronounced example of infrastructural privilege, a third lane was not added to the section of expressway that runs roughly from southeast to northwest behind the Club Waikiki, even though an extra lane was added to the rest of this stretch of the expressway. Three lanes of southeast-bound traffic now pass between the club and a narrow (less than fifty-meter strip) of beach, and two lanes of northwest-bound traffic are squeezed behind the club and nestled right up against the base of the cliffs. The result is a bottleneck that causes traffic congestion during peak commuting hours. Commenting on this situation, Raúl, the surfer and ecologist who had conducted environmental assessments for the APCV, remarked that the "government normally would drive over anybody to do what they want." In the case of Club Waikiki, the individuals who pay thousands of dollars to be annual members have considerable influence in the city's economy and politics. Furthermore, because the club's concession predates the creation of the Costa Verde project and the expressway, it received special consideration.

These disparities are indicative of broader spatial inequalities in the development of the Costa Verde's infrastructure. At the time of writing, there were only five functional pedestrian bridges along the coast. This is not just an issue of beach access, but also safety, because these bridges and staircases double as evacuation routes for tsunamis in this seismically active area. There was a bridge in San Isidro that was still without stairs to connect it to the cliffs and the beach because EMAPE had built a bridge that the district municipality did not want for fear that tourists and residents from other districts would use it to access a local coastal park. There were also projects in Barranco and Miraflores that EMAPE had begun work on several years earlier that also stood half-finished. In Barranco, for example, there was a pedestrian bridge that was abandoned before it had been finished. EMAPE had hired a subcontractor to build the bridge to create a new connection between Barranco and Barranquito beach below but had to halt construction when local officers reported that the bridge was unsafe.

Race-class politics surrounded the pedestrian bridge that EMAPE constructed over the expressway in San Isidro. The municipal government of San Isidro did not want the bridge and so chose to not build stairs that connected the bridge with the cliff tops or the beach. Raúl referred to this as a "bridge to nowhere." According to him, the "underlying reason" for not finishing the bridge was that the residents of San Isidro

> do not want people coming to their area [because] they will leave garbage. That is one reason. Another reason is that they just do not want people to come. [They think] 'it's our park, there are ten of us using it, we do not want to share it.' So, they didn't build the bridge. It is [also] because there is no plan [in the APCV] that accounted for the limitation that the municipalities had the power to just say no [to a proposed project].

San Isidro is one of the most socially and economically exclusive districts in Lima and, as Raúl put it, has a noticeably "gated spirit." José Antonio, an expert in sustainability who also had conducted environmental assessments for the APCV, echoed this sentiment when he remarked in a 2015 interview that "San Isidro has many rich people, which is why there is no [pedestrian] bridge, exclusion is more prevalent in San Isidro." While it is the wealthiest (per capita) district along the Costa Verde, it has the least developed portion of coast. Part of this is because the waves along the northern stretch of the Costa Verde are very strong and dangerous for swimming. This portion of the Costa Verde has been extended farther into the ocean than the southern half and, while not suitable for bathers, has led to a large shelf that the APCV has envisioned as an ideal site for an extensive park system. However, this also has to do with class and that municipal officials in San Isidro do not want to attract people to their stretch of the Costa Verde.

During the summer season, residents from Lima's poorer districts use the zone's beaches, especially those in Chorrillos. The city's elites long abandoned the area as a site for beachgoing recreation to avoid the influx of migrants and the increasingly polluted water. The exception to this is the historical enclaves that exist along the Costa Verde, such as the Club Waikiki and the Yacht Club in Chorrillos, whose gated compounds shelter the city's wealthy residents from their physical and social surroundings, and which have received special protection in the area's development. Furthermore, the most popular beaches and parks of the Costa Verde are separated from public access points along the tops of the cliffs by six lanes of traffic, walled medians, and an ongoing dearth of public transportation. These patterns indicate how elite discourses of race-class difference and material practices have coproduced the spatial inequalities of the Costa Verde's infrastructure.

A COAST THAT CAN NO LONGER BE SAVED?

In August 2018, surfers and other recreational users of Miraflores's stretch of the Costa Verde protested ongoing coastal construction. This time the protestors, loosely organized by the Facebook group Costa Verde de Todos (Costa Verde for All), opposed the expansion of the pedestrian walkway that threatened to reduce the size of Redondo beach, located just past Playa Makaha as one travels southeast along the expressway. *El Comercio*'s (2018) coverage of the protest lead with a photograph of a surfer with sunglasses and hooded sweatshirt holding a boogie board with the slogan "Salvemos la Costa Verde" (Let's Save the Costa Verde) on it. In a statement on its Facebook page, the group argued that construction so close to the waves only served to "destroy our beaches," and that "one day we will wake to find a Costa Verde that can no longer be saved" (*El Comercio* 2018). Protests evolved to the point where surfers and other recreational users were not just opposing infrastructural expansion for cars but also pedestrian infrastructure that they saw as threatening to the coastal environment.

The waves that surfers enjoy and access to them are environmental services provided by the Costa Verde's infrastructure. Surfers feared that road expansion would destroy this condition by potentially altering where the waves hit the beach or changing the contours of the coastal floor, thus threatening the potential of popular surf areas to create the kind of waves that surfers needed. City officials countered surfers' defense of this enactment of the Costa Verde's environment with an enactment of coastal infrastructure that they claimed would balance the transportation and recreational needs of all of Lima's residents. Exploring the tensions between these enactments reveals the complex ways in which racialized, classed, and gendered inequalities have been entwined with the politics and materiality of Lima's coastal environment. Surfers' protests created a sense of cross-class solidarity based on their shared experiences of immersion in the ocean and riding waves. Yet they defended a prior enactment of the city's coast that subtly drew on and reinforced historically rooted racialized, classed, and gendered spatial oppositions. Similarly, while city officials and APCV planners sought to improve recreational access and decrease traffic congestion for more of the city's residents, their efforts largely reinforced long-standing circuits of exclusion. This dynamic underscores how much cultural and social inequalities are inscribed in the zone's materiality and the degree to which they have been maintained across different enactments of Lima's coastal environment.

The persistence of these inequalities seems to stand in contrast to the instability of the ocean and Lima's coast. The ocean is in a constant state of movement, and these movements, both regular and unpredictable, are forever reshaping the coast: exposing or flooding land, moving sand and gravel from one place to another, eroding the foundations of roads and walkways, and battering piers and docks. Lima's unstable cliffs regularly shed rocks and sand down into the ocean, adding to the mix and altering the shifting zones of contact between land and sea. Surfers and city officials have engaged in processes of trying to "fix" this zone of movement into a definitive coastline (Gillis 2014), albeit for different ends. Surfers have tried to preserve certain physical conditions to produce waves, one of the most unstable of oceanic phenomena. City officials have attempted to create a coastline with established borders between sea and land, beaches and roads, and so on. These efforts to fix the coast are regularly upset by the instability of the ocean, requiring new efforts to extend beaches, repave roads, and protect surf breaks. Rather than undoing entrenched inequalities, these efforts by surfers and city officials repeatedly have folded those inequalities back into the enactments of the city's coastal environment. In the coming decades, these enactments likely will be further undermined by an increasingly unstable ocean and projected sea level rises that could submerge the Costa Verde's beaches and roads and alter where the city's historic waves break. Ongoing analyses of the material inequalities of Lima's coastal environment will be critical for assessing whether future enactments of the zone's infrastructure achieve greater justice in their distribution of environmental services.

CHAPTER 2

PLASTIC OCEAN

THE artisanal fishing wharf in Chorrillos is located on the far southeastern end of the Costa Verde, sandwiched between the popular Playa Agua Dulce to the north and the walled complex of the Lima Yacht Club to the south (see map 2). The wharf is comprised of a set of low buildings, a concrete pier, and an open-sided fish market next to a small parking lot. On the afternoon of September 8, 2019, I crossed the concrete parking lot, heading toward the covered fish market to see if anyone I knew was around. There were a few people with tables of fish out, but the wharf was quiet. During summer, especially on the weekends, there are tourists on the neighboring beaches, people stopping into the restaurants and kiosks that line the dock for lunch or dinner, and in the evenings, there are shoppers in the market looking for fish. During the austral winter months, everything slows down. The sun stays hidden behind clouds and water temperatures drop. I exited the fish market on the side opposite to the parking lot and headed over to the covered area where there are usually fishers mending their nets and talking. On my way I ran into Lorenzo, a fisher and boat builder, whom I had known since I first started doing research on the wharf in 2012. Lorenzo was in his mid-fifties, but a recent spate of health issues had aged him considerably since I last had seen him. We chatted for a while about the fishing, a boat he was restoring, and the general state of business on the wharf. He told me that Luis, whom he knew was a longtime friend of mine, was cleaning up the beach. I looked over, but I did not see him right away in the distance. Lorenzo pointed to a row of old boats that were being stored along the beach, and then I saw two men with a wheelbarrow and rakes. I thanked Lorenzo, told him I would circle back later to talk to him more, and walked over toward the beach to say hello to Luis. I crossed back through the fish market and went down a small, sandy slope on the edge of the parking lot that led to the beach.

When I first started working in Chorrillos, this area had been full of old boats, many of which still had owners but were no longer usable. The people who owned them lacked the money to repair them but had nowhere else to store them. For years the municipal government and the central state ministry responsible for oversight of the dock pressured the local fishing association to clean up the boats.[1] Over the past few years, the association had slowly moved the boats, working with the municipal government to tow them once the owners had been identified and notified. The beach was more open than it had been even just the year before and it was also noticeably clear of debris. Although it sits next to one of the most popular beaches, which attracts hundreds of people each day in summer, the small strip of beach next to the dock has not been used for recreation. There is a well-known freshwater spring that bubbles up from the sand there, which is why the area is called Playa Agua Dulce (Fresh Water beach). Locals with limited means use it to bathe and wash their clothes, but that is the extent of its use. Much of this has to do with the fact that the beach was often covered with seaweed. Playa Agua Dulce sits at the southern end of the bay and the circular currents that move water through the area are at their slowest there, and so debris and seaweed accumulate where the water does not move fast enough to push them along.

As I walked closer to the boats, I could make out Luis's face. He was taking a break and smoking a cigarette while he leaned against one of the old boats that was still left on the beach. It struck me how "clean" the beach was—it was not covered in the usual seaweed and trash but looked sandy like the other surrounding beaches. Luis and I exchanged greetings and hugs and we quickly got caught up, talking about all that had happened in the past year. I asked Luis what he was up to, and he gestured to his wheelbarrow, which was full of garbage, most of it plastic, and said that the local fishing association had been working on cleaning up the beach. These efforts were motivated in part by government pressure and in part by fishers' desire to see if they could attract more tourists, who might then spend money on the dock on fish, boat rides, or food. Luis finished his cigarette and gathered his rake. He asked the other fisher who was with him to push the wheelbarrow back to the shed where it was stored. As we walked back to the dock together, he commented on how much better he thought the beach looked but also lamented the fact that there was a constant stream of garbage showing up, more so than just a decade before. Local fishers regularly had to rake the beach for garbage if they had any hope of keeping it clean. He thought that the problem was that people threw too much away and often dumped it into the ocean instead of tossing it in a trash bin. He was hopeful that a new ban on single-use plastic bags in Lima would help to slow the tide of plastic waste that washed up on Playa Agua Dulce every day (see figure 8).

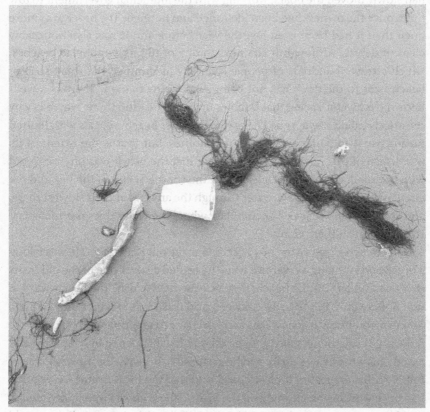

FIGURE 8 Plastic garbage, a Styrofoam cup, and seaweed that had washed onto the Playa Agua Dulce in Chorrillos. Photo by Maximilian Viatori.

Luis's frustration with plastic pollution was not unique to him or to his local beach. In the last few years plastic ocean waste has emerged as a global environmental concern, and Lima recently has received attention as having some of the most garbage-filled waters and beaches in South America. In 2014, Ocean Conservancy, an NGO that focuses on international campaigns to reduce marine pollution, announced that Playa Carpayo was the most polluted beach in South America. The small strip of coast is located about twenty kilometers northwest of Playa Aqua Dulce in the port city of Callao (see map 2). Playa Carpayo had a higher trash per kilometer ratio (eighty metric tons per kilometer) than any other beach surveyed on the continent (*El Comercio* 2014). Some global media services featured the announcement, presenting it as an indication of the alarming degree of coastal pollution that has occurred around the world in the past decade. Lima's daily media outlets also ran the news. However, the state of Playa Carpayo came as no surprise to the city's residents. Each year Peru's health ministry conducts a survey of beaches around the country, and Playa Carpayo consistently has ranked first among the most contaminated shorelines. Arturo Alfaro, president of the Peruvian NGO Vida, told a reporter from the newspaper *El Comercio* (2014) that he had been cleaning up waste on Playa Carpayo for close to fifteen years, and the amount of detritus he found had only increased from one year to the next. When Playa Carpayo's status as the country's most contaminated beach was reconfirmed the following year, Alfaro noted that the trash that accumulated on the shore was composed primarily of consumer plastic and wood from local construction (*El Comercio* 2016a). Of particular concern, he pointed out, was "micro trash" from the plastic that could break into small particles, and which could "be consumed by marine fauna."

Luis's and Alfaro's comments indicate some of the ways in which people invoke certain relationships to understand visible plastic waste on Lima's beaches. Luis suggested that recurring plastic waste was the result of people being careless about how much they threw away and where, an issue that required government action to correct. Similarly, Alfaro noted that poor consumer choices and illegal construction dumping were to blame for coastal trash while suggesting that what washed up on Lima's beaches was only the tip of the iceberg—it was a visible marker of a broader web of plastic contamination in the ocean.

In this chapter, I examine the different sets of social and material relationships that people invoke to establish the fact of marine pollution in Lima and assign blame or responsibility for its presence as well as prescribe appropriate measures for dealing with it. Waste that circulates in Lima's waters and is deposited on its beaches links and crosses multiple social assemblages at once. Yet I argue that dominant readings of ocean waste strip away and obscure relationships of care and responsibility in ways that reproduce enduring social inequalities, making it seem that "out of place" waste is the result of people who are supposedly "out of place" in Lima. This is a dynamic that transcends current concerns with plastic ocean waste and is critical for thinking about how plastic waste has become infused with particular social and cultural meanings in Lima. There is a long history in Lima of elite anxiety about the composition of the city's seawater, and local elites have long made dubious links between the area's environmental and supposedly social contamination. Over that past fifty years, Lima's population has grown by a multiple of five (or more) as impoverished, often Indigenous, migrants from the Andean highlands have moved to the city to escape civil war and economic crisis. As Daniella Gandolfo (2009) makes clear in her ethnography of urban renewal in Lima, the city's cultural, political, and economic elites have viewed this migration as an "invasion." Once a sanctuary for elite recreation, Lima's central coast has become a site for popular recreation as well as a free sink for dumping the city's growing sewage and construction waste. In the ensuing years, Lima's seawater and beaches have become objects of an elite gaze in which the facts of ocean or beach waste invoke a whole set of material and semantic relationships that reinforce a link between environmental contamination and its perceived social marginalization and enable a host of government interventions and public shaming.

How do people establish the meaning of different forms of ocean waste? Whom do people hold responsible for the appearance of ocean waste that is supposed to be "elsewhere"? Is the presence of plastic waste or sewage bacteria the product of a global problem, the failing of state disposal systems, or the behavior of local consumers? In addition to questions of scale and responsibility, I ask what kinds of actions people demand or undertake in the presence of waste that is "out of place." I explore these questions by tracing how state officials, government scientists, local media elites, beachgoers, and artisanal fishers, such as Luis, have responded to the existence of ocean-borne waste in Lima's waters and on the city's beaches. A critical aspect of this exploration is understanding how waste circulates in the Pacific Ocean in ways that cross geographic and social boundaries and links people and places in distinctly unequal ways.

CIRCULATION

Waste circulates in the ocean in both predictable and unexpected ways that result in the movement of items such as plastic trash across large distances and their accumulation and concentration in particular ocean spaces. The circulation of ocean waste is distinct from, but inherently linked to, the circulation of commodities around the world. Environmental anthropologists have shown how the circulation (and concomitant valuation) of commodities relies upon the alienation of natural resources from noncapitalist social relationships.[2] These processes of circulation also involve discarding unwanted substances as part of the process of generating value. For the past two centuries, the world's oceans have been used as free sinks where the unwanted waste of global capitalist production and urbanization was dumped for free.

Before 1972, there were no significant international agreements on or limitations to what could be dumped in the ocean. Industrialized countries intentionally discharged all manner of things into the ocean, including "radioactive wastes, sewage sludge, and discarded chemical and biological weapons" (Schenker 1973, 33). Growing public awareness and concern over the dumping of unused military waste and the emergence of dead zones in the waters off major coastal cities, such as New York, contributed to the creation of several international agreements on ocean dumping in the 1970s (Schenker 1973). Foremost among these was the International Maritime Organization's "Convention on the Prevention of Marine Pollution by Dumping of Wastes and Other Matter 1972," which is often referred to as the "London Convention." This convention took effect in 1975 and was ratified by eighty-seven countries around the world, including Peru. The London Convention effectively ended the legal dumping of radioactive and industrial waste directly into the oceans. An updated version in 2006, known as the "London Protocol," banned the dumping of most waste at sea without prior permitting.

However, such agreements do not cover waste that is dumped or leached into rivers, which then makes its way to the ocean, nor can they prohibit ongoing illegal, intentional dumping. Most of the waste that makes its way to the ocean is from human activities on land.[3] Rivers are important vehicles for transporting this waste from continental landmasses to the world's oceans. Much of the estimated eight million tons of plastic that is deposited each year into the oceans comes from rivers. Human-produced waste also makes its way from land to the sea via numerous points around the world's coasts where it is dumped directly into the ocean, such as through sewage discharges. In addition to these land-based sources of waste, offshore human activities also generate ocean waste. For instance, commercial fishing boats often lose or discard large nylon nets. These "ghost nets" are not only a significant source of plastic pollution but they also inadvertently gather other waste and ensnare sea creatures.

In his overview of anthropological research on waste, Joshua Reno (2015, 561) notes that most waste management is "absential" in that it is aimed at making waste invisible by moving it "elsewhere." Despite international antidumping agreements, the world's oceans continue to be used as vehicles for making various forms of waste invisible by absorbing them and moving them "elsewhere" at little or no cost. However, waste that is discharged in one part of the ocean rarely stays in that spot because it is moved by the ongoing circulations of the ocean. These circulations are the products of ocean currents operating at global, regional, and local scales. Currents are the generally predictable, directional movements of water in the ocean that are the combined results of the earth's rotation, prevailing surface winds, tides, and differences in the temperature and salinity of masses of water.[4] The South Pacific Ocean between Australia and South America is ringed by four major surface currents—the Antarctic Circumpolar Current to the south, the Peru Current to the east, the South Equatorial Current to the north, and the East Australia Current to the west. These currents play a critical role in the circulation of nutrients, creatures, and waste, as well as in regional and global weather patterns. Surface currents result from wind-created drag on the ocean's surface and thus roughly follow the direction of prevailing winds. However, because of the earth's rotation in the southern hemisphere, they curve at about a forty-five-degree angle to the left of the wind's direction.

The movements of these major currents create an enormous area of slowly turning water known as the South Pacific Gyre, which is one of five major gyres—large, stable systems of "rotating ocean currents"—in the world's oceans (https://oceanservice.noaa.gov/facts/gyre.html). The oceanic pole of inaccessibility (also known as Point Nemo)—the point on earth that is farthest from land—is located in the South Pacific Gyre, which is also the world's largest ocean desert (see map 1). There is little upwelling (the movement of deep water to the surface) and a lack of dust blown from nearby land masses, which results in scant nutrients to support life in the gyre. Because it is the point farthest from inhabited land and major shipping routes, space agencies around the world have used Point Nemo as a dumping spot for larger space craft, satellites, and space stations that do not burn up completely on reentry. International space debris now lays on the ocean floor in the center of the South Pacific Gyre.

In 2018, a scientific expedition discovered that space junk was not all that had accumulated in the South Pacific Gyre. At the center of the gyre there was a floating collection of garbage that measured three million square kilometers, making it larger in surface area than Mexico. Scientists noted that a third of the fish they had surveyed had evidence of plastic consumption and that the plastic they found had traveled from Peru and Chile as well as Australia and New Zealand (Mayo 2018). Plastic and other debris get caught by the swirling currents of the gyre and slowly move to the middle, where they accumulate and break down into smaller particles. For years this process occurred out of sight in the most remote part of the Pacific Ocean. This was one major example of how ocean currents rendered human waste "invisible" by moving it out of sight and slowly transformed it into smaller and smaller bits that were less visible (but more insidious as they infiltrated the ecosystem). However, the discovery of this clearly visible patch, along with larger and better-known garbage patches in the North Pacific Ocean, has underscored that the ability of the world's oceans to continue performing this service clearly has come undone.

Modern carbon capitalism has reshaped the very nature of oceans by making them more acidic and filling them with petroleum-based plastic waste. Global plastic production has doubled in the last two decades, with packaging comprising the greatest single use of plastic around the world. Despite growing recognition that the world is awash in plastic waste, production is likely to increase in the coming decade as oil companies look to offset decreased fuel demand by increasing plastics production and as cheap fracked natural gas in the United States is turned into plastics for export.[5] However, oceans remain outside the control of human systems. Currents circulate ocean waste in ways that are not dictated by and indeed often undermine human management systems. As Reno (2015, 565) points out, "Waste can also circulate and bite back as a result of nonhuman flows and divides." The discovery of garbage patches in the world's ocean gyres has raised widescale alarm about the quantities of human-produced waste that now circulate in the ocean. Ocean garbage patches remain physically distant and internationally complex problems (Whose responsibility is it to clean up global plastic in international waters, anyway?), which people experience primarily through highly mediated environmental campaigns. In contrast, the growing abundance of human waste in coastal zones presents a more pressing issue for people working and living in those areas, as well as local governments. Plastic debris and sewage bacteria that were supposed to remain invisible and stay elsewhere have accumulated in overwhelming quantities in the "wrong" places, such as the beaches in Lima.

Lima has undergone rapid urbanization in recent decades. In 1960, Lima's population was less than two million—it is now eleven million. This dramatic expansion has taxed a waste disposal system that was created decades before to accommodate the needs of a much smaller city. Furthermore, much of the city's growth has occurred on its geographic "periphery," driven by what Lima's elites often refer to as "invasions" of "informal" housing (Gandolfo 2014). The growing ring of new neighborhoods around the city's center are linked to sanitation infrastructure in patchy and unequal ways, with most of the newer settlements lacking access to formal disposal services. There are only four official landfills in the city, and these dumps can take only a fraction of the total waste produced each day by the city's residents. The only solution that many of the city's local governments and residents have is to engage in illegal dumping, which is an extensive and daily occurrence throughout the city. Much of the beach waste in Lima comes from garbage that is dumped into the Rímac, Chillón, and Lurín Rivers. Runoff from illegal dumping is also a major source of water contamination in rivers and, subsequently, Lima's coastal waters. Additionally, millions of gallons of mostly untreated or undertreated sewage are dumped by the city's sewage collectors—which are constantly behind capacity and unable to keep up with the city's population—into Lima's waters each day.

An intricate system of currents circulates this waste in the waters off Lima's coast, dispersing it in some areas and concentrating it in others. Between the edge of the continental shelf and the coast, seawater is moved by coastal currents, which play a critical role in the "transport and dispersal" of "nutrients, pollutants, and sediments" as well as fish and crustacean larvae (Gelfenbaum 2005, 259).[6] The most significant current for the movement of seawater off Lima's coast is the Peru Coastal Current, which is a cold-water, equator-bound surface current that comprises the eastern edge of the Peru Current.[7] Waste that is discharged along Lima's coast generally flows northward because of the Peru Coastal Current. However, the outflow of the city's rivers as well as the movement of tides and the area's geography also impact the circulation of waste on a local scale. There is a strong ocean-bound current near La Perla in Callao that carries waste and pollutants out into the Peru Current. In the summer, when the city's rivers are flowing at a higher rate, their discharges are pushed farther out and help to push waste away from the coast (Correa et al. 2008, 181–82). During the rest of the year river discharges are weaker and stay closer to the shore, which means that effluent from them is trapped and pushed back against the coast by the Peru Coastal Current. In Lima, a system of breakwaters was constructed to prevent coastal erosion by absorbing and dissipating the strength of incoming waves. They also help to create slow, circular currents in the bay, in places such as the water off the Playa Agua Dulce in Chorrillos or the Playa Carpayo in Callao, where an eddy current accumulates and traps waste, like a miniature version of the South Pacific Gyre.

Increased quantities of plastic refuse and sewage waste circulating in Lima's waters (and the Pacific Ocean more generally) have led to increased concentrations of waste not only on Playa Carpayo but all along Lima's and Callao's shores. What happens when this waste stops circulating and is made visible, either as garbage on a beach or the published results of government bacterial testing? "Waste" is not a de facto category that simply describes the material process of subtracting physical components with no use value from commodities and daily human life. The identification of something as waste is a socially mediated process through which associations and meanings are ascribed to or deleted from various substances—visible or invisible—that are interpreted in particular social contexts as waste, filth, or toxins. This dynamic underscores the importance of considering social worlds for establishing what is waste—How is something established as being "out of place" (Douglas 1966), who has the authority to establish this fact (Gandolfo 2009), who has the ability to decide what happens to waste (Alexander and Reno 2012), and how do particular groups of people or places come to be associated with waste (Millar 2018)?[8] The moments in which ocean waste becomes visible or its presence is established are pivotal moments for uncovering how different groups of people interpret its meaning by framing and producing it within existing languages, discourses, and practices of different, but often overlapping, social assemblages.[9] They are also critical moments in which relationships of inequality are established as actors with greater social capital assert dominant interpretations of ocean waste that map its presence in accordance with existing social boundaries and attributions of responsibility. Such readings rely on processes of translation (Gal 2015) that omit critical aspects of, decontextualize, and promote ignorance about the ways that less powerful social actors, such as artisanal fishers, interpret and act on ocean waste and their reasons for doing so.[10]

UBIQUITY

The circulation of plastic waste exceeds important aspects of cultural politics and power in Peru, while it also reinforces significant components of existing inequalities. Microscopic plastic particles now circulate in ocean creatures, Antarctic ice, and even rain. The ubiquity of ocean plastic in all its forms surpasses state control as well as human efforts to clean it up. Cheap plastic has made a whole new set of capitalist exchanges possible while threatening the reproduction of life on a planetary scale. Efforts to address plastic pollution in Peru (as throughout much of the world) have focused primarily on cleaning up visible plastic trash on beaches and encouraging consumers to avoid single-use plastics, such as grocery bags and straws. While such campaigns have raised important awareness about plastic waste and pressured the Peruvian state to act on the issue, they also reinforce long-standing beliefs about "filth" and class in Lima as well as obscure the structural inequalities that limit different consumers' abilities to make choices about the plastic they use.

In Peru, NGOs run by people with considerable social capital have driven awareness and action on ocean plastic waste. Until recently, Peru has not had any national laws that dealt directly with the issue of plastic waste in the ocean. Local environmental activists have taken it upon themselves to coordinate with transnational environmental NGOs to coordinate beach cleanups and awareness campaigns, and pressure local and national governments in Peru to deal with plastic waste. The NGO Vida, run by Arturo Alfaro, has been at the forefront of these efforts. In 1999, Peru began participating in the Ocean Conservancy's International Coastal Cleanup initiative. Vida coordinated with the Peruvian Navy to organize annual beach cleanups around the country. Vida's staff recruit thousands of volunteers from Lima's *pueblos jóvenes* ("young towns," or informal settlements), schools, and universities as part of an effort to raise awareness about the problems with single-use plastics. As part of these cleanups, Vida volunteers also record the kinds and quantities of trash that are removed during its annual cleanup days. These results are then aggregated, summarized, and published in Ocean Conservancy's annual cleanup reports.[11] Vida's reports have demonstrated that, year in and year out, plastic has been the largest single category of waste on Peru's beaches, especially single-use bags and bottles. As Alfaro has stated in numerous published interviews, the purpose of these efforts is to put pressure on Peru's government to expand and subsidize recycling, to incentivize people to not throw away plastic waste, and to pass laws to reduce or ban the use of such plastics with the end goal of reducing the impact that plastic waste has on already-threatened marine life.

In recent years, a new generation of antiplastic campaigners have linked Vida's concerns for protecting Peru's marine environment from plastic contamination with concerns for social justice. Foremost among these has been the social enterprise Life Out of Plastic (LOOP). LOOP was founded in Lima in 2011 by Irene Hofmeijer and Nadia Balducci, who have sought to tackle the issue of plastic ocean waste in Peru and around the world by combining climate activism with gender empowerment. LOOP's team of coordinators and campaign leaders is comprised entirely of women. LOOP's team conduct sustainability workshops with Peruvian corporations and run social media campaigns aimed at raising awareness about plastic pollution and consumer as well as corporate responsibility. The enterprise works with women-run organizations to produce consumer goods—primarily tote bags that can replace disposable plastic shopping bags—from upcycled plastic bottles that have been converted into fabric. LOOP sells these items at their small headquarters and in several upscale boutiques in Lima and sells them to corporate sponsors who are interested in using them for green branding.

These initiatives reflect contemporary approaches to the "green" economy, which stress the idea that by buying the "right" kind of commodity consumers can initiate a whole chain of events that results in positive impacts for environments and the people who live or work in them.[12] Recycling plastic ocean waste has become a new, popular component of this economy. Green companies as well as corporations seeking to boost their environmental credentials are now offering everything from fashion sneakers to sunglasses to office chairs to single-use plastic bottles (really) made from recycled ocean plastic. LOOP staff present their tote bags and other products as "merchandising alternatives" for individuals or companies that are inspired to help conserve the ocean as well as promote environmental sustainability and social empowerment for the women who make these commodities. LOOP's credibility and brand as an alternative, green merchandizing enterprise have been established through its environmental campaigning, at the heart of which are its beach cleanup days.

Since 2013, LOOP has coordinated an annual beach cleanup campaign called "Hazla por tu playa" (Do it for your beach). In a relatively short period of time, "Hazla por tu playa" has become an international event that mobilizes approximately ten thousand volunteers in eleven countries in the Americas and Europe as well as every province in Peru. Like Vida, these volunteers not only clean up plastic waste along beaches but also record and publicly report the kinds of waste they collect. Marysol Naveda, a campaign director for LOOP since 2015, commented on the significance of these cleanup days in a 2019 interview posted to the Lima-based Conservamos por Naturaleza, a website curated by the Sociedad Peruana de Derecho Ambiental (SPDA, Peruvian Society of Environmental Law). After LOOP's volunteers helped to gather twenty metric tons of garbage from Peru's beaches, Naveda commented that

> the sea gives us energy, it soaks us with calm, and gives us life. Because of this, I decided to help it and teach others its importance in our lives. Each [piece of] garbage that is collected in the clean-ups invites us to reflect on how fortunate we are to live in a country that has the privilege to have a sea so close to it, which infects us with its happiness and refreshes us each summer, gives us food, and teaches us about the diversity that lives in it. (https://www.conservamospornaturaleza.org/noticia/dia-mar-peruano-marysol-naveda/)

These comments echo the goals on LOOP's website, such as inspiring "people to live a life in harmony with the ocean" and "empowering citizens to take action against plastic contamination" (http://loop.pe).

This vision creates a direct link between LOOP's potential volunteers and consumers with the Pacific Ocean by reading the latter as a space of recreation and a wild nature that needs care and protection from land-generated waste. This vision has garnered broad resonance throughout

Lima's elite social circles. In 2018 a high-end restaurant in the city partnered with Cerveza Corona on a "plastic ceviche" campaign. Customers at the restaurant were served ceviche—the "national" dish of Peru, which consists of fish tossed with lime, onions, and peppers—that was made entirely out of plastic. The customers' responses were circulated on social media. Since 2017, the municipal government of Miraflores has organized a 5K run, "Lima corre sin plástico" (Lima runs without plastic), to "create consciousness about care for the environment through the minimal use of plastic."[13] These efforts regularly gain positive coverage in Lima's local news media, and both LOOP and Vida played important roles in pressing municipal governments in Lima and Peru's state government to adopt official measures to reduce single-use plastics. In 2018, the Peruvian state passed a new law to regulate and phase out certain single-use plastics over a three-year period. The law prohibited businesses, such as grocery stores and restaurants, from distributing free plastic bags, plastic straws, and Styrofoam containers to consumers and instituted a tax on consumers who wanted plastic bags. The law also implemented a gradual ban on the importation, production, or distribution of plastic bags made of polymers that do not degrade easily. In 2019, the coastal district of Miraflores also passed a municipal ordinance that prohibited businesses from handing out single-use plastics on the first Wednesday of each month.

The success of antiplastic campaigns is worth noting in a country where the state has a long history of violent opposition to environmental activism. The ongoing criminalization and killings of activists have earned the country a reputation as a deadly place for environmentalists, especially Indigenous activists opposing extractive industries (and water contamination) in the Andes and Amazonian lowlands. The success of antiplastic campaigns is due in large part to how they have dovetailed with existing race-class geographies of coastal Lima and ongoing concerns with the contamination of those spaces. Visions of the ocean as a space for recreation and a nature in need of protection, such as those promoted by Vida and LOOP, obscure the complex race-class history of the ocean and people's unequal access to it in Lima (see chapter 1).

During the colonial era, the city's center was established on the Rímac River, away from the coast. Elite residents in Lima imagined the city's core to be the epicenter of power, whiteness, and urban culture—all of which decreased in potency the farther one moved from Lima's center (Panfichi

1995; Poole 1997). For much of the colonial era, the city's coast was a kind of hinterland, where Indigenous fishing communities existed outside the gaze of city officials and clergy (Flores Galindo 1991). Beginning in the late eighteenth century, wealthy residents traveled to the coast for recreation, eventually building summer homes and later resorts, such as the Lima Yacht Club. The imagined position of Lima's coast in elite race-class geographies changed in the twentieth century as a result of ongoing migration from the rest of the country, which resulted in a third of the national population living in Lima and thus collapsed elite distinctions between urban, white "national" culture and rural, Indigenous tradition. As Shane Greene (2016, 76) points out, Lima's elites had to rework these oppositions to confront this new reality and constantly sought ways (consumptive, spatial, bodily, and linguistic) to distinguish themselves from the city's masses, who they racialized as "cholos/as" (Indigenous people supposedly "out of place" in an urban environment). In response to urban migration, elites retreated to their beach homes and resorts on Lima's coast, making the districts such as Miraflores and San Isidro into the new, exclusive residential zones of the city. This move was accompanied by the development of this portion of the coast into a strip of human-made beaches connected to the coastal districts by a new expressway. Increased sewage in coastal waters from the city's booming population, increased car traffic, and trash along the beaches have threatened the image of the coast as a natural refuge. In response, residents of Lima's coastal districts regularly have decried the state of the zone's beaches and pressured the state to protect the area.

The issue of plastic beach waste fits neatly into this dynamic. Beach cleanups target the small (relative to that in other parts of the ocean) amount of highly visible plastic waste that washes up on Lima's beaches. Such cleanups perform the symbolic act of making local beaches less visibly "dirty" in addition to removing signs of the informal economies and urban "filth" (Gandolfo 2009) that surround the coastal districts, but which still make their way to the area's beaches via the city's rivers and ocean currents. Plastic bags, forks, straws, and plates are part and parcel of Lima's informal street-vendor economy and, like the sewage that teems through the area's waters, are yet another indication for local elites that their spaces of recreation have been despoiled by migrants who do not "belong" in the city.

Official statements and local media coverage of plastic ocean waste, beach cleanups, and the new law promote this interpretation. The dominant discourse surrounding the issue has emphasized consumer education, rather than highlighting how and why plastic has become such a central aspect of carbon capitalism in Peru and around the world. Commenting on plastic waste on Lima's beaches, Arturo Alfaro, the president of Vida, recently noted that various forms of plastic "end up in the ocean because of poor management of solid waste and a lack of awareness and citizen environmental education" (*Publimetro* 2018). While Peru's new law includes rolling restrictions on the production of certain kinds of plastic, media coverage of the law has stressed its importance for changing "Peruvians' 'chip' in regard to the excessive use of non-reusable bags" (Mayo 2018). Martín Vizcarra, Peru's then-president, asserted that the passage of the law would "change the comportment of our society to be friendlier to the environment" and argued that "we need to change the mentality" of Peruvians (*La República* 2018b). Awareness campaigns, such as Vida's and LOOP's, take this same focus of encouraging individual Peruvians to make better choices and recycle single-use plastics instead of throwing them away in order to, in the words of LOOP's website, "care for the oceans."[14] However, there has been only a very limited recycling capacity in Lima (much less the rest of Peru)—only certain numbered plastics can be recycled in Lima and only in certain (primarily wealthy, coastal) municipalities. Only a small portion of Lima's (mostly white-elite) residents can participate in the environmental citizenship that NGO- and government-backed antiplastic campaigns have promoted, which are based on caring for the ocean by taking individual responsibility to make "good" personal choices.

Antiplastic campaigners argue that this is a means of encouraging people to do what they can now and putting pressure on a reluctant state to expand capacity for recycling. By focusing on individual choices it also obscures the structural limitations that prevent the majority of Lima's residents from not only recycling but having their trash formally disposed of in official garbage dumps. Antiplastic campaigns that link care for the ocean as a recreational nature with responsible environmental citizens who properly dispose of their garbage subtly invoke and reinforce discourses of race-class, hygiene, and coastal contamination in Lima. These discourses are clearly apparent in the oceanic circulation of sewage in Lima and the discursive and material relationships that government officials and elite residents call into action to frame this waste as a product of Lima's lower classes.

CONTAMINATION

Plastic waste has emerged within global environmental discourse as one of the most pressing environmental issues facing the world's oceans. In contrast, the circulation of sewage and garbage do not have the same kind of global resonance, and many of Lima's residents see the contamination that emanates from them as a more local issue, one that clearly signifies issues in the city's social constitution and geography to a greater degree than plastic waste. Oceanic contamination, especially from sewage, carries with it a significantly greater perception of social filth—of bodily waste that should be distanced from people and made invisible as quickly as possible.

For many of Lima's elites, the ongoing presence of sewage in Lima's waters and solid waste garbage on its beaches have emerged as clear indicators of multiple social ills. First, elites add such contamination to ongoing criticism that state and municipal governments have failed to meet the basic responsibility of disposing of human waste and trash effectively. Second, elites often interpret such failings as the result of an influx of race-class Others from the provinces who have overwhelmed and informalized the city's infrastructure, resulting in coastal sewage contamination and the despoiling of local recreational spaces. Third, elites often have argued that such contamination has been intensified by a "deficiency" of "culture" among the city's impoverished residents, whose supposed lack of social education has meant that they see no problem with engaging in a host of behaviors that add to the contamination of Lima's waters and beaches. The city's elites and many government officials have read the circulation of ocean contamination in ways that are intensely racialized and classed.

Nowhere is this more apparent than the area where I began this chapter— the beaches surrounding the fishers' wharf in Chorrillos. The Playa Agua Dulce and Playa Pescadores are some of the most frequented beaches in Lima. Unlike much of the rocky coast in the rest of Lima, the beaches in Chorrillos are wide and sandy in large part because the slower, circular moving water in this part of the bay helps to deposit and maintain human-deposited sand on these beaches. Thousands of people use the area each summer. Many of these beachgoers are people who cannot afford to leave the city for their ocean recreation. However, the area is also used by local sports associations for training and borders the Lima Yacht Club, one of the most socially exclusive resort clubs in Lima. Urban elites often deride the area for being polluted, dirty, and neglected. Lima's television and newspaper reporters regularly feature the wharf and surrounding beaches as examples of government neglect and indicators of the lack of hygiene among the city's impoverished residents.

One such instance occurred on February 18, 2018, when the local television station TV Perú broadcast a story about the appearance of worms on the Playa Pescadores.[15] The story featured images of a bucket of seawater and sand that was full of small, wriggling white critters. A reporter for the station repeatedly pointed to and counted the number of worms he found on the beach or were being dug up by children as they played in the sand. Images of the beach showed that it was full of people, several of whom the reporter stopped to ask their opinions about the worms. One woman, who appeared surprised, replied that she did not know that there were worms on the beach. A man surmised that the small worms could get into children's mouths, noses, and ears, causing them illness. The reporter noted that he did not know the origins of the worms. Indeed, at no point in the broadcast did the reporter identify the worms. However, he assumed that they could be from people throwing their food trash in the water or leaving it on the beach. In response to the discovery, the Dirección General de Salud Ambiental e Inocuidad Alimentaria (DIGESA, General Directorate of Environmental Health and Food Safety) momentarily declared the beach unfit for recreation. The following day Silvana Sam, the director of DIGESA, reported to several news crews that she and her staff had "not seen" any worms and that they had done tests of the water at the Playa Pescadores, which confirmed that it was safe again for swimming and recreation. She also explained that there were various reasons why the worms could have shown up, such as a decaying animal, but that DIGESA staff did not find anything that would have been a clear source of the worms.[16]

In a separate interview, a lab director for DIGESA explained its criteria for deciding whether a beach is apt for bathing: water quality (bacteria levels need to be within an acceptable range), cleanness of the beach (which should not have any residue or contamination), and the presence of functioning and clean services for personal hygiene.[17] She emphasized that Playa Pescadores met the three criteria and, therefore, was acceptable for bathing. When asked why the worms appeared, she offered this: "It is evident that there were unhygienic conditions because we see these strange bodies in the sand. They could have entered for various reasons. It could have been that the sea brought in some animal that was decomposing, or some bather left garbage, and we could guess that this was the reason because already the following day, hours later, they were gone." Despite these findings, or nonfindings, as it were, word about the worms and contamination of the beach continued to circulate in Lima's media in ways that highlighted the race-class alterity of the area as a space of degradation, poor hygiene, and low-brow cultural practices.

The day after DIGESA's announcement that the beach was safe for swimming, a late-night talk show, *La Noche es Mía*, ran a sensationalized exposé titled "They Wash Clothes in Agua Dulce," with a subtitle of "The Last Straw, They Don't Just Leave Trash, Now They Wash Clothes."[18] The segment was introduced by the show's two hosts, a man and a woman sitting in a television studio who bantered about going to the beach. The man asked his cohost where she liked to go to the beach, to which she replied, "Punta Hermosa"—a beach community south of Lima that is popular among the city's elite. In response, he laughed and called her a "pituca"—a "snob," in Lima slang, which carries specific race-class connotations (see chapter 1). After some back and forth, he said to her, barely containing his laughter, "You should go to Agua Dulce where there are worms in the sea." The worms were found on the neighboring Playa Pescadores, not Agua Dulce. But here the beaches were used interchangeably to signal the social and cultural alterity of the zone. After some more banter, the male host added, "In Agua Dulce, they are washing clothes. And the sea, how is it doing?" The show then cut to a phone video that a viewer had submitted of people washing clothes at one of the freshwater springs along the northern stretch of the beach, which led the show to send a reporter and a camera crew to see what was going on. The show also alerted the police.

The broadcast then jumped to footage of two women wading in a freshwater pool with clothes around them drying on the rocks and a shirtless man standing near a truck. The reporter approached them and asked, accusingly, what they were doing. The man replied several times that they were just "taking water from the spring" because they did not have any at their house in San Juan de Lurigancho, the most populous district of Lima and one with extensive poverty. Within elite-imagined geographies of the city, the district is often associated with crime and symbolizes the problems of the city's rapid expansion. As the camera focused on the man, viewers could hear the reporter's voice saying things such as, "Who does this [beach] belong to, mister?"

and "You are invading the beach." The reporter later stated, with dramatic music playing in the background and images of laundry brushes and soaking clothes, that they captured images of people washing clothes on the beach because they had been alerted by local bathers who were indignant that part of this "beach of the people had been taken" by these "planet aggressors" who were contaminating the water with their detergent and soap. The reporter engaged in repeated acts of public shaming, at one point grabbing one of the empty packs of laundry soap the women were using and holding it up to the camera while saying, "This is what is contaminating our beaches." At the end of the segment, when the view cut back to the studio and the male host, all he said was "My poor little country."

This commentary is emblematic of elite gazes of Lima's urban coastal geography that frame contamination as the direct result of the poor choices and cultural practices of the city's impoverished residents. Within this gaze, the beaches where white-elites once engaged in practices of bathing and bodily cleansing that marked their social status are now viewed (with indignation) as areas where people wash their clothes, eat lunch, and presumably throw their waste into the ocean. This view obscures the reality that there is no way that water contamination in Lima's waters could be the result of a few people washing their clothes! Levels of solid waste and bacteria are produced by various sources, such as illegal trash dumping by municipal governments or construction companies. Arguably the most significant source of contamination is Lima's aging and overburdened sewage system that spews tons of waste into the ocean every hour. Everyone, regardless of social status, contributes to the production and circulation of human waste through Lima's sewage system. The ocean along Lima's coast is part of this system. Waste is dumped into the ocean every hour of every day, and the ocean's currents circulate this waste and the bacteria that emanate from it, concentrating it in some areas and dispersing it in others. This circulation of waste is largely invisible in day-to-day life, especially for most residents who do not spend time working, surfing, or swimming in the water. Even for those individuals, the bacteria itself is invisible, only its effects—in the forms of skin rashes, eye infections, or gastrointestinal illnesses—are usually apparent.

DIGESA's water testing momentarily stops the circulation of this waste and makes it visible in the form of a narrow range of test results primarily for coliform bacteria, which is used as a proxy of overall water quality. This process fixes the circulation of waste in a specific place and a particular moment in time, closely associating specific beaches with the filth of sewage, while absolving others. DIGESA has records of its beach quality testing that date to 1986, when it began monitoring twelve beaches in Lima for water quality. By 2002, DIGESA had expanded its monitoring to its current number of 234 beaches around the country.[19] On its website, DIGESA cites UN conferences on the environment and sustainable development as a critical factor that led to the creation of the beach-monitoring program. Testing also reflected elite concerns with local water quality in Lima. In 1990, only one beach had water quality that DIGESA reported to be "very good"—the majority of beaches surveyed were classified as having "bad" water quality, which meant that they had between 1,000 and 4,000 Most Probable Number (MPN) per 100 ml of thermotolerant coliform (CT).[20] Thermotolerant bacteria can reproduce at high temperatures (e.g., 37–45 degrees Celsius) and although they are found throughout the environment, they are present in high numbers in human and animal feces and are used as an indicator of sewage contamination in Peru and in water testing programs around the world (WHO 2017).[21] Coliform makes seawater social—not only do thermotolerant coliform come primarily from people and their sewage but the presence of thermotolerant bacteria becomes a social indicator of particular beaches and areas, and of the sea in Lima in general. In this context, bacteria are translated into a marker of social contamination.

DIGESA checks the water quality of Lima's beaches every month during the summer bathing season and reports its findings online. These results circulate widely and are featured in local newspaper and television stations' lists of beaches that are reported to be *apta* (fit) or *no apta* (unfit) for swimming. DIGESA also uses a system of flags to mark the status of individual beaches. Red flags that read *no saludable* (not healthy) are planted at beaches, marking them as no-go zones for swimming, surfing, and other water-based recreation. At the outset of the summer of 2020, DIGESA certified twenty-five beaches in Lima as *saludable* (healthy), while forty-four were considered *no saludable*. DIGESA provided updated information about each beach.[22] One of the beaches listed as unfit for bathing was Playa Pescadores, because even though the water quality was acceptable and there were functioning hygiene services, the level of cleanliness on the beach was deemed to be unacceptable. As the DIGESA official noted above, the presence of waterborne bacteria is one of three factors that the office uses to determine beach quality. The others are functioning bathrooms and the presence or absence of solid waste on the beach itself. While bacteria are invisible indicators of social filth that the state makes visible through testing, elites and state officials have long associated hygienic practices with indices of race-class status in Lima.

In January 2019, DIGESA again declared all the beaches in Chorrillos to be unfit for bathing because of the presence of garbage on the shore. On January 8, ATV Noticias, a local station, ran an extended report on the situation, which featured a reporter on site at the wharf in Chorrillos.[23] At the outset of the segment, the reporter pointed to a large pile of garbage near the old boats and showed that there were seagulls and pigeons feasting on the trash, which was spilling out of plastic bags onto the beach. The reporter explained that garbage trucks from the municipality had not been picking up the trash and that young people training on the beach had to run past the garbage. The camera then cut to footage of teenagers from a local cycling club jogging past the garbage on their way to the adjoining yacht club. The reporter walked down onto the beach next to the wharf and showed the garbage that had washed up on shore, from old tires to plastic food containers. At one point, the reporter reeled at what he described as the foul smell of the beach. The anchorperson for the show offered voiced-over commentary from a studio in Lima and occasionally was shown using a split screen. She repeatedly exclaimed that the beach was a *basurero* (dump) and lamented that it was one of the most frequented of the Costa Verde's beaches. While the camera panned over images of garbage on the beach, the anchorperson stated with exasperation that the "absolute contamination" of the area was an "embarrassment." As she was saying that, the camera cut to previously recorded footage of the beach full of people and jumped from one shot to another of ambulant food vendors and people sitting on the beach eating snacks. The reporter then responded that the area was a "source of contamination" in part because local currents concentrate and deposit garbage on the beach next to the wharf, and in part because so many people go to the beach and leave all of their food garbage there, resulting in a "a completely contaminated ocean." The anchorperson echoed this, exclaiming that the area was a "source of infection and absolute contamination for children and athletes, for everyone who comes to Agua Dulce." The camera focused on a lone surfer paddling out on his board, while the anchor said, "How sad! Imagine it!" and the reporter noted that the surfer was paddling his board "amid trash" because, as the reporter inferred, the surfer "had become accustomed to it." The anchorperson finished by calling on Augusto Miyashiro, the former mayor of Chorrillos, to do something about the situation and resolve the problems that the municipality was having with its sanitation services and Fabiola Muñoz, the minister of the environment, to look at the images of the beach and act.

The beaches in Chorrillos are often on the list of waters that are unfit for swimming because of high bacteria levels and waste on the beaches. For the many residents of Lima who do not have the financial means to leave the city for beach recreation, the Agua Dulce and Pescadores beaches are their best options for public recreation. This represents a significant example of how impoverished people are often exposed to greater environmental harm and toxicity, even in recreational activities. Elites in Lima conflate the presence of impoverished residents flocking to Chorrillos's polluted beaches during the summer as a sign of shame for the city and an indication of the cultural alterity of the city's poor, who supposedly do not know any better and make bad choices about where they swim, while also treating these areas badly by leaving their trash there. This reading of ocean contamination clearly obscures the structural factors—such as a lack of proper landfills or adequate sewage processing facilities—that produce excess, untreated sewage, and garbage in places such as Chorrillos. This reading also obscures significant inequalities in mobility and the fact that most of Lima's population is unable to do what the city's wealthy residents have done in recent decades—flee to more pristine beach communities south of the city for their summer recreation.

Finally, elite interpretations of ocean contamination deny the knowledge that people who spend time in the water in Chorrillos may have not only about pollution but about the broader ecosystem as well. Elite interpretations obscure this knowledge by promoting the idea that poor people make bad choices about where they swim because they are ignorant. These interpretations reduce Lima's coastal areas to recreational spaces that are threatened by the sewage and trash of impoverished residents. Elite residents and government officials regularly have levied such accusations against local artisanal fishers in Chorrillos and throughout Peru. In a report on the state of marine waste in Peru prepared for the Comisión Permanente del Pacífico Sur (Permanent Commission of the South Pacific), Vida's president Arturo Alfaro (2007, 86–87) detailed the structural issues in Peru that contributed to marine waste, such as the ongoing lack of sufficient treatment for Lima's sewage. At the end of the report, Alfaro (2007, 94) provided an analysis of the situation and suggestions for future action, focusing on three things: the inefficiency of municipal garbage collection, a lack of regulation over ocean dumping, and "environmental education for artisanal fishers and operators in docks and ports." Alfaro justified the last with a one-sentence statement that fishers are "frequently observed" throwing things into the ocean they no longer "find useful."

The knowledge and experiences of local artisanal fishers reveal how wrong these elite assumptions are. Fishers in Chorrillos see waste as one of many things that circulates in the bay's water that they must consider as they work to navigate and help to reproduce the local ecology. They talk about the bay as a place where multiple beings make their lives—fishers and vendors, but also fish, shellfish, sea lions, birds, and so on. Fishers read the water in ways that take this into account, focusing on the color of the water and what it tells them about when and where fish might be moving, what temperature the water is, and how much it is contaminated. These readings enable forms of care in which environmental, cultural, and economic relationships are bound together and recreated on a daily basis. These forms of care are critical for reproducing local coastal ecologies, but they are largely obscured by elite readings of waste circulation along Lima's coast.

THE COLOR OF WATER

On May 17, 2018, I woke to the bed and walls in my room shaking. It took a moment for me to realize what was happening, but once I did, I shot out of bed and ran to the small terrace outside my room. The shaking stopped in a few seconds, and I went back into the room, quickly showered, got dressed, and headed out to see what was going on at the wharf. The TV was on in the bakery where I stopped to get breakfast, and according to the news, the earthquake had been a 5.5 on the Richter scale. The epicenter was just south of Lima near the small city of Mala. There were no reports of deaths or major damage, but apparently the ocean had withdrawn fifteen meters from its usual limit on the beaches near Mala. Sources from the Peruvian navy and the Instituto Geofísico del Perú (Geophysical Institute of Peru) reported that there was not a threat of a tsunami, but that they would continue to monitor the situation. After digesting the morning's news, I decided to walk to the wharf instead of taking a taxi. Walking would give me a chance to watch the ocean and see if there was any noticeable damage to buildings or streets.

In a little bit less than an hour I was at the dock. The ocean was calm. It was the beginning of the winter season. The sky was a uniform gray, and it was chilly near the water. The dock was quiet. I made my way through the wharf toward a group of three fishers I knew who were huddled together on one of the concrete benches near the beach. They were all dressed in warm clothes—heavy jackets on top of sweaters and stocking caps. When I have gone out fishing, I always have been struck by how cold it is on the open water, even during the summer. I greeted the fishers and sat down with them. They all were complaining that the fishing was bad, and it was not worth going out that day. The weather had been poor, and the water was cold, which meant that few fish were moving into the bay. There were some *pejerrey* (*Odontesthes regia*, Peruvian silverside), a small fish that likes cold water and comes very close to shore during the winter. There were also limited amounts of *lorna* (*Sciaena deliciosa*, drum) and *lisa* (*Mugil cephalus*, striped mullet), equally common local staples. The best fishing was at night, so one of them commented that he would head out later to put out his nets and see if he could catch anything.

Conversations like this are daily occurrences among fishers on the wharf. They represent important means through which fishers engage with, interpret, and modify knowledge about the ocean. Fishers see the ocean as a constantly changing seascape, one that they must learn how to read to make a living through their navigations of the physical space of the ocean and the myriad ecological relationships that comprise it. Fishers talk about the ocean as an active entity that engages them while they engage with it. It is an entity that both enables their lives and threatens it, binding them in a relationship that requires knowledge, care, and respect. A lifelong Chorrillos fisher, César, put it this way: "The sea pulls, well, it pulled me [in] because I could have left and studied something else, but from an early age I had to go to work in fishing. I liked it. Listen, even though it has worked me over and my friends have died [at sea]." Fishers and vendors often talk about the dock and the ocean as their real homes, the places where they feel most relaxed and where they find refuge from the bustle of the city. They often comment that when they are in their houses, they feel restless and all they can think about is getting back to the water. Luis once said that "the sea restores one's life here. I would like to be in the water before being in my house. I am used to being here at sea. I have lived here for forty-two years of my life." He went on, saying that for him the most important thing is to get out into the ocean, because "you feel better, in the water you are entertained. You go out and see the animals."

Fishers see the ocean as their home and refuge, but they also think about it as the territory of different creatures that engage in active relationships with them. Species of fish constantly are on the move—they come and go as seasons change and as water conditions improve or deteriorate, warming or cooling with shifting currents. Fishers' knowledge about these circulations and changes is grounded in their daily practices of engagement with the wind, ocean, waves, animals, fish, and each other. Through these engagements individual fishers learn to read the water and update these readings according to changing conditions. "Everything is already included there," Luis once told me, pointing to his head. "When you are walking from your house [to the dock], you already leave thinking where you can go. That is right. That is how fishing is. There are others who do not know and sometimes are lucky and find a little place [where the fish are]. But the creatures run, they do not stay on one side, they run there, they run here." Knowing where to find a good catch relies on constantly updated interpretations of the water and weather conditions for different seasons or during shifts from one season to another. Domingo, who has fished Chorrillos for close to fifty years, explained to me that "each fish has its season." "The season for lisa is beginning," he said, because "the lisa enter during the warm water season [and] lorna is [when] waters are cold." On that specific day, Domingo complained that fishing was not possible, because the "sea is rough, it's not possible with this current." Pointing out to the bay, he said, "Look at how many boats are anchored. Some have gone out, but only a few. Because there are not many fish. It seemed like it wanted to improve about a month ago. It seemed like the fishing wanted to improve, but then these waters entered and cooled everything. There was another color of water [that came in]." What was he going to do? "I will watch now and see if something comes in," he commented, explaining that "first this water comes in and then after it, the fish."

Fishers emphasize the importance of the color of the water as a means of interpreting changes and understanding when conditions are favorable (or not). Fishers use color to read water temperature, turbidity, seasonal changes, and pollution—all of which help them to think below the surface and anticipate what is happening with the daily or seasonal movement of different fish, creatures, and contaminants. Luis put it this way during one of our conversations: "Every day you go out and every day you are looking at the environment, where more or less you are going to go fishing." He added that "the color of the water is important, the color of the water changes. You realize this and you have to keep looking for that water." Similarly, César reinforced the importance of watching the color of the water in the bay, because, as he put it, "Every fish comes with its waters." He elaborated on this in greater detail, noting as an example:

> Around the bend [there in the bay], where the *corvina* [*Cilus gilberti,* corvina drum] enters, you can see the water is a green color. This is the little color that brings the corvina. There you can get them. As my uncle told you, every fish goes with its waters. If you see medium red, a little red, [it is] warm. There is the lisa. You already know. If it is red, red, it is because it has some mud. From experience the fisher already knows that if he sees these waters they are good. He already knows that he will net some fish. Sometimes if the water appears white, it would be cold. There is nothing [in white water], you will not take anything. Sometimes, the water is cold but only to a certain depth. Down to a certain depth, but below it is warm. There is lorna.

These comments were from a conversation with César in 2018, the year after a coastal El Niño brought unseasonal warming and flooding to coastal Peru (see chapter 3). César explained that the water in the bay was much too red for fishing—it meant that there was too much mud and debris in the water. At the outset of the warming, there was some good lisa fishing, but then once the water became full of effluent from the local rivers that were flooding, there was too much in the water, even for lisa. He and other fishers had to head farther out to look for better water. Following the warming, he noted that the water had changed to white. There was too much white water that had "not left many fish."

Fishers' knowledge of changing water conditions is critical for navigating an increasingly compromised local ecology, and fishers are constantly modifying and adapting this knowledge to read these changes in efforts to maintain their livelihoods. Urban pollution and industrial overfishing combined with climate change have led to declines in local fish populations in Chorrillos over the past fifty years. One might assume that given the current situation of precarity that artisanal fishers face, that they would pursue their own best interests by taking as many fish as possible to earn more money, thus leading to a crash in the local ecology. That is not what has happened. Declines in local fishing combined with the growing cost of living in Lima and the low social and economic value placed on manual fishing labor in the city's political economy have made it difficult to make it as a fisher.[24] In response to this situation, artisanal fishers in Chorrillos have placed increased emphasis on care of the local ecology in their conversations not only with me but with each other, as they have discussed the state of the local fishery. Fishers in Chorrillos often told me how many spawning grounds there were in the bay in Chorrillos, also noting that there used to be even more when conditions were better. They talked about the importance of avoiding those spawning grounds during the seasons in which different species reproduced—complaining that larger artisanal boats that were not from Chorrillos or small industrial boats ignored this when they sometimes passed through the bay scooping up whatever they could to fill their holds. Unlike industrial boats, artisanal fishers' livelihoods are based primarily on a local fishery and what it can produce. Fishing is not just an economic activity; it is also an ecological and a cultural one.[25] Fishing provides people who lack social capital in Lima's political economy with a sense of dignity and autonomy. Fishers and vendors in Chorrillos talk about the ocean as a second home because it is a place where that dignity and autonomy is created, enabled, and renewed on a daily basis.[26] Care for local fish populations and for the ocean is not purely motivated by economic interest—they feel a personal responsibility to the place.

Ana was a vendor who had worked on the dock for a decade and had helped her father, a local shellfish diver, while she was growing up in Chorrillos. She summed up the contrast between industrial and artisanal approaches, saying that "the fish industry sucks up and destroys everything [right down to] the little [fish]. They take everything." But artisanal fishers are "conscious, because if you know you are going to kill juveniles, when you come to fish [again] you will find nothing." Describing how he approached care for the local ecology, César once elaborated on this responsibility, saying,

Yes, I take care of it. I take care of it. There are people who throw plastic [into the ocean]. I pick it up. There are people who throw boards. I get them out and take them over there [to the garbage]. Everything I pick up in my net, everything that is trash and that will not break down, I take and put it in a bag and throw it out over there [in the trash]. I do not throw stuff in the sea. Even better, I take out things that are in the sea. Why would I contaminate the sea?

César explained that he does not "clean" the beach, he "cares" for it. For him, cleaning was something that one does for pay, such as a municipal trash worker who sweeps up garbage only because he or she is paid to do it. In contrast, care was something that he did out of respect and a connection to a particular place and his feelings for it. "No one has taught us how to take care of things," he remarked, "it is just what one knows."

There are limits to what fishers can do to care for their bay's degraded ecology. The complex attitudes and understandings that fishers have about pollution, especially invisible sewage bacteria contamination, reflect this reality. Most of the fishers I have known and interviewed over the years have acknowledged that sewage and other urban contaminants were a problem and tried to adapt to it. During the summer months, when warm water temperatures promoted the growth of bacteria in nearshore waters, many fishers would head out or they said they would target fish species that moved into the bay and then moved out, as opposed to fish who stayed close to shore.[27] Luis once told me that some fishers would target the area near the La Chira discharge because some species of fish would gather there to feed on the waste. He refused to do that and said that none of the fishers he knew in Chorrillos would do it either because of the health issues and the responsibility they felt toward the people who were going to buy or eat the fish they caught, which often included their own family members. Fishing near La Chira is an extreme measure. The reality of day-to-day fishing and the choices that fishers make about where they fish and what they catch is more complex.

Government health officials have told fishers and divers that certain fish and shellfish from the bay are not safe to eat because of local contamination. Despite such warnings, fishers have continued to harvest these species and sell them. There are real limits on the choices fishers can make about what they catch and sell and under what conditions, given that the local waters on which they rely are environmentally contaminated. Luis and many other fishers tried to minimize the impacts of this by arguing that levels of contamination in the bay were probably not that bad, given that the socially exclusive Yacht Club was right next door, and some of its members used the

same waters to sail or swim (althou
or sat in beach chairs looking out c
even told me that they thought th
health. One pointed out an olde
had done so for as long as the fi
that he knew an older fisher v
and never got sick.

Fishers constantly draw
able to them through their daily pr
to assess and reassess the risk that largely invis
to them, to local fauna, to fish consumers, or to beachgoe
know there is bacterial contamination in Lima's near-shore waters, the
tion they are always assessing is: Just how bad is it, really? As Luis pointed
out, he and the fishers he knows would not fish right near the sewage discharge, because they knew contamination levels would be too high to safely
consume fish. What about the water farther from the discharge that sur-
rounds the wharf? What about in winter, when the water is colder and there
is more movement in the bay versus the summer? These are questions that
fishers reevaluate using their experiences of what the water is doing, what
color it is during what seasons, how healthy fish look when they are caught,
what happens to the people around them who regularly eat fish and spend
time in the water, and what they need to earn on a given day to cover their
expenses and have enough to live. Drawing on these diverse sources of data,
fishers often conclude that water contamination in Chorrillos is not as bad
as government officials claim. Fishers' and their families' livelihoods rely on
people coming to the dock not only to buy fish but also use the dock and the
beach. Furthermore, fishers and vendors do not have the social or economic
capital simply to move to another place to find better economic or ecological
conditions—such mobility is something that is a privilege of the city's social
and economic elites, who have moved their beach homes and resorts farther
and farther away from the city. Fishers have had to accept that certain levels
of contamination are not only unavoidable but also out of their control.

This attitude often has been mistaken as complacency by government
officials and Lima's elites, who have targeted the fishing wharf in Chorrillos
as an eyesore and a site of contamination and pressured the local fishing
association to do more to clean up the area. During the period when I was
doing research, city and state officials pressured fishers to improve the dock's

wastewater system
to provide the n
were stuck in
not being a
three fis

.[29] However, fishers retorted that officials were not willing
cessary services or money for such improvements, so fishers
a constant cycle of being reprimanded by the government but
ble to do anything to resolve the situation. In an interview in 2013,
hers expressed frustration with this dynamic.

FISHER 1: When they see improvements [to the area, they say,] "Look, this
    beach has the beach area, the little walkway, [which are] all beautiful,
    everything beautiful. And this, what's this [referring to the wharf]?"
FISHER 2: Every day it was full of boats and [they were] buried over there
    and the walkway was full of trash.
FISHER 3: Full of trash.
FISHER 2: We cleaned it, we took out the boats and moved them over there
    [pointing to an area away from the beach]
FISHER 1: Before [this part of the beach] was full of old boats.
FISHER 3: Little by little we have to do what can be done.

They complained that they had done their part to take care of the wharf and
the bay—they had done "what can be done" given the resources that they
had and the scope of the problem.

Fishers' ways of caring for the wharf and the bay overlap with and are
informed by state regulations and pressure from officials. Government officials neither recognized this care nor provided fishers with the necessary
resources to undertake large development projects on the wharf, such as
rebuilding the wastewater system from the fish market, which dumped
directly into the bay near the beach. State practices of monitoring water quality and elite depictions of garbage on the area's beaches make most aspects
of fishers' care invisible through the processes of translating and scaling up
that officials and local elites use to translate local instances of pollution into
indicators of broader environmental, governmental, and social problems.

State water monitoring isolates certain facts of water quality, such as coliform bacteria content, to establish consistent measures of contamination
across time and space, which can be scaled up from local testing sites to
government labs to national reporting (and can be effectively communicated
to global scientific communities). For this process, measurable aspects of
water contamination in Chorrillos must be decontextualized and isolated
from the web of relationships that fishers understand and work to maintain.

State water monitoring does not document this understanding or work. State reporting on water quality in Chorrillos only indicates if the water is unfit for swimming because there is too much bacteria or there is too much solid waste on the beach. It does not (and cannot) report that local fishers or other people who regularly use the area have developed ways of reading the water that help them to recognize when it may be more polluted and use this information to modify their activities, or that they have engaged in regular cleanings of the beach, but the lack of municipal trash services in Lima means that the tide of plastic waste or local food garbage is too much for them to keep up with on a daily basis. Similarly, elite media shaming of impoverished fishers and beachgoers is only possible if such relationships of local knowledge and care are obscured and ignored when instances of local contamination or garbage are scaled up from Chorrillos and reported in broadcasts that circulate throughout Lima or Peru or around the world (for example, via YouTube or social media). Elite framings of ocean contamination as indicators of social filth misattribute responsibility for such contamination to local people in ways that obscure not only the limitations that such local actors have in dealing with extralocal contamination but also the role those elite residents play in producing sewage waste and garbage that circulates in the ocean and the responsibility that they have as individuals with greater social capital to do something about it.

WASTE/WATER

The appearance and recognition of ocean waste represent critical moments in which relationships of power and inequality are produced and reinforced through the symbolic frameworks that different people use to attach meaning to such waste and the ways in which they translate these meanings from one context or scale to another. When scaling up or down the issue of coastal waste, state officials and elite commentators blame local fishers or beachgoers for Lima's contamination, while obscuring the structural inequalities and systemic inadequacies in the city's (and the world's) waste infrastructure, which are the culprits for increased ocean garbage. As the fact of sewage pollution gets scaled up from local fishers' approaches to the presence of such pollution to state government tests for specific bacteria to media reports on the safety of Lima's beaches, the knowledge and care that fishers employ to navigate their compromised ecology is undercut and stripped away. This process of translation also cuts out broader relationships of accumulation and circulation that produced such waste in the first place and unequally exposed different groups of people to it based on their socioeconomic position within Lima's urban political economy. It is only through such translations that elite recounting of coastal pollution can assign responsibility for "out of place" waste with supposedly "out of place" people, the people who presumably lack the "culture" to care for local coastal ecologies and themselves by picking up their trash, not using so much disposable plastic, or simply going elsewhere.

This dynamic is readily apparent in the ways that state and municipal government officials and local environmental groups have rescaled and translated the global issue of ocean-borne plastics into national- and local-level campaigns targeted at changing the consumptive and hygienic practices of individual Peruvians. Such discourses subtly reinforce and call into existence long-standing elite discourses that link geophysical contamination with social filth and blame environmental contamination on socially marginalized people. State government systems of monitoring beaches to decide which are "apt" for recreation as well as local media coverage of beach infestations and garbage often include the public shaming of people who use the areas despite their contamination. Elite assumptions and discourses about ocean waste overlook the intricate ways in which impoverished artisanal fishers, who are often the targets of elite scorn regarding the filth of the beaches in Chorrillos, engage in various forms of care and relationships of responsibility for the more-than-human web that comprises the local ecology.

The reproduction of such inequalities in how ocean waste is understood is significant not only for thinking about how social and ecological dynamics are linked around waste in Peru. In the past decade, the issue of ocean waste and contamination has risen to the forefront of global environmental campaigns to save the ocean. Such campaigns have sought to address plastic waste through the invocation of different kinds of green economy solutions, such as LOOP's upcycling project, or proposals for geoengineering, such as Ocean Cleanup's attempts to gather floating waste with a barrier and net system. Such schemes have become dominant ways of responding not only to plastic pollution but to other global environmental and climate issues as well.[30] The problem is that both reduce issues such as ocean waste to a narrow set of economic and technological considerations while obscuring the complex biological, social, political, and historical relationships that comprise ocean ecologies (and which are tenuously held together in artisanal fishers' interpretations of different circulations in Lima's waters).[31] Moreover, such schemes also enable forms of environmental care that reproduce inequalities regarding who can participate (e.g., who has the capital necessary to engage in the green economy), who wields the technology necessary for geoengineering, and who decides what issues or what places require care (among other things).

CHAPTER 3

PRECARIOUS WEATHER

I was hot when I visited Lima during the first two weeks of March 2017. At the end of Peru's austral summer the days are normally sunny and warm. That year they were sweltering. Warming waters from an El Niño Costero (coastal El Niño) raised temperatures several degrees Celsius above average temperatures. On the morning of March 15, I stood under the roof of the fish market on the wharf in Chorrillos. Fishers were spending most of their days selling fish or mending nets in the shaded areas of the wharf and going out to fish during the evening or at night. I was talking to Enrique, a young fisher, when he motioned over to one of the cleaning tables where there were fish arranged for sale. Enrique pointed to small pile of fish that I had not seen before in the market. They were long and thin with silvery-blue sides and pointed mouths full of small teeth. I asked him what they were, and he responded *marao ojón*. Agujon needlefish (*Tylosurus pacificus*) are open-ocean fish normally found in tropical waters off the coast of northern Peru (see figure 9). However, they were showing up, at least in small numbers, in Lima's usually cold waters because of the coastal warming. Just a few days before, Enrique had waved me over to a bucket of water and pulled out a *langosta* (*Panulirus gracilis*, lobster). These lobsters normally range from Baja California to northern Peru, but during El Niño warming cycles can be found as far south as Pucusana, a small port just south of Lima.

FIGURE 9 Needlefish in the fish market on the Chorrillos wharf in March 2017. Photo by Maximilian Viatori.

Coastal warming presents numerous challenges for artisanal fishers in Lima. Fish that prefer colder water and are popular with consumers disappear, while fish that like warm water show up in such abundance that prices are depressed to the point that fishers often cannot sell them for a profit. After spending several hours talking about this situation with Enrique, I decided it was time for me to head back to my hostel and get ready for my flight out of Lima later that night. I often stayed at a hostel in a quiet neighborhood in the outer edge of the district of Miraflores, near where it meets the centrally located district of Surquillo. The hostel was about six kilometers from the dock. I walked first to a restaurant in the nearby district of Barranco and then slowly made my way to the hostel, trying to enjoy my last bits of Lima's summer sun.

It was early evening when the hostel's owner knocked on the door to my room and said that the driver I had hired to take me to the airport had called. I had asked him to pick me up at 9 p.m. so that I could get to the airport with enough time to check in for my 1 a.m. flight. Normally, the twenty-kilometer ride from the hostel to the airport in Callao takes about forty-five minutes. However, the driver suggested that he pick me up as soon as possible. Traffic to and from the airport was moving at a snail's pace, and he thought it might take us several hours to get there. Gridlock has been an ongoing problem in Lima, where the number of cars expands each year. Traffic delays that evening were not the result of normal congestion. They were the product of *huaicos*.

A huaico is a flash flood that is caused by heavy rains that carry mud, rocks, debris, and anything else in their path downstream, creating a fast-moving wall of sludge that scours riverbanks, floods roads, and destroys houses and bridges before spewing a brown slurry into the ocean. The surface temperature of the Pacific Ocean along Peru's coast was unusually warm in January, February, and March 2017, which created the conditions for torrential rains. Coastal cities in northern Peru were devastated by the flooding, which left thousands of people without homes and cut off from aid because of collapsed bridges and destroyed roads. From January to early March, rains that were heavier than they had been in almost twenty years fell in the mountain districts of eastern Lima Province. The capital city of Lima sits on a thin ribbon of coastal desert between the Andes mountains and the Pacific Ocean. Approximately fifty kilometers east of the city, the Rímac River and the Chillón River emerge from the mountains and begin their steep descents to Lima's urban core before emptying into the Pacific Ocean. Beginning in January, the town of Chosica, where the main stem of the Rímac River begins, suffered a series of huaicos that flooded streets and buildings, filling them with mud and debris. The steep, arid western slopes of the mountains outside of Lima are largely devoid of vegetation that would help to hold the sandy, rocky soil in place. Normally this is not a problem, given the scant amount of rain that these areas receive in an average year. During weather anomalies, such as the one that occurred in early 2017, downpours trigger landslides. On March 14, torrential rains in Chosica lasted for almost nine hours. Huaicos erupted from four ravines, destroying homes and bridges and flooding the main highway that connects the town to Lima. Downriver, the Rímac River and the Huaycoloro River, which joins the Rímac about fifteen kilometers west of central Lima, swelled. On March 15, the Rímac River spilled its banks in Lima and Callao and flooded neighborhoods, parks, and roads.

The Rímac River forms the boundary between Lima and Callao, where the international airport is located. As rush-hour traffic encountered ever-growing flooding, streets in central Lima and Callao ground to a halt. The next day Lima's media featured images of the recently constructed Puente Talavera, a pedestrian bridge that connected El Agustino and San Juan de Lurigancho, which had collapsed and fallen into the Rímac River. The most iconic and widely circulating images of the huaicos were those of Evangelina Chamorro Díaz, a thirty-two-year-old woman who was swept up in a mudslide on the outskirts of Lima. A brief video clip circulated around the world of Chamorro emerging from a pool of detritus, covered from head to toe in tan mud like a human-sized clay figure. According to reports, Chamorro survived the experience largely unscathed and was celebrated in Lima's media and by local and national politicians as a symbol of Peruvian bravery and courage in the face of the natural disaster.

Flooding, displacements, and the threat of diseases continued in northern Peru, while in Lima water service was cut off in many parts of the city and schools were closed for over a week. The unfolding disaster led to a range of responses both within and outside of Peru. Among them were calls for calm by the president, Pedro Pablo Kuczynski, who tried to reassure Peruvians that the flooding was not a disaster and that the central government would be able to quickly handle damage control and reconstruction. Rival politicians criticized the central state for being slow in its response and pointed out that regional governments had not spent sufficiently or transparently on disaster preparation. Others questioned why government meteorologists and scientists had not been able to predict the torrential rains, especially in a country that experienced regular oceanic warming events that had caused numerous natural disasters in previous decades and centuries. Some analysts outside of Peru claimed that the disaster was evidence that the Peruvian government had not done enough to plan for climate change–related disasters. Urban planners and development specialists pointed out that the worst destruction in Lima was a result of rampant informal settlement along the city's flood plains.

In this chapter, I examine how different actors talked about Peru's 2017 coastal El Niño in their efforts to define it, identify appropriate responses to it, and assign blame for its destructive effects. While such warming events regularly occur in the eastern Pacific, this episode of localized warming caught government scientists and officials off guard, leading to debates over how to classify and respond to it. Through analyses of scientific reports and discussions, media coverage of the coastal El Niño, and ethnographic data, I trace how the oceanic and atmospheric event came to be a sociopolitical event through varying interactions, engagements, predictions, and experiences of its physical effects. Central to my analysis is an exploration of how different actors established the scale, temporality, and impacts of the coastal El Niño. Was it predictable, and if so, how far in advance? Did the event represent a crisis that required deep changes to Peruvian politics or society? Was the event an isolated disaster? Was it part of a recurring cycle? How long would the impacts of the disaster last?

These questions are important departures for not only thinking about how people experienced the 2017 coastal El Niño but also as a way of exploring how people make sense of weather amid the unfolding climate crisis, when meteorological unpredictability and instability have become the norm. Anthropologists studying the relationships between social life and the atmosphere have emphasized the importance of examining how people talk about "nature," "weather," and "climate."[1] People use these concepts to group numerous natural phenomena and cultural experiences in historically specific ways. Tim Choy (2011, 145) argues that considering the different human and material entities that are brought together in an abstraction like "air" or "atmosphere" might help to "imagine a collective condition that is neither particular nor universal." Thinking about the 2017 coastal El Niño as a climate event makes it possible to pull together and examine numerous oceanic, atmospheric, piscatorial, geological, and human relationships (among others) across a wide swath of air, land, and water. At the same time, "coastal El Niño" is also a semantic container that is quickly overloaded with meaning and becomes incapable of holding these myriad relationships in view. Ultimately, meteorologists, politicians, fishers, and anthropologists must rely on metaphors to think about and examine the collective and individual aspects of the 2017 coastal El Niño by focusing on specific features of the event and claiming that they represent significant indicators of the larger entity. As with all metaphors, these ways of framing the event derive their power and meaning from the ability to forefront particular connections and relationships at the cost of others.[2] Furthermore, not all metaphors are created equally—some circulate more widely because the people who articulate them have greater social or institutional capital.

These challenges of representation and analysis are not unique to the 2017 coastal El Niño. They are indicative of broader challenges in analyzing the myriad actors and entities that are arranged in unequal relationships within concepts such as "climate." While representing these relationships in their ontological fullness is impossible, anthropologists and other social scientists have the intellectual tools to study the cultural histories whereby different actors produce and advance metaphors for thinking about El Niños, weather, or climate (O'Reilly et al. 2020). Mark Hulme (2015) argues that humans have relied on the metaphor of climate to imagine stability when thinking about constantly changing and unpredictable weather. The climate crisis has destroyed this idea of climate as a metaphor of long-range atmospheric stability and predictable patterns. The result, Hulme (2015) argues, is that people must develop new metaphors for reorienting their relationships to climate and the actions they take that affect it. Such tumultuous moments represent opportunities for state authorities or other powerful actors to further images of the global biosphere in ways that, for example, reinforce the state as an "essential cog" (Zee 2020) in the functioning of the earth's climate or put forth a "nationalized vision of planetary danger" (Masco 2010, 9).

My analysis of the 2017 coastal El Niño reveals how inequalities were produced at multiple scales in the production of knowledge about El Niño events, their forecasting and decision-making about such forecasts, as well as how the impacts of these events were experienced unequally and narrated differently by various actors. These discursive framings of the 2017 coastal El Niño show how different actors advanced political claims or legitimated specific (non)responses to the event by making selective connections between different scales while also obscuring critical aspects of these interrelations. I begin with an analysis of how, at the "national" scale of meteorological services, Peruvian scientists framed the 2017 coastal El Niño and their difficulty predicting its impacts as a problem of technical definitions and a need for better models, research, and technology to prevent future disasters through better forecasting. This emphasis on better forecasting obscured the reality that much of the damage that occurred was the result not of poor meteorological knowledge but increased socioeconomic vulnerability and precarity in Peru's urban coastal zones. Peru's president and state officials framed the coastal El Niño as an event that could not be predicted but was one that was well within the response capabilities of the state. The president and his cabinet talked about the events' impacts as being regional and localized in nature and argued against the declaration of a national state of emergency. In contrast, media commentators in the national capital and opposition politicians framed the disaster as a crisis that resulted from deeply rooted government ineptitude and corruption as well as widespread societal deficiencies that could only be solved with an overhaul of the Peruvian state.

These interpretations of the scale of the 2017 coastal El Niño all relied on and were rooted in the widespread mediation of the most visible impacts of the disaster: flooding rivers, houses being swept away, sunken bridges, and temporary tent cities housing coastal residents. These interpretations also relied on selective connections of instances of suffering with responses or mistakes by international and national meteorologists and state, regional, and municipal officials to advance their claims to scientific and political authority. These selective connections also obscured critical and widespread aspects of the suffering, which was overwhelmingly endured by impoverished Peruvians. In the final portion of this chapter, I examine the impact of the 2017 event on Peruvian fisheries, focusing on the experiences of artisanal fishers in Lima. Peru's industrial fishery for anchoveta did well in 2017 and increased catches following the coastal El Niño. However, artisanal fishers were negatively impacted during the event. Those in the north lost months of work as equipment and infrastructure were damaged. Fishers in Lima did not suffer this kind of damage. Media reports noted that catches of some species were up, which was a boon for consumers because it meant depressed fish prices. It also added economic precarity for fishers. In their discussions of the event, artisanal fishers framed the coastal El Niño not as an aberration or the result of key mistakes by officials, but as part of ongoing climatic and economic fluctuations that fishers saw as challenging their livelihoods and pushing them into increased precarity. This precarity was obscured as politicians, meteorologists, and media commentators scaled up and down in their competing analyses of the coastal El Niño. Understanding this precarity is essential for revealing how natural disasters and shifting weather patterns reproduce and deepen extant spatial inequalities, both in their short- and long-term impacts.

OSCILLATION

The use of the term El Niño to refer to oceanic warming was first documented in Peru in the late nineteenth century.[3] Fishers in northern Peru referred to the warm seasonal current that appeared each year usually in December as El Niño (which in this context, meant "the Christ child"). Since the late nineteenth century, the concept of El Niño has been expanded from localized understandings of cyclical warming to a basin-wide oceanic-atmospheric phenomenon—the El Niño–Southern Oscillation (ENSO)—that became an object of scientific knowledge and meteorological forecasting and a highly mediated concept that circulates globally among weather news consumers.[4] Certain ideas about what constitutes an El Niño event have become scientifically and meteorologically codified, while others have been ignored or marginalized (Cushman 2004b).[5] One result of this is that basin-wide monitoring and forecasting systems are oriented to identify and predict warming events that develop in the equatorial Pacific. But the 2017 event was different. It did not emerge how a "normal" El Niño does. It developed quickly along the far eastern edge of the Pacific Ocean in a way that made it difficult for existing models to forecast.

To understand this "coastal" El Niño, I sought out a weather expert to discuss the significance of the El Niño phenomenon in Peru and the challenges of predicting different El Niño events. I asked to meet with one of the meteorologists in the Servicio Nacional de Meteorología e Hidrología del Perú (SENAMHI, National Meteorology and Hydrology Service of Peru). SENAMHI is the national government agency that is responsible for providing meteorological and hydrological services, such as the provision of daily public weather forecasts, and coordinates with other national and international meteorological services to forecast regional events, such as El Niños.[6] In September 2019, I took a taxi from the dock in Chorrillos across the city to the district of Jesús María, about fifteen kilometers from the wharf, where SENAMHI's offices are located. My appointment was at five o'clock, and bumper-to-bumper traffic had already started to build in central Lima. After the taxi dropped me off, I walked to a gated entrance where a security guard escorted me to an office where a secretary asked about the details of my appointment. Once she confirmed my appointment time, she asked for my passport so she that could record my information and invited me to have a seat. While I sat and waited, I looked at the posters on the wall, one of which outlined the multiple impacts—from public health to politics—that the weather has on human life. After about fifteen minutes, the secretary informed me that the meteorologist was ready to see me, and she directed me across an inner courtyard to another building that I entered, ascended three flights of stairs, and then after a few wrong turns, eventually found the correct office.

I sat down across from Juan Manuel's large, wooden desk and told him that I was interested in learning more about the difference between a "normal" El Niño (if there is such a thing) and the "coastal" El Niño that hit Peru in 2017. Over the course of an hour, we sat and talked about Pacific weather systems and looked at a series of maps on his computer screen that showed morphing red-orange-yellow blobs (representing warming sea surface temperatures) in different parts of the Pacific Ocean. Juan Manuel explained that the term El Niño is problematic because it is used by forecasters in the United States to refer to warming conditions in a particular part of the Pacific Ocean, whereas in Peru the term is often also used to describe coastal warming generally.

Predicting ENSO events has become an important and regular practice among meteorological and oceanographic services across the Pacific Basin with the United States' National Oceanic and Atmospheric Association (NOAA) playing a central role in monitoring ENSO and distributing data throughout the region.[7] NOAA uses indices for specific El Niño zones in the equatorial Pacific to track climatic changes.[8] Zones 1 and 2 are usually considered one region (1+2)—Zone 1 is the area off the coast of Peru, and Zone 2 covers the Ecuadorian coast out to the Galapagos Islands (see map 1). Warming in these zones is linked with torrential rains along the Ecuadorian and Peruvian coasts and, although it is not always the case, warming in these zones sometimes precedes basin-wide warming. However, the weather in these zones is the most difficult to predict because it is more susceptible to fluctuations in regional weather patterns. Because of this these zones are not tracked by NOAA's ENSO models. Beginning in the 1980s, NOAA's scientists focused their attention on what happened in Zone 3 in the central equatorial Pacific because warming (or cooling) in this zone appeared to produce the widest range of teleconnections (long-distance impacts) in North and South America. In contrast, Zone 4 in the western equatorial Pacific usually does not undergo a large temperature shift during El Niño events, nor does it have as great an impact on climate

in North or South America, with teleconnections relegated mostly to the
western United States and Canada.[9] Weather forecasters from NOAA
look for above-average sea surface temperatures in El Niño region 3.4 and
declare El Niño warming when average temperatures are higher than normal for three consecutive months. This warming usually leads to warmer,
dryer temperatures in parts of the United States and wetter conditions in
others. As such warming moves across the Pacific Ocean and nears Peru's
coast, it usually produces heavy rains and flooding in the northern part of
the country.

Juan Manuel noted that this is not always the case. For example, the
"super" El Niño of 2015 and 2016 did not generate heavy rains in Peru. Temperatures in Peru were higher than normal, but it was dry. In contrast, the
2017 coastal El Niño brought significant rains and flooding to the north while
the central Pacific was exhibiting colder than average temperatures, leading
NOAA to declare La Niña conditions. In Peru, the 2017 event was referred
to and experienced as an El Niño because of the warmer than normal temperatures and the heavy rains that led to extensive flooding, especially in the
northern part of the country. As Juan Manuel explained, the 2017 coastal
El Niño resulted from warming in a different part of the ocean than a typical ENSO event. Instead of warming in Zone 3.4, the 2017 coastal El Niño
resulted from warming in Zone 1+2, located along the Peruvian coast. This
warming was not the product of changes in the west to east movement of
water and winds that drive ENSO. Rather, the 2017 coastal El Niño occurred
because of a shift in north to south winds along the Peruvian coast that created an intensification of the Intertropical Convergence Zone (ITC) off the
coast of Ecuador and northern Peru, which produces warm sea surface temperatures that result in wetter than normal weather for the Peruvian coast. In
contrast to an ENSO event, Juan Manuel explained that a coastal El Niño is
harder to predict for two reasons. First, global forecasting models for ENSO
are not designed to predict coastal El Niños, given their focus on conditions
in the central Pacific and the teleconnections that result from them. Second,
the conditions that lead to a coastal El Niño develop very quickly over the
course of a few weeks in January and February and then end just as quickly
(in contrast to ENSO warming, which usually develops over months). By
April, the strength of the sun in the southern hemisphere is weakened and
is not able to warm the ocean surface enough to maintain above-average sea
surface temperatures.

Meteorologists Ken Takahashi and Alejandra G. Martínez (2017) under-score the importance of recognizing the diversity of "El Niño" phenomena when thinking about impacts on the far eastern Pacific and Peru's coast. Drawing on a historical analysis of the strong 1925 El Niño and comparing it to the other two strongest warming events of the twentieth century, they argue that there are two "El Niños" that have significant effects on Peru's weather but that both emerge from quite different dynamics. There is the El Niño that is the warm phase of ENSO, in which warming in the central equatorial Pacific and changes in the southern oscillation produce a series of teleconnections, including serious impacts on the Ecuadorian and Peru-vian coasts. Then there is the coastal El Niño, which is comprised of coastal warming with "cold to neutral conditions in the rest of the equatorial Pacific" (Takahashi and Martínez 2017, 17).

This research emerged out of Peruvian scientists' efforts to monitor con-ditions along the Peruvian coast because of the local impacts of sea surface temperatures in this region on local weather (Takahashi, Mosquera, and Reupo 2014). Since the late 1990s, NOAA scientists have focused on Zone 3.4 as the most important zone for predicting ENSO events (see map 1). Ivan Ramírez and Fernando Briones (2017, 490) argue that it is "not always the best area for observing other varieties of El Niño that develop or ecological impacts that may concentrate along the coasts of northern Peru and south-ern Ecuador." NOAA's monitoring system creates significant disparities in what is monitored and what knowledge about ENSO is produced. This is further complicated by the "fact that many countries, including Peru and Ecuador, rely on the NOAA ENSO alert system and forecast models that estimate the probability of El Niño occurrence" (491). In response to this situation, in 2012 Peru's Comité Multisectorial Encargado del Estudio Nacio-nal del Fenómeno El Niño (ENFEN, Multisectorial Committee in Charge of the National Study of the El Niño Phenomenon) implemented the Índice Costero El Niño (ICEN, Coastal El Niño Index) to have an agreed-upon index for tracking changes along the coast. Using data on anomalies in sea surface temperatures in zones 1+2, ENFEN issues reports every two weeks that note consecutive temperature anomalies, provide predictions, and issue alerts regarding unfolding coastal warming or cooling.

During the 2017 coastal El Niño, ENFEN issued regular updates, predic-tions, and alerts. However, it was not able to predict the severity of the 2017 event "soon enough to allow lead time for an early warning" (Ramírez and

Briones 2017, 490). ENFEN issued its first official communication of 2017 on January 16, predicting that conditions would be between neutral and weak warming along the Peruvian coast during summer with a 30 percent chance of a weak coastal El Niño developing (ENFEN 2017a). Two weeks later in its January 24 report, ENFEN issued a coastal El Niño watch, noting that "favorable conditions exist for a weak El Niño Costero event in the present summer" (ENFEN 2017b). On February 2, ENFEN reported that the "watch" had been updated to an "alert" because conditions had developed that favored a coastal El Niño, but it maintained that the coastal El Niño was likely to be weak (ENFEN 2017c). At this point, heavy rains, flooding, and huaicos were already occurring in northern coastal regions, leading to bridge collapses, displacements, and deaths. The subsequent ENFEN report maintained the alert and predicted the continuation of a "weak" coastal El Niño into March with a high likelihood of heavy rains in northern Peru (ENFEN 2017d). It was not until March 2 that ENFEN issued a report upgrading the coastal El Niño's probable magnitude from "weak" to "between weak and moderate" with a "high probability of heavy rains in the north" (ENFEN 2017e). In its March 16 report, ENFEN reported that the coastal El Niño was of "moderate magnitude" (ENFEN 2017f) and predicted the continuation of this moderate coastal El Niño into May with the ongoing probability of heavy rains in the coastal zone from Tumbes to Lambayeque decreasing during the month of April. It was not until June that ENFEN reported a state of "no alert."

In a special technical report issued in July 2017, ENFEN's scientists summarized the challenges that the coastal El Niño had posed for their monitoring and predictions. The report begins by noting that during January of that year "the surface temperature of the ocean increased abruptly, against the predictions of ENFEN and international climate models" (ENFEN 2017g, 1). Although the ICEN classified the 2017 coastal El Niño as "moderate" regarding its temperature anomalies, in terms of its impacts from rain and flooding ENFEN's scientists argued that it "could be considered the third most intense 'El Niño Phenomenon' of the last one hundred years in Peru" (ENFEN 2017g, 1). Some meteorological stations in northern Peru recorded their highest or second-highest ever rainfall amounts in February—rainfall amounts that were similar to the destructive 1982–83 El Niño (20). The report's authors concluded with recommendations for improving the prediction of future events and preparing for their impacts, such as increasing "the temporal and spatial coverage of in situ oceanographic, meteorological and biological piscatorial monitoring along the coast"; supporting "the operation and maintenance of the international observational system in the eastern Pacific Ocean"; promoting expanded research cooperation with Peru's universities; and improving government decision-making in relation to "probabilistic predictions of El Niño or La Niña" (29).

These recommendations emanated from ENFEN's mission to monitor warming or cooling events in the Pacific Ocean that affect Peru's weather and make public predictions about them. These recommendations also reflected broader public discussions about the 2017 coastal El Niño, during which media outlets and public figures questioned why Peru's meteorologists had not been able to predict the event with greater accuracy or more advance notice. An editorial in *El Comercio* in May 2017 asked, "What lessons have the recent coastal El Niño phenomenon taught us?" (Mendoza Riofrío 2017). The blunt response that the author provided was that there was a critical "lack of forecasting." Such commentaries emphasized the importance of improved forecasts for predicting climate events such as the coastal El Niño and its negative impacts in the belief that earlier warning would lead to government and citizen actions to prepare for the event and thus mitigate the disaster.

However, anthropologists and sociologists who study weather and natural disasters have noted that there are significant challenges to this argument.[10] It overlooks the importance of how the authority of predictions is viewed by consumers of such information. One of the challenges that meteorologists have is conveying predictions that are based on statistical probabilities to public audiences with enough certainty to make them appear likely (Fine 2007). If meteorological predictions seem to be too uncertain, they risk undermining the authority of the scientists who are issuing them and the prediction itself.[11] Ramírez and Briones (2017, 491) argue that the conflicting forecasts that emerged during the 2017 coastal El Niño may also have undermined the authority of government meteorological information, thus muddling risk preparation. Media reports on the coastal El Niño, especially in late January and February, reflect public confusion over how to make sense of what exactly was going on. For example, an article in *La República* (2017a) in early February stated that the event was "not El Niño, but it seems like it." An article in *El Comercio* noted that "this year an El Niño phenomenon was not expected, and although at the moment the ocean warming conditions would permit the Instituto Nacional de Defensa Civil [INDECI, National Institute of Civil Defense] to presume that it [was occurring] . . . the specialists still cannot confirm it." The article quoted Sheyla Yauri, a specialist from INDECI, as saying that "with these anomalies we could say that it is an El Niño, but still we cannot establish this conclusively. It could also be from isolated or seasonal warming" (*El Comercio* 2017a).

Moreover, issuing better predictions does not mean that people will or can respond to them in ways that mitigate the negative consequences of El Niño events. Reflecting on the first few decades of ENSO forecasting, Michael Glantz (2001, 122) argues that there was "an overemphasis by researchers on developing a capability to forecast El Niño's onset" and not enough emphasis on helping "society to figure out how best to use the El Niño information that [research] has already produced." The belief that improving forecasts will mitigate future El Niño–related disasters overlooks the fact that much of the damage from previous disasters resulted from uneven development that made a significant portion of Peru's population vulnerable to the worst impacts of El Niño flooding. A report on the impacts of the coastal El Niño prepared by a consortium of development organizations notes that increased urbanization of coastal areas by impoverished migrants in the past twenty years has led to the development of high-risk areas such as floodplains and river corridors (Venkateswaran, MacClune, and Enriquez 2019, 13). During normal years such areas are dry, which has enabled the construction of densely populated urban settlements and infrastructure, but during heavy El Niño rains and flooding these areas are vulnerable to extensive damage (13). This vulnerability was compounded by the fact that once the government made people aware of the danger posed by the coastal El Niño, many were reluctant to leave their homes because they often were unsure about what their options were or felt that they did not have anywhere else to go (35). Improved forecasts can help reduce the impacts of weather events in coastal Peru but only if the state has the capacity and authority to respond quickly and provide vulnerable populations with the resources they needed to evacuate, relocate, and reconstruct.

DISASTER AUTHORITY

Public discourse in Peru surrounding the coastal El Niño was dominated by discussions about not only the state government's difficulty forecasting the event but also its slow and limited response to the unfolding disaster. An editorial published in *El Comercio* on April 6 reflected the key components of such critiques (Caramanica 2017). The author lamented that "decade after decade, history repeats itself: hundreds of lives lost, hundreds of thousands of displaced people and thousands of millions of soles spent on reconstruction." Despite this recurrent nature of El Niño events, the Peruvian state continued to be incapable of "manag[ing] the effects of a predictable phenomenon." Many Peruvians saw the lack of long-range predictions for the coastal El Niño and the damage that ensued as emblematic of the state's failings. The president and his officials countered such perceptions by reassuring Peruvians that the state had the resources necessary to mount an adequate response, that there was not an imminent national crisis, and that the main threat to disaster response and reconstruction was ongoing corruption in regional and local governments.

What was at stake in public discourse was whether the coastal El Niño should be considered a natural and political "crisis." Janet Roitman (2014, 3) argues the idea of "crisis" is a knowledge claim and a call to normativity that designates a particular event as a watershed, a break from the past that can be used to anchor a new, different future in which normativity can be restored.[12] Roberto Barrios (2017, 152) notes that public discussions of "socially disruptive geophysical phenomena" tend to focus on the question: "What went wrong?" This has the effect of framing natural disasters as crises that result from "errors or accidents that are aberrations of the normal operation of things" (152) rather than being the products of historical inequalities that make certain populations or spaces more vulnerable to the effects of geophysical phenomena, such as El Niño flooding. There is a long history of natural disasters in Peru, especially those caused by earthquakes and El Niño flooding.[13] In addition to being geophysical phenomena, Charles Walker (2008) argues that such events brought under scrutiny existing spatial relationships, social divides, and political authority. Natural disasters presented opportunities for projecting state authority, as foundations for questioning the capacity of the state to care for its citizens, or as moments when new political subjectivities emerged or were suppressed in the reconstruction of physical and social infrastructure.[14] The 2017 coastal El Niño occurred at a time in which Peruvians' belief in the authority of the state was exceptionally low, and for many the disaster represented a clear moment that laid bare the failings not only of the government of Pedro Pablo Kuczynski but of the whole Peruvian political system as well.

The 2017 coastal El Niño caught off guard an already embattled president whose public authority was faltering. A center-right economist and technocrat who had held positions at the World Bank and International Monetary Fund, Kuczynski was elected to the presidency in 2016 promising to rid the Peruvian state of endemic corruption. Peru's congress, which was controlled by the Fuerza Popular opposition party led by Keiko Fujimori (the daughter of former president Alberto Fujimori who was convicted and imprisoned for human rights abuses) repeatedly thwarted Kuczynski. In the months before the coastal El Niño the congress and the executive became embroiled in a conflict over a new airport in Chinchero, a small city near Machu Picchu, Peru's most important tourist attraction. Opposition lawmakers disputed the recently revised contractual terms for the airport's construction and demanded that Martín Vizcarra, then minister of transportation, be questioned at length over the issue. As part of his ministerial position, Vizcarra was tasked with overseeing the government response to El Niño flooding and reconstruction. Evoking discourses of national unity, the congress suspended its investigation of Vizcarra during March and April.[15]

Kuczynski responded to growing concern over flooding and damage in northern Peru with public statements of authority and calm to bolster the image of the state as a capable, efficient actor. He reassured Peruvians that there was no need to worry about the problems caused by the coastal El Niño because the central government had resources to overcome all of them. Additionally, he made boilerplate calls for unity amid adversity, asking that political divisions and rancor be put aside so that the country could focus on overcoming the immediate disaster. He also resisted declaring a state of emergency—a position that drew growing national (and even some international) ire. While rivers in Lima were overflowing and much of northern coastal Peru was flooded, he stated on national television that his government would only "declare an emergency where one really exists" (*La República* 2017b). He exhorted Peruvians to be patient, explaining that "in Peru there is money. The government is taking care [of it]. We have to have faith in the officials that we have elected." Two days later, on a visit to affected areas in the north, the President restated his position, arguing that it was "still not necessary to declare a [state of] emergency" (*La República* 2017d). He responded to critics by saying that the recent weather had surprised everyone. "No one would have predicted rain of this magnitude at a time when there was not a true El Niño," he noted, adding that "these are coastal rains" and thus implying that this was not a real El Niño event. The president told reporters that confronting the disaster was not a problem of money, but of organization and ensuring that the Pan-American Highway was opened so that aid and commerce could flow (*La República* 2017f).

On March 17, Kuczynski finally relented and declared a state of emergency. However, he resisted doing so for the whole country, opting instead to declare states of emergency for the eleven regions most affected by rains and flooding. During a March 21 interview with CNN, the president asserted that declaring a state of emergency for all of Peru would be tantamount to "opening the door to corruption" because regional and municipal governments "will undertake works without competition or bidding."[16] He added that "lamentably, the other huaico that we have had in the last months is one of corruption." Kuczynski emphasized that the coastal El Niño was a result of broad and increasingly normal changes caused by global warming and the state had adequate resources to deal with it. He repeatedly attempted to frame the disaster as something that was well within the capabilities of the central state government and did not represent a crisis that required a significant departure from what his government was doing. Indeed, as his comments above suggest, he tried to argue that his government's approach to the disaster was part and parcel of his overall fight against endemic corruption.

Kuczynski was not successful in convincing Peruvians of the effectiveness of his actions. During the month of March, his already low national approval rating fell by more than five percent. Those affected by the disaster, especially in the north, decried a lack of government support and presence, complaining that both were in short supply after two months of rains and flooding (*La República* 2017g). Many political and cultural elites commented in national media outlets that the lack of government planning and response to the disaster revealed ongoing problems in Peruvian society, politics, and urban development. In Lima's media, critics lambasted the government's ongoing "culture of reaction."

In an editorial published in *El Comercio*, Alfredo Torres (2017) remarked that Peru was a "country of huaicos and earthquakes," and these regular occurrences should not lead to such widespread destruction. The problem, he argued, was that the state needed to invest in better urban planning, affordable housing, and flood-resistant infrastructure, and spend less time fighting over how to react to the crisis. An editorial in *La República* asserted that the coastal El Niño "revealed" that the "state was broken" (*La República* 2017c).

"How many times are there huaicos in Chosica?" the author asked, replying that "I do not have the number, but I think it is almost every year. They are recurrent phenomena, and we lack foresight." The editorial highlighted not only what the author saw as ongoing problems with state priorities but enduring discrepancies in Peru's political geography, where Lima's elites have long imagined their city to be the political, economic, and cultural center of the country. The author argued that "the state would be better prepared if sometimes it rained in Lima with the force of an El Niño in the north."

These and other commentators interpreted the disaster as a crisis that emanated from enduring geographical inequalities in urban development and government spending. In their explanations of these inequalities and their relation to damage from the coastal El Niño, commentators often fell back on and reinforced elite discourses of provincial ineptitude and urban informality to decry what they saw as the current state of things. Commentators in Lima's media outlets engaged in finger wagging at regional governments, pointing out that regional and municipal governments were responsible for underspending on disaster prevention and mitigation. As one editorial in *El Comercio* (2017b) noted, "In 2016, the regional governments of Lambayeque, Ica, Piura and La Libertad—where 75% of those affected are concentrated—only spent 64.4%, 67.5%, 68.2%, and 76.6% of their budget [allocated] for emergency preparation." Many public figures used the damage from the coastal El Niño to decry what they saw as ongoing problems with Peru's culture of "informality." In Lima, "informality" has become central to elite preoccupations with the rapid expansion of the city, which has transformed critical aspects of Lima's economy, social composition, and cultural geography. The idea of informality—the supposedly messy, unregulated, and unplanned quality of the neighborhoods created by new arrivals to the city— has come to stand in elite discourse as a proxy for the race-class alterity of Lima's shantytowns (Gandolfo 2009). Numerous editorials in *El Comercio* emphasized the lack of planning in Lima's urban development as the primary cause of damage in the city. One asserted that readers should not "blame the rain," but rather the state and municipal governments for allowing uncontrolled building and failing to ensure adequate disaster prevention in the city's development (*El Comercio* 2017c). Another, by Patricio Valderrama, asserted that "our problem is the overexposure of people in zones where a river should be able to flood or a huaico to run" (*El Comercio* 2017d). He argued that "we are paying the bill for almost four decades of no territorial planning and informality in the entire urban environment." He recognized widescale spatial inequalities that existed in Peru and Lima while simultaneously avoiding any discussion of the underlying structural factors that contributed to them. Instead, he and other media elites drew on discourses of informality to explain the vulnerability of residents living in areas with a high risk for flooding.

As the rains from the coastal El Niño began to ebb, national public discourse shifted from debates about who or what to blame for the disaster to how reconstruction should proceed in its aftermath. Debates about the political and social meaning of the disaster continued. Critics of the president argued that the disaster revealed the ongoing incapacity of the state to deal effectively with such problems and necessitated sweeping changes in Peru's political culture. Numerous editorials in *El Comercio* emphasized the need to adopt a "culture of prevention" (Prialé 2017) that prioritized the state's capacity to reduce the impact of future natural disasters through saving, better planning, and flood mitigation. Critics argued that, along with affected regions of Peru, the Peruvian state needed to be reconstructed as well. José Ugaz (2017) asserted that the destruction caused by the coastal El Niño was equal to that caused by endemic corruption, with the latter making the former worse. "As with the El Niño phenomenon, the problem of corruption in Peru is not episodic, it is recurring, structural and systemic," he wrote, adding that both required a "sustainable" solution. "The disaster has exposed the grave deficiencies of [political] decentralization in our country," remarked Alonso Segura (2017), who argued that the situation required the construction of a new institutional "capacity in the Peruvian state." The president and his cabinet members countered that, if done correctly, reconstruction represented a potential moment to break from Peru's past of corruption and mismanagement.

Pablo de la Flor, the state official in charge of reconstruction, told *El Comercio* that the "disaster laid bare the worst of Peru—the improvisation and poor quality of [public] works completed, in many cases, with corrupt means" (*El Comercio* 2017f). In his many public statements on the matter, Kuczynski emphasized his intention to move away from these histories of corruption, arguing that "reconstruction means doing things better than before." He also sought to temper expectations, cautioning that it could not "transform into a demand for everything that has not been done in 200 years" (*La República* 2017h).

As the months passed, Peruvians in affected areas experienced a significant gap between Kuczynski's promise of efficient reconstruction and what was (or was not) happening on the ground. State reconstruction prioritized transportation infrastructure over housing and favored resettlement as a strategy for areas that were deemed "unmitigable" (Venkateswaran, Mac-Clune, and Enriquez 2017, 1). Local communities were not only left out of the recovery planning process but also faced difficulties getting necessary resources from municipal and regional governments. In Trujillo and other coastal communities, families were moved from tent cities to prefabricated houses but told that they only had six months to stay, leaving them in a state of precarity that was worse than what they experienced before the floods (Gallegos 2017). At the end of 2017, there were still people in Piura living in emergency shelters without electricity or potable water, who had not been able to return to their homes. As one local mayor told *La República*: "We've gone nine months and the reconstruction has not started, this [year of] 2017 was only announcements."

Residents of some affected communities staged protests in attempts to draw public attention to their situation and pressure the government to do more to help them reconstruct. In September and October 2017, people in Chosica, where huaicos swept away numerous houses earlier in the year, coordinated community meetings and marches to pressure the state to do a better job of helping to rebuild and prepare for the next floods. They demanded more help with cleaning drainage canals, clearing the River Huaycoloro of debris, and cleaning geodynamic netting that is used to help contain flooding. These measures were necessary for ensuring that during the upcoming seasonal rains, the water would drain quickly and effectively and not back up and flood the town (*La República* 2017j). Residents of Huarmey blocked the Pan-American Highway for two days to draw attention to the lack of reconstruction that had occurred in the town (*La República* 2017i).

One year after flooding, approximately 5 percent of the government's reconstruction budget had been spent, most of it on infrastructure. For those who were most impacted by the coastal El Niño, reconstruction resulted in a state of ongoing precarity. This reality was largely obscured in national-level public discourse, as debates between the president and his adversaries focused on whether the coastal El Niño event represented a crisis. While briefly highlighting ongoing inequalities and geographical disparities, elite commentators did so to support their divergent political projects and desires in ways that largely reinforced ongoing disparities. National-level political discourse about the disaster obfuscated the on-the-ground realities of challenges that climatic events produced for impoverished people in Peru. In contrast, artisanal fishers in Lima talked about the coastal El Niño as part of an ongoing and interlinked cycle of climatic and economic forces that exacerbated the precarity of their situations.

FISHING EL NIÑO COSTERO

On March 21, 2017, *La República* (2017e) ran an article informing its readers that the "coastal el Niño also has positive effects, among them the greater availability of warm-water fish." The warming event had replaced the normally cold waters found along Lima's coast with warmer water, which attracted a range of popular table fish, such as *caballa* (*Scomber japonicus*, chub mackerel) and lisa. During March the availability of these two species in Lima's fish markets had almost doubled in respect to the former and more than quintupled for the latter. The bonus for fish buyers in the city was that prices for these fish were much lower than normal. Other media reports reiterated the suggestion that El Niño Costero had been a boon for coastal artisanal fishers and fish consumers (*El Comercio* 2017e).[17]

The reality for artisanal fishers in Lima was more complicated. They were spared the kind of destruction to critical infrastructure or personal belongings that hampered artisanal fishing in the north for much of 2017.[18] However, changing ocean conditions caused by the coastal El Niño along with market pressures contributed to fishers' ongoing economic precarity in subtle but significant ways. This was an issue that was obscured in public discourse and analysis of the coastal El Niño, which framed the event as a disaster-crisis whose immediate impacts were exacerbated by a lack of forecasting and inadequate government planning and response. For artisanal fishers in Lima the coastal El Niño was not a crisis that stood outside of "normal" time or the regular functioning of things. They experienced the event as part of an ongoing cycle of climate and market fluctuations that repeatedly have pushed them to the brink of economic insolvency. This perspective is critical for highlighting how geophysical phenomena work within and contribute to ongoing precarities caused by broader structural inequalities.

There are roughly four hundred fishers, fish vendors, and food kiosk operators in Chorrillos who make a living from the local, near-shore fishery.[19] The market for fish from Chorrillos is small and highly individualized. Vendors and kiosk operators sell fish and prepared food to people from the area who frequent it for tourism, mostly during the summer and on weekends. Fishers who work on the dock sell their fish directly to consumers either at the daily evening market located on the dock or through personal agreements that they have with regular buyers, such as local restaurant owners. Within Lima's political economy, the manual labor that fishers and fish vendors perform is devalued, which means that they receive little compensation for their work. On average, fishers in Chorrillos make less than Peru's official minimum wage (which is relatively low compared to other countries in the region). Add to this the high cost of living in the city and ongoing fluctuations in catches because of seasonal and climatic changes as well as constantly shifting prices of different fish that are affected by changes in local, regional, and sometimes global markets. In recent decades depredation by larger boats based in Callao as well as increased pollution from Lima's sewage discharges has further impacted Chorrillos's near-shore fishery. All of this has contributed to the ongoing economic precarity that fishers and fish vendors face daily. While the pay is low and inconsistent, the men and women I have come to know over years of studying life on the dock in Chorrillos prefer to continue working there because it affords greater individual autonomy and dignity than doing menial, wage work in the city (such as construction or domestic service). Nonetheless, in recent years, fishers and vendors have told me such dignity has been slowly undermined by the growing economic precarity of their situation.[20]

As the coastal El Niño unfolded in March 2017, I spent a week in Chorrillos talking to fishers about their catches and the unusually warm, late summer weather that Lima was experiencing. Each day the sun shone brightly and I could feel the heat building off the pavement and sandy cliffs by midday. The waters in the bay were noticeably hotter than normal and the fishers I knew all complained about the fishing and the market for fish. Luis, who grew up fishing in Chorrillos, said that the lisa had been in and fishing for them was good since they preferred warmer, summer waters. However, by March he said that fishing for the popular catch had slowed. Perhaps it was because the waters had warmed too much, he thought. However, he surmised that the more likely cause was all the mud that was being dumped into Lima's coastal waters by the local rivers that were flooded with dirt and debris from the huaicos. Most fishers spent the hot afternoons mending their nets or resting under awnings or tarps and then went out at night when the water was cooler and fish were more active and moving closer in toward shore. Enrique, a younger fisher who had worked on the dock for almost fifteen years, told me that there was *coco* (*Paralonchurus peruanus*, Peruvian banded croaker). However, he said that prices were so low that it was not worth going out for them. Fishers routinely complained that they could not earn any money from the fish they were catching because the market was so saturated with coco and lorna that the going price was only one or two soles (about three to six dollars) per kilo of fish. Much of what the fishers in Chorrillos caught that week they took home so that their families at least had something to eat even though they were not earning cash.

In follow-up interviews in 2018 about the impacts of the coastal El Niño on fishing in Chorrillos, fishers commented on the economic challenges that such climatic events present for them and how they add to their precarity. Luis said that "there are phenomena that are good and others that are not. The one from this year left some fishing." He expanded on this, noting that "it had been a while since we saw *ayanque* [*Cynoscion analis*, Peruvian weakfish], good lisa." However, he said that in general the coastal El Niño was "not that good" for fishing because it did not "bring many species of fish like other years." While some species showed up in abundance, their sheer numbers pushed down the prices of these fish, to the point that they were not profitable. Artisanal fishers land a wide diversity of fish during different seasons. Consumers come to the dock looking for certain species of fish at different times of year. During the coastal El Niño consumers had the benefit of buying a narrow range of fish for very low prices. It also meant that other favored fish were not available, and many times when consumers could not find those fish, they left the market without buying anything. This situation led Luis to comment that the coastal El Niño created "disasters for all." By invoking the idea of "disaster," Luis subtly linked the difficulties that artisanal fishers experienced during the coastal El Niño with the suffering of flood victims and displaced people. He did not do so in a way that attempted to make them all equivalent, but rather to make visible the negative impacts of the phenomenon on artisanal fishers in Chorrillos.

Marcos, another local fisher, has spent most of his adult working life in Chorrillos. He said that "the fishing was good" during the coastal El Niño but added that "when the fishing is good, it also brings bad things." He explained that events such as occurred in 2017 bring "a good number of fish" to the bay. "But when there is a lot, who benefits?" he asked, responding to his own question, "Well, the people benefit," not the fishers. When there are more fish, there are more fish landed and more competition, which drives down the prices. Marcos added that "when El Niño goes, there is nothing left . . . because when the El Niño current leaves another current enters, but the fish take a while to come in on this current, the pejerrey for example, wait two years to return, crabs sometimes five years." "Because of this you have to save," Marcos commented, "because there are going to be months that follow when there is nothing." The problem, though, is that it is nearly impossible for fishers to save during the warm months because of low fish prices.

Mercedes, a fish vendor who had worked on the wharf for more than four decades, summed up the challenges of trying to make even a small profit under such conditions. She said that "if there is a lot of fish, the price goes down." Often when the price is too low, she added that fishers do not "get back what they put in" because they have to "pay for gas, pay for the fishing trip, the transportation, and other things." In Marcos's experience, operating costs also tended to be higher during El Niño years. One of the problems caused by the coastal El Niño (and in Marcos's experience, other events, such as the 1997–98 El Niño) is that "when the rivers flood, the sea fills with mud and the fish do not come close to shore, they go farther out." The increased sediment means that the water "loses its oxygen" and, Marcos noted, "the mud sticks to the nets and makes it easier for the fish to see them." This means more trips farther from shore to find clear water and hence higher gasoline consumption, which is a significant cost for artisanal fishers and contributes to their economic loses.

Marcos linked the struggles of Chorrillos's artisanal fishers during and right after the coastal El Niño to what he saw as broader, ongoing climatic and socioeconomic problems. He commented on the fact that the coastal El Niño was not "expected" but remarked that "that is how it is with nature—unexpected." This was increasingly true, he believed, with the onset of climate change, which he noted affects "the currents, everything." "There is not the same [amount of] fish as in years before," he said, because "it seems that humans are doing something that is not good," and "these currents do not enter as they did in the past." Mercedes remarked that "the life of a fisher is sad" because regardless of year-to-year fluctuations, the quality of fishing in

Chorrillos and other Peruvian ports had declined significantly. "There were a lot of fish before," she said, "and fish of every kind," naming ten different species that used to be found in the bay in greater frequency. "But now," she concluded, "there is not even a fourth [of what existed]."

This situation has put artisanal fishers and vendors in an increasingly difficult position. Jósefina was one of several people who for a small fee cleaned fish that people bought in the market, and her partner was a local artisanal fisher. The problem in fishing, she remarked, was that "when there are fish, you earn just enough. But when there aren't fish, you are left with nothing, just an [empty] pocket." "And all day you kill yourself at sea," she added. Marcos remarked that fishers know how to be patient, how to wait for better fishing, and how to look for other things to do for work. "When there is no fishing, well then, you dedicate yourself to something else," he said but quickly added that there are not many good options for fishers who lack social capital in the city's labor economy. Like so many other fishers in Chorrillos, Marcos said that he preferred not to leave the dock for work because he did not "like it when someone tells me to go here, go there, do this." "I will go and work, because I always work," he said, but when you work in the city "they treat you like a *huevón* [idiot]." He added that employers could do that because "in Peru there is no job stability."

In their discussions of the 2017 coastal El Niño, artisanal fishers and vendors in Chorrillos linked the event to broader dynamics, foremost among them climate change and the political economy of labor in Lima, the combination of which resulted in a "disaster" for them in terms of exacerbating their ongoing precarity. Artisanal fishers highlighted the ways in which geophysical phenomena such as the coastal El Niño interacted with existing political ecologies that relied upon (and reproduced) extant inequalities. Rather than creating a "crisis" that represented a sharp break with the past, for artisanal fishers the coastal El Niño was part of an ongoing crisis of precarity that constantly threatened their livelihoods.

This slow-moving crisis was invisible in elite media, political, and scientific discourses about the coastal El Niño, which focused on the dramatic effects of the flooding and infrastructural damage that precipitated a national "crisis" and required different actions to prevent or mitigate future crises. Peru's president focused on the coastal El Niño as an unpredictable weather aberration, but one whose effects were not worthy of a national emergency declaration that would jeopardize his political project. Opposition politicians and elite media commentators linked highly mediated images of suffering with the idea that the coastal El Niño represented a crisis that required a deep transformation of the state. As they scaled up and down from basin-wide, to national, regional, or local levels, elite commentators selectively linked aspects of the event in ways that denied the ongoing precarity of impoverished producers. By framing the "crisis" as the product of poor mete-orological predictions, government corruption, or state inadequacy, elite dis-courses obscured the central role that deeply rooted inequalities in Peru's coastal political ecologies played in producing the unequal (and disastrous, dramatic, or slow-moving) impacts that the coastal El Niño had on vulner-able populations of people. The increased precarity of artisanal fishers was something that, if they recognized it at all, government officials and media commentators could chalk up to the "normal" state of things for the city's impoverished fishers.

WEATHERING INEQUALITY

What is the importance of the 2017 coastal El Niño for thinking about how people experience and are affected by the unfolding climate crisis in dif-ferent and unequal ways? Recent meteorological research suggests that the world's warming climate will likely increase the variability of ENSO.[21] Such variability could make forecasting El Niño events more challenging and lead to greater cycles of destruction in places such as Peru.

Examining different interpretations of the 2017 coastal El Niño in Peru demonstrates the importance of analyzing the ways that people talk about cli-mate and weather disasters and link them to perceptions of the normal func-tioning of life, historical time, and political authority for understanding how such phenomena become socially meaningful events. Analyzing the specific metaphors that different actors used to read the 2017 coastal El Niño reveals how they connected specific components of multidimensional climate phe-nomenon in ways that obscured and perpetuated significant inequalities. People in Peru produced a range of representations of the coastal El Niño event. Each of these representations was "situated" (Haraway 1988) in and made sense of by a specific set of cultural, social, and institutional knowledge practices. However, certain ways of representing and knowing the coastal El Niño circulated more widely than others and were scaled up as "national" representations of the event because they were enabled by or reinforced the authority of state governance, elite counterpolitics, or dominant regimes of representation. National politicians and media elites narrated the coastal El Niño in ways that foregrounded facts that supported their claims that it was not a national disaster or that it was a "crisis" that required specific state actions, while obscuring the ways in which the event engaged with and perpetuated long-standing political ecological disparities. The latter was something that artisanal fishers in Chorrillos highlighted in their reading of the event, although their lack of political influence and social capital prevented this reading from "scaling up" and circulating more widely.

This dynamic is not unique to the 2017 coastal El Niño or to Peru but is a critical aspect of broader discussions of "climate" around the world. Anthropologists have the ability to study the cultural dynamics and histories of how particular readings of climate are produced and by whom, and what they emphasize and at whose expense. Inserting such analyses of power and inequality into readings of climate is critical for revealing how extant inequalities are obscured and reproduced not only by climatic events and their material impacts but by the ways in which powerful actors narrate them and identify appropriate responses to them.

CHAPTER 4

SQUID LIFE

O NE warm, sunny afternoon in March 2014, I stood talking to a group of fishers on the dock in Chorrillos. We passed a bottle of soda and a glass around taking sips as we watched a crew unload crates of *pota* (*Dosidicus gigas*, jumbo squid) from a boat anchored in the harbor. The boat was one of only a few larger artisanal boats in Chorrillos designed for fishing the high seas. Larger boats are not able to unload on the small dock, so it anchored in the harbor while two men used a smaller rowboat to relay crates of squid from the boat to the shallow water just off the beach. Two other men waited to take the crates on their shoulders and carry them about twenty-five meters from the rowboat to a stone wall. Atop the stone wall were two more men, who took each of the crates, loaded down with forty or fifty kilos of squid, whose tentacles dangled from the sides and swayed as they were moved, onto a cart. They rolled the crates to a refrigerated truck that was parked next to the small, covered fish market. The men lifted the squid into the truck where they covered each crate with ice to keep the squid fresh.

Unloading the catch took several hours because the boat had brought in several metric tons of squid. This time-consuming relay is typical of artisanal fishing in much of Peru, which relies on the manual labor of men and women whose work is devalued within the country's urban and rural political economies as unskilled and informal. Peruvian law defines artisanal fishers as individuals who use small wooden boats (and manual labor) to catch fish for direct human consumption (as opposed to fish that will be processed into meal). Low pay, ever-changing markets, and high risks have made artisanal fishing a difficult way to make a living. On boats such as the one that was unloading in Chorrillos, a captain and crew of six men would spend a week over fifty nautical miles or more from shore. They would eat, sleep, and work on the small, open wooden deck of the boat with no protection from the elements, staying up all night to fish with lanterns and jig lines when the squid were most active near the surface. Fishers often talked about the aggressive nature of the large squid, which could grow to well over a meter long and to weights of twenty-five or more kilos. The fishers described the difficulty of landing squid at night, commenting on how the squid thrashed around as the fishers tried to pull them aboard, gripping the fishers with their tentacles and spraying them with water and ink.

On the docks of Lima some of the entanglements of squid and human life are obvious, while others are less so and require an examination of the broader, Pacific Basin—wide historical development and political ecology of the jumbo squid fishery to make them apparent. Thirty years ago, fishers did not target jumbo squid. Captures of the species now represent the largest cephalopod fishery in the global seafood trade (McClure 2015).[1] Artisanal fishers in Peru account for roughly half of the global trade in jumbo squid. The squid fishery has become the country's second-most important fishery behind anchoveta (*Engraulis ringens*, Peruvian anchoveta). The fleet of boats pursuing squid off Peru's coast has become "so extensive and concentrated, that the light emission from the jigging vessels is detectable from space via satellite imagery" (Jereb and Roper 2010, 304). Artisanal boats that are used for pursuing open ocean species such as *perico* (*Coryphaena hippurus*, mahi-mahi) and *bonito* (*Sarda chiliensis*, also known as bonito in English), can shift easily to jigging for squid. For artisanal fishers in Chorrillos, squid fishing has provided a boost when small concentrations appear off Peru's central coast and other species are not as readily available. In northern Peru, jumbo squid have led to the development of a sector of several hundred artisanal fishers who specialize in the pursuit of squid for processing and export.

Peru's squid fishery emerged out of the aftermath of a crisis in Peru's industrial fisheries in the 1970s and 1980s, when overfishing and two strong El Niño events in the span of a decade led to crashes in anchoveta and other traditional capture species. In response, the Peruvian state charged its marine biology institute with evaluating the potential of other species for new capture fisheries. With help and encouragement from the Japanese government, which was looking for new squid stocks to supplement declines in its own overfished stocks, biologists and fisheries managers "discovered" the jumbo squid and established the first exploratory fisheries for the species in the late 1980s and early 1990s. Foreign industrial boats initially dominated Peru's jumbo squid fishery. However, artisanal fishers, who had been summarily excluded from the anchoveta fishery, slowly took over the squid fishery, and in 2011, state officials reserved jumbo squid catches for artisanal fishers as a means of fostering development of the sector. This level of state support for an artisanal fishery is uncommon around the world, where industrial fleets have been prioritized in fisheries regulations. However, the Peruvian state has not been able to protect its artisanal jumbo squid fishery from growing incursions by foreign boats into Peruvian waters or the massing of Chinese squid boats in international waters just outside of Peru's exclusive economic zone (EEZ).

Peru's jumbo squid fishery provides important insight into how to theorize the (un)making of life amid environmental and climatic changes. These jumbo squid are, to use anthropologist Anna Tsing's (2017, 16) terminology, "weedy." They are aggressive and highly adaptable and able to shift population dynamics quickly in response to changing environmental conditions. This is one of the reasons why this "non-selective predator with a wide trophic range and a high consumption rate" (Ibañez et al. 2015, 406) has doubled its range in the Pacific Ocean in the last two decades (see map 1) and why its populations have declined quickly in reaction to temperature shifts caused by recent El Niño events. Tsing (2015, 6) argues that such processes of "re-assemblage" and "auto-rewilding" are essential for understanding how various species find their way into and interact in damaged landscapes, creating both potential for hope and alarming outcomes. She argues that amid the "numbing speed of capital's mobility," the liveliness of "auto-rewilding" is the best chance for species survival while weedy species "often kill the chances of other, less aggressive and disturbance-loving species" (Tsing 2017, 6, 9). In her analysis of these dynamics, Tsing (7) emphasizes the importance of using landscape to highlight "the gathering of human and nonhuman trajectories" in certain spaces.

I draw on Tsing's ideas about weediness and space by tracing the shifting relationships among squid, fish, and people in a rapidly changing Pacific oceanscape. I do so to analyze the ways in which Peru's jumbo squid fishery has been made possible by a "world-ecology" (Moore 2015) produced and momentarily sustained by a specific configuration of nature, capital, and politics in the Pacific Ocean. My analysis demonstrates the importance of historical ecology for understanding how to make sense of when and why certain species become "weedy" within a "scape." A species is only weedy until science and capital can find a way to put it to work and use it to generate value. After all, a weed is a plant that is unwanted in a particular landscape. Within the eyes of fishers, fisheries scientists, and government regulators, jumbo squid began as a "weed"—a species that was caught only accidentally because there was no market for it and a species that was assumed to impact negatively established commercial species, such as Peruvian anchoveta. Overfishing of other species and changes in global seafood markets led government fisheries scientists and managers to take another look at jumbo squid. In the process, the species shifted from being a weed to a commodity, which has generated a new jumbo squid extractive industry while creating the potential conditions for its undoing.

My argument in this chapter follows two main strands. First, I explore the development of government-sponsored fisheries science on jumbo squid and its role in identifying the species as an uncommodified form of life that could be converted into an extractable commodity. Second, I examine the myriad ecological, political, and economic engagements in the eastern Pacific's oceanscape that have produced Peru's jumbo squid fishery. Following these two intertwined processes and histories reveals how the research that established the basis for managing the squid fishery in Peru has obscured broader processes of multispecies (un)making that have occurred and continue to evolve in the eastern Pacific Ocean. This approach has blinded state regulators (among others) to the ecopolitics of squid extraction in Peru that both produces and imperils the human and nonhuman lifeworlds on which it depends. The solution to this blindness is an approach that maintains in constant view the natural, political, and economic processes that have combined to produce a historically specific squid world ecology in the eastern Pacific. At the end of the chapter, I return to the dock in Chorrillos to explore how the experiences of artisanal fishers provide such a view of the entanglements of squid extraction and the importance of attending to them for thinking about how and why Pacific world ecologies have changed and how they contain the potential for dramatic future changes.

LIMITS

Changes in Pacific Ocean ecologies, global consumption trends, and marine science led to new encounters among jumbo squid, fisheries biologists, artisanal and industrial fishers, and government officials in recent decades.[2] These encounters made the jumbo squid fishery possible and created new ways of classifying human and nonhuman life, new relationships of production and consumption, and new forms of labor and environmental struggle. As a result of the decline of other species and changing ecological conditions, jumbo squid went from a mysterious and largely ignored creature to an object of fisheries science and government regulation. This change led to novel relationships of prey and predation between squid populations and Peruvian, Japanese, Korean, and Chinese fishers. The development of an artisanal squid fishery in Peru also led to new relationships of knowledge and oversight between largely impoverished artisanal fishers, who had been historically marginalized in the production of fisheries commodities for global consumption, and state officials. The squid fishery created new ground for political contestation and the articulation of class inequalities among the state, industrial fishing corporations, and artisanal fishers, thus demonstrating how extractive regimes reorder existing ecological assemblages and life to generate the tenuous conditions for capital accumulation and in the process create the conditions for future environmental change.

Peru's jumbo squid fishery could be described as what anthropologist Eben Kirksey (2015, 1–3) calls an "emergent ecolog[y]"—a "novel" assemblage that has resulted from ecological destruction and degradation as well as species losses, additions, and invasions. Studying such emergent ecologies is critical for understanding "present multispecies communities, as well as possible futures" (5). Jason Moore (2015, 2) argues that understanding such ecologies and contemplating their futures is not possible without careful attention to the role that capitalism plays as a *way of organizing nature.* Moore (2015, 3) asserts that capitalism must be conceived as a *world-ecology* that joins the "accumulation of capital, the pursuit of power, and the co-production of nature in dialectical unity." The implication of this is that rather than destroy nature, capitalism works *through* nature" by finding ways to make it "work harder and harder—for free, or at a very low cost" (13) (emphases in the original). World ecologies set limits on the ability of historical natures to produce value, thus creating the conditions for future crises of accumulation and ecological change.

Science and the production of scientific knowledge play important roles in identifying and establishing claims to natures that can be commodified for capital accumulation. An extensive body of research has shown the intricate ways in which scientific knowledge has been enabled by, entwined with, and served myriad regimes of imperial power, biopolitics, and capital.[3] However, the implementation of scientific management rarely has been a straightforward process. The rationality and authority of scientific regimes have been challenged by the complex nature of the subjects that state-sponsored scientists have tried to make into the objects of their knowledge practices (Vaughn 2017). In his work on rangeland science in the western United States, Nathan Sayre (2017) examines the limitations of state-sponsored science for understanding and effectively managing rangeland ecologies. Sayre (2017, 2) argues that rangelands are "sites where the separate and combined efforts of capital, science, and the state meet their limits" because they are vast, ecologically variable, and socially marginal. Rangeland science emerged in early twentieth century as a presumably apolitical means of overcoming ecological crises and making rational decisions about maximizing land use. However, the "vast extent of western rangelands" greatly "exceeded what was financially, logistically, and technologically feasible in terms of data collection and research" (24). The authority of range science was rooted not in its efficacy but its ability to erase "signs of extra- or nonscientific influences and assumptions" (24). Rangeland science was oriented to a national scale of analysis, which obscured not only the importance of global markets and the demands they placed on ranchers but also the incredible ecological variation that exists among rangelands in the United States. Consequently, almost all of the range development projects implemented throughout the mid-twentieth century were "abject failures" with myriad ecological consequences (20).

Ocean ecologies have presented equally—if not more—vexing contexts for the implementation of modern fisheries science.[4] The Pacific Ocean (and oceans and seas generally) is a three-dimensional space that is characterized by predictable patterns and regular changes as well as considerable variation.[5] It is comprised of different vertical and horizontal zones, where varying levels of light penetration, oxygen saturation, and currents (among other factors) support different webs of life. Near-coast areas are generally more biologically diverse than the open ocean. Great upwelling systems, such as the Peru Current, which pushes cold water along much of Peru's and Chile's coasts, make portions of the ocean more productive (in terms of fish biomass) than others. Not only is there exceptional variability in the ocean's constantly changing biophysical conditions, but the creatures who inhabit its many spaces are often on the move. Many ocean creatures do not stay in one place, nor do they adhere to national and international boundaries. They move, not only in depth but also in distance across ocean space. Such variation pushes fisheries science to its very limits, challenging its ability to know and serve as the basis for managing the extraction of individual species. Fisheries scientists have dealt with the immense variation of the ocean and its creatures by restricting their analyses and the parameters of the knowable to a relatively narrow range of variables about key species—What are the characteristics of their basic biology (food, reproduction, migration), and under what conditions and where can they be most easily extracted?—at the scale of the "national."

Jumbo squid populations are especially revealing of these limits of state-sponsored fisheries science, given their adaptability, plasticity on both an individual and population level, and constant movements. Jumbo squid occupy "an important role in marine food webs as both predator and prey" (Alegre et al. 2014, 1). Jumbo squid are preyed upon by large ocean-going creatures, such as sperm whales ("whose diet consists of 100 percent jumbo squid" in this part of the world), sharks, and swordfish (Ibañez et al. 2015, 407). As predators, jumbo squid are not choosy. They consume a wide range of fish, mollusk, and squid species. The squid will target and decimate schools of commercially significant species such as hake (*Merluccius gayi*), jack mackerel (*Trachurus murphyi*), sardine (*Sardinops sagax*), and ancho-veta (*Engraulis ringens*) when the right ocean conditions are available (405). Jumbo squid are such voracious eaters that some studies have noted a high rate of cannibalism among the species, with other jumbo squid comprising almost half of the stomach contents of individuals sampled during certain times of the year.[6]

This eating is necessary to sustain the squid's rapid growth rate. Jumbo squid have relatively short life spans of one to two years, depending on ocean conditions. Nonetheless, they can attain lengths of over two meters and weights of up to fifty kilograms. This requires the squid to undertake regular vertical and horizontal migrations, moving from depths of over six hundred meters during the day to the surface at night and sometimes swimming up to one hundred kilometers in the matter of a few days in search of prey (William et al. 2006). Given their rapid growth, short lives, and ability to reproduce several times in a year, jumbo squid can change size on a population level to adjust to shifts in water temperature. They are smaller during warm water conditions, but larger when water temperatures drop, a population adaptation that enables individuals to undertake "longer migration distances" (Ibañez et al. 2015, 405). This plasticity has been significant for helping jumbo squid not only adapt to regular temperature shifts produced by the El Niño–Southern Oscillation (ENSO, see chapter 3) but also adjust to and thrive under broader climatic and ecological changes.

The decline in recent decades of many prey species, such as sharks, is but one factor that has contributed to the growth of jumbo squid populations. In addition to decreased predation of squid, recent increases in cephalopod populations in the eastern Pacific Ocean (and around the world) are likely due to climate change and decreased competition for food in areas where overfishing of competing species has occurred (Doubleday et al. 2016; Hoving et al. 2013). The jumbo squid's range has expanded dramatically in recent decades—historically it was from Mexico to central Chile, but now they are often found from Alaska to southern Chile (see map 1). "These fast-growing adaptable creatures," notes squid biologist Alexander Arkhipkin (2016), "are perfectly equipped to exploit the gaps left by extreme climate changes and overfishing."

The conditions under which jumbo squid populations have thrived are tenuous, and ongoing climate change may stretch the species to the limits of its adaptability. The world's oceans are becoming warmer, more acidic, and less oxygenated—trends that will worsen in the coming century if no dramatic measures are taken to reduce carbon emissions. Existing research suggests that these three factors are likely to have a negative impact on squid in general, and jumbo squid in particular.[7] Squid require a high amount of oxygen to move because they use jet propulsion, which has a high metabolic cost, yet they have a lower "oxygen-carrying capacity" than most fishes (Seibel et al. 2016, 420). Their blood is very sensitive to pH changes and is not as efficient as many fishes at taking up oxygen. Squid specialists Brad Seibel and Rui Rosa (2008) hypothesize that to balance their high metabolic rates and oxygen demands with their bodies' limited ability to take up oxygen, jumbo squid undergo daily vertical migrations. During the day the squid dive deep to the edge of the ocean's oxygen minimum zone (OMZ, the depths of the ocean—usually in the range of two hundred to a thousand meters—at which oxygen saturation is lowest) where they undergo metabolic suppression to slow down their bodies' metabolically costly functions (Seibel 2015). At night the squid moves back to the surface, thus "maximizing its oxygen extraction capabilities" in oxygen-rich waters of the upper ocean (Seibel 2016, 421).

Seibel (2015, 419) argues that it is probable that warmer waters limit jumbo squids' ability to absorb oxygen and increase the likelihood of asphyxiation because "warming waters reduce oxygen availability and elevate metabolic oxygen demand." Furthermore, the expansion of OMZs upward in the water column may force jumbo squid to "occupy a narrower and shallower night-time vertical distribution that will improve the nighttime foraging efficiency of its own vertebrate predators" (170). Seibel (2015) cautions that these out-comes have been confirmed in short-term studies, but the long-term outlook for jumbo squid is unclear. He suggests that the squid may be able to adapt by hatching earlier, reproducing more quickly, living shorter lives, and mov-ing into more amenable climates, as jumbo squid have done recently with migrations to the north Pacific Ocean (Seibel 2016). In any case, jumbo squid populations will likely shift and change dramatically in the coming decades with massive alterations in the Pacific Ocean's temperature and chemistry.

The conditions for squid's future are already present in the eastern Pacific Ocean's world ecology. The expansion of jumbo squid has been produced by historically specific political ecologies, which have used the ocean as a giant carbon sink and treated myriad fish species as "cheap natures" (Moore and Patel 2017) for unsustainable extraction. The same conditions have created new changes that may threaten the very existence of jumbo squid populations in the eastern Pacific Ocean. Reconfigurations of capitalist world ecologies in the Pacific Ocean have both made possible and simultaneously imperiled the precarious multispecies networks that make Peru's jumbo squid fishery possible, and have thus significantly reor-dered squid-human relationships at multiple scales. However, government-sponsored fisheries science has approached jumbo squid populations as a technical problem that can be solved by focusing on a narrow range of biological characteristics—"discovering" key unknowns about the species that can serve as a rational foundation for fisheries management—among squid populations in Peru's "national" waters. This approach has obscured the fact that the rise of jumbo squid populations is the product of unique extractive ecologies and that contemporary jumbo squid fisheries have been driven by global market demands as well as domestic politics (the employment of artisanal fishers). State-sponsored fisheries science and policy potentially contribute to a new, emergent ecological crisis, such as a crash in jumbo squid populations.

ABUNDANCE

Prior to 1990, jumbo squid were an afterthought for marine biologists, fisheries managers, and fishers, who concerned themselves with studying, regulating, and catching marine life forms that had been identified as objects of commodification, such as anchoveta or bonito. There was no market demand for the squid and no need to work out its migrations, reproductive cycles, habitat, and feeding behavior to develop schemes for converting squid life into value through extraction and management.[8]

This not to say that the squid was unknown to scientists or fishers. Latin American and European naturalists identified jumbo squid as early as the late eighteenth century and produced detailed descriptions of the bodily characteristics of squid that had washed ashore. Like all squid, the jumbo squid has three main body parts: eight arms and two feeding tentacles, a head with round eyes, and a long, muscular mantle that houses its primary organs. On each side of the jumbo squid's mantle there are two large fins that flap as the squid moves through the water by creating a jet of water that propels it forward, giving the impression that it is flying.[9] French naturalist Alcides d'Orbigny (1835, 1845) is credited with being the first to assign the species of the jumbo squid, which he encountered in his travels through South America between 1826 and 1833, as *gigas*. Danish zoologist Japetus Steenstrup (1857) proposed the genus *Dosidicus* for the squid, and subsequent zoologists synonymized the various names given to the species to arrive at *Dosidicus gigas* (Pfeffer 1884; Berry 1912). Commenting on *Dosidicus gigas* in his review of cephalopod literature, S. Stillman Berry (1912, 301, 304) marveled at how "robust and massive" the individual specimen he examined was of this "powerful species."

Marine biologists later established that the jumbo squid were one of the "most abundant" invertebrate marine species in the Pacific Ocean (Ibañez et al. 2015). However, mystery continued throughout much of the twentieth century about basic aspects of the squid's life, behavior, and range. What scientific knowledge did exist on these squid was anecdotal, derived from fishers' encounters with the *diablo rojo* (red devil), as the squid is known in parts of Latin America, because it uses color cells in its skin to flash red and white when feeding and because fishers reported that the squid was aggressive and would attack people. The jumbo squid only garnered scientific attention when they became a problem, as was the case in Concepción, Chile, where large numbers of squid died from time to time and clogged the city's beaches.

Biologists working in Chile published several reports of these squid beachings in the 1930s and 1950s (Schneider 1930; Wilhelm 1930). Ottmar Wilhelm (1954) described the massive number of squid that would sometimes arrive in the bay of Talcahuano toward the end of Chile's austral summer, die, and then create a local sanitation problem because of the hundreds of rotting corpses. In his description of the problem, Wilhelm (1954, 199) hypothesized that these mass die-offs might be the product of mating migration, noting that many of the dead squid had spent ovaries and lacked eggs that were in formation. While he thought this provided some understanding of the species' reproductive cycle, there were "still many unknowns" about the squid's biological characteristics (197). Autopsies of the stranded squid had provided important information about their diet. In the squids' stomachs, Wilhelm and his colleagues found crabs and other unidentified mollusks, fish, and jumbo squid, thus demonstrating the significance of cannibalism in the squids' diet.

Important questions still remained about the squids' migration in pursuit of food, the effect that water temperatures and currents had on the squids' movements and life cycles, and the impacts that chemical pollution from nearby rivers might have on squid entering Talcahuano's bay. Knowledge of these phenomena, Wilhelm argued, were critical for finding a means of controlling squid populations to avert the negative impacts of squid deaths. "In the meantime," he suggested that "it is worth taking advantage of this enormity of dead squid for industrial purposes," using them as fertilizer, for example (201). Wilhelm concluded that science might transform "an unpleasant problem into a source of wealth and well-being." Before the century was over, jumbo squid became subjects of more extensive fisheries science, which identified the species as a potential commodity for extraction and regulation. While Chilean fishers contributed to the squid's extraction, the global epicenter of this fishery became Peru.

DISCOVERING SQUID

During the 1950s and 1960s, Peru experienced a boom in anchoveta fishmeal production, which led to the rapid industrialization of a sector of the country's fishing fleet and the country's "Blue Revolution" (Bailey 1985; Wintersteen 2021). By 1964, the country became the largest single exporter of fishmeal in the world. The engine of Peru's fishing industry was the tiny Peruvian anchoveta, which fishers caught in record numbers to supply industrialized countries with fishmeal. However, overfishing and a strong El Niño event in 1972–73 led to a collapse of anchoveta stocks, which did not return to their pre-1972 levels until the mid-1990s. In response to this crisis, the fishmeal industry underwent a significant reorganization. The military government of President Juan Velasco Alvarado nationalized the industry to save it from bankruptcy. His government cut roughly half of the boats and laborers working in the industry, thus helping to consolidate and downsize the fishmeal industry to make it smaller, more efficient, and better able to extract a profit from diminished anchoveta stocks. The government also encouraged the thousands of workers left unemployed by these reorganizations to enter the artisanal, food-fish fleet as part of the government's overall strategies for promoting food import substitutions (Caravedo Molinari 1977). As Peru's overall economic situation worsened in the 1980s, the artisanal fishing sector absorbed growing numbers of impoverished Peruvians who were left unemployed by industry restructuring or were migrants who had recently arrived in coastal cities from the highlands. By the 1990s, this bifurcation became legally codified, with catches of anchoveta for "indirect human consumption" (fishmeal) reserved for the industrial fleet, while artisanal fishers were authorized to use wooden boats with nonmechanized nets to fish only for species intended for "direct human consumption" (in other words, table fish, not anchoveta for meal).[10]

These reorganizations made the emergence of Peru's jumbo squid fishery possible. As a result of ongoing crises in the anchoveta fishery, government officials and biologists sought new species that could sustain the expanding capacities of existing industrial and artisanal fleets. In the late 1970s and early 1980s, sardine (*Sardinops sagax*) stocks became more plentiful, and the government encouraged anchoveta boats to pursue the species until sardine numbers showed signs of overfishing and closed seasons were instituted. The Instituto del Mar del Perú (IMARPE, the Marine Institute of Peru) played a central role in this process as it continued to refine its methods for monitoring stocks and conducted more and more studies on species other than anchoveta to begin generating baseline population data about important food species, as well as investigating whether different species presented new opportunities for extraction. Jumbo squid were one such species.

Between 1961 and 1988, Peruvian fishers never landed more than nine hundred metric tons of jumbo squid in a single year (Mariátegui and Taipe 1996, 11). Throughout much of the 1970s, the government did not even bother to record landings of the squid. Initial studies suggested little promise for jumbo squid as a target species. IMARPE scientists conducted an experimental catch survey of the squid's populations between September 1979 and April 1980 using a Peruvian fishing boat for the first half of the survey and a Japanese boat for the second half.[11] In their report, IMARPE scientists Carlos Benites and Violeta Valdivieso (1986, 110) noted that the purpose of the survey was to better understand how jumbo squid populations had been affected by the recent boom and bust in anchoveta fishing. While "excessive fishing and the changes that have occurred in the marine ecosystem" led to a decline in anchoveta and an increase in other pelagic species, the "effects on cephalopods" was "not that clear" (110).

They reported that assessing the state of squid was important given a growing global interest in the species and "an important expansion of their markets" (110). The scientists caught squid at 128 stations over the course of their study, landing approximately eighteen tons of jumbo squid (108). What they found was that the squid were more readily available and easier to catch at night using lanterns and jigs and that the greatest concentrations of the species were in the central and northern portions of the coast. The scientists also sampled the stomach contents of the squid they caught, since little was known about their diet. Many fishers and scientists believed that they preyed on anchoveta and that recent declines in the fish might explain the drop in jumbo squid bycatch in the 1970s. These samples revealed that jumbo squid were eating small pelagic fish, fish eggs, crustaceans, and other squid (119). The scientists reported that cannibalism represented an important form of sustenance for the squid. They also noted that anchoveta did not appear in the squid's stomachs.

Benites's and Valdivieso's report suggested little promise for the development of a jumbo squid fishery in Peru. Despite six months of sampling during what was normally the high season for fishing in Peru, the scientists reported that levels of the squid were low along the Peruvian coast. They surmised that the "low availability" of jumbo squid in Peruvian waters might be due to declines in anchoveta stocks and that much of the population may have migrated north in search of better conditions, as evidenced by increased landings of the squid in Mexico (119–20).

Despite this assessment, growing interest in the species by Japanese and South Korean governments and their respective fishing industries led to more work to examine the potential of jumbo squid stocks for extraction. Fishers in these countries did not target jumbo squid because of the high concentration of ammonium chloride in their meat (Arkhipkin et al. 2015, R209). Declines in squid species traditionally targeted for Japanese and South Korean squid consumption, combined with new processing methods for removing ammonium chloride in squid meat, fueled interest in jumbo squid as a target species (R209). In 1989, the Japanese Marine Fishery Resources Research Center (JAMARC) paired with IMARPE to do a new survey of Peru's jumbo squid populations. The first of these studies, conducted in December 1989, found "good concentrations of the resource" along the Peruvian coast north of Callao, especially off Paita (Rubio and Salazar 1992, 9). The authors of the survey surmised that water temperature was critical in the recruitment of jumbo squid, noting that the "distribution of the resource seems to be influenced by the convergence of currents of surface ocean water (20 to 21 degrees Celsius) and coastal waters (17.8 to 19.6 degrees Celsius)" (9).

While earlier studies used terms such as "cephalopods" and "squid" in addition to scientific names to refer to the squid surveyed, in their report on the 1989 survey, Juan Rubio and Carlos Salazar consistently refer to jumbo squid as "the resource." In addition to supplying basic scientific information about squid populations, such as their distribution in the water column, the report's authors also provided technical information about the methods they used for capturing squid (jigs versus nets), the specifications of equipment (down to the wattages of the lights used for jigging), and best practices for preserving squid during transport (such as squid to ice ratios) (5–6). The use of such language and the inclusion of this technical information signaled the shifting status of jumbo squid from occasional bycatch and scientific unknown to an object of technical knowledge and a nature to be commodified. In addition to scientific and technical research on jumbo squid, between 1989 and 1991, the Peruvian government also authorized Japanese, South Korean, and Soviet boats to participate in experimental jumbo squid fishing seasons (Mariátegui and Taipe 1996, 5). This experimental fishery resulted in the largest catches of jumbo squid at the time. Soviet boats reported landing over nineteen-thousand metric tons of the squid during this two-year period, confirming that there was a high biomass of the species in Peruvian waters (5).

Based on these catches and data from scientific studies, in April 1991 the Peruvian government issued its first call for companies to bid on quotas for an experimental commercial jumbo squid fishery. In 1991, what was then the Ministerio de Pesquería (Ministry of Fisheries) licensed thirty-one industrial boats with automatic jigging stations to capture jumbo squid. With only one exception (a Peruvian industrial boat), these boats were all owned by Japanese and South Korean companies. Peruvian artisanal fishers were exempted from the quota and allowed to fish for the squid on a daily basis, given that they could not (and indeed did not) land many squid on any given day because they were limited legally to the use of small wooden boats and manual capture technologies. The noticeably foreign nature of the squid fishery prompted complaints from some in Peru's industrial fisheries sector that the squid fishery was benefiting only foreign boats, which had to pay a nominal fee to the Peruvian government for each ton of jumbo squid landed. The minister of fisheries responded that Peruvian boats and processing plants did not have the capacity to "exploit this resource in large quantities and, furthermore, could not invest in a product that shows up in the Peruvian sea on a temporal basis" (*El Comercio* 1992a, 1992b). Peruvian officials remained skeptical about the economic potential of jumbo squid, whose market price both in Peru and abroad remained very low. Officials initially saw jumbo squid as a low-risk opportunity to extract limited rent from foreign companies.

However, the foreign jigging fleet quickly demonstrated the potential of the fishery for growth. Prior to 1989, less than 1,000 metric tons of jumbo squid were reported by fishers in Peru each year. By 1994, licensed jigging boats, which numbered sixty-six, had landed over 160,000 metric tons of jumbo squid (Mariátegui and Taipei 1996). The success of foreign squid boats prompted Peruvian officials to institute measures to stimulate the domestic fishery for jumbo squid. In 1994, the Ministry of Fisheries issued a "Management Plan for Jumbo Squid" (RM 155–94-PE) with the objective of achieving a "rational and sustained exploitation of jumbo squid" and "maximiz[ing] the economic benefits deriving from exploitation of the resource." The management plan established vessel quotas for all foreign boats and Peruvian boats with hold capacities over thirty tons (depending on conditions, total catch was to be set between 100,000 to 200,000 metric tons). Such boats were also prohibited from pursuing squid closer than thirty nautical miles from shore to ensure that they did not interfere with artisanal boats or industrial anchoveta boats, both of whom tended to operate closer to shore. The regulations also created provisions for encouraging an artisanal fishery for jumbo squid, which the authors of the management plan stressed were "underexploited in Peru's jurisdictional waters." In support of the new management plan, in 1994 IMARPE began acoustic surveys for jumbo squid, adapting techniques used since the 1960s to estimate anchoveta populations, to better assess squid populations and set annual quotas based on scientific data about jumbo squid populations.

WATERY FRONTIERS

One of the key components of IMARPE's exploratory studies of jumbo squid were maps of the species' distribution in Peruvian waters. All but two of the squid studies that IMARPE scientists published in the 1980s and 1990s included maps that detailed where biologists had found squid and in what concentrations. Maps have functioned for a long time as technologies of territory making, as means through which spaces and the natural resources in them become known so that they can be claimed by empires, states, or corporations (Dym and Offen 2011). An essential aspect of this process is what James Scott (1998, 2–4, 30) refers to as "simplification," whereby complex places are reduced to abstract spaces that highlight the presence of certain borders, people, or features, while ignoring others. Through this process of eliminating unnecessary information and highlighting desired objects of power, maps "make the local situation legible to an outsider" (45). This is a critical process through which natures and lifeworlds are converted into natural resources that are ready for extraction and commodification. As a "technology of conquest" (Moore and Patel 2017, 55), maps play a critical role in bringing into being new ecological relationships. "The transformative power resides not in the map, of course, but rather in the power possessed by those who deploy the perspective of that particular map," and who can wield that power to "ensure that the logic of [the] map prevails" (Scott 1998, 87).

The maps that IMARPE scientists produced and included in their published reports reduced the complexity of the eastern Pacific Ocean's ecology to render jumbo squid visible to other scientists, government regulators, and fishing companies, making squid life an object of state regulatory practice and extraction. In IMARPE reports on jumbo squid populations, scientists presented maps of their findings as no-nonsense representations of the scientific data that they collected. As with all maps, the relationship between what is portrayed and what is left out is critical for interpreting their purpose and thinking about how these maps served as guides for how the eastern Pacific Ocean's squid life could be transformed into a commodity. IMARPE's scientists portrayed the eastern Pacific Ocean as a flat, homogeneous zone that was featureless—a white blank that was punctuated only by markings that symbolized the coordinates of squid catches.

On the first of these maps, published in Benites and Valdivieso's (1986) report of IMARPE's first exploratory study of jumbo squid populations, the ocean was separated from the land by a thin, black line that traced Peru's coast (and which included small portions of those of Ecuador and Chile). Otherwise, the maritime and terrestrial spaces were indistinguishable—they were featureless blank expanses that showed no geographic relief, predominant currents, or texture of any kind. Along the coast, the names of Peru's key ports were written perpendicular to the coastline. The ocean space was dotted with circles, squares, and triangles, some empty and some filled in black. These small shapes marked the coordinates of the ship's stops and how much squid was caught at each stop. An empty circle marked the lowest density (105 kilograms or less) and a black triangle marked the highest density (more than 525 kilograms). The resulting effect was that Benites and Valdivieso (1986, 134) presented squid populations as dispersed throughout the eastern Pacific Ocean off Peru's shore. While a greater concentration of circles, dots, and triangles was located off the coast of northern Peru, there were markers throughout the country's ocean territory. The coordinates provided on the outer edge of the map enabled the reader to locate the longitude and latitude of each test cite depicted. Although the report suggested that concentrations of squid were not high enough to support a viable fishery, the report's map depicted an ocean space that was peppered with squid populations in reach of Peru's major fishing ports.

Subsequent IMARPE reports documented improved densities of squid, especially off Peru's northern coast, and the way in which the authors chose to depict squid populations changed. Instead of representing squid catches as scattered data points, IMARPE scientists in the 1990s showed squid populations as solid zones whose varying concentrations were designated by different shadings (horizontal hatching versus vertical hatching versus black). These zones appeared on the maps as a kind of ocean topography—as layers that radiated out from high points of squid concentration. Furthermore, the zones were bounded by dotted and solid lines that created the impression of a squid territory that was marked out from the white, blank ocean expanse that surrounded it.[12] The effect created an image of a maritime frontier—a newly discovered squid archipelago located near Peru's coast. IMARPE's squid maps provided cartographic information about where the best concentrations of squid life existed, with the ultimate end goal of converting these lives into commodities.[13]

Early maps, such as the one provided by Rubio and Salazar (1992, 24), lacked movement. They depicted the squid frontier in a static relationship to the coast and portrayed the space between this frontier and coastal fishing ports as a blank ocean.[14] These maps emphasized ease of access and a lack of impediments to movement—such as existing zones of extensive fishing, high-traffic shipping routes, or, beginning in 1992, exclusive fishing zones for artisanal boats. While Mariátegui and Taipe's (1996, 16–18) survey of jumbo squid distributions in Peruvian waters preserved these spatial representations, they added time depth to their visual depictions of the squid population by providing sequences of maps that showed the concentration of jumbo squid populations during different seasons or years (see also Mariátegui et al. 2000). Through a series of three maps, Mariátegui and Taipe show how concentrations of squid slowly moved north between 1991 and 1993. There were also areas of concentration off the southern coast that existed in mid-1991, disappeared in 1992, and reappeared in 1993. While these maps persisted in showing squid populations as bounded territories, they suggested the importance of thinking about how and why these territories moved for more efficient, targeted extraction.

While earlier surveys showed the changing nature of squid territories, they consistently indicated that the greatest concentrations were off the country's northern coast. Subsequent studies focused attention on this area and sought to explain concentrations of squid populations by studying their relationship to variables such as ocean salinity and temperature. The maps that IMARPE scientists produced for their reports became increasingly localized. Rather than depicting all squid populations in relation to the whole of Peru's national coastline, they zoomed in on the eastern Pacific off the northern coast, usually from Salvaverry to Puerto Pizarro, close to the border with Ecuador. These maps provided greater detail about the most commercially important squid populations and sought to map their subtle variations in relationship to variables that regulators and fishers could use to predict relative abundance from one season or year to the next. In their study of squid populations off the coast between Paita and Puerto Pizarro, Francisco Ganoza et al. (1997) included a series of maps that represented squid populations as bounded, shaded islands of abundance. Mapped onto these zones were solid lines that designated salinity in one map and in another, surface water temperatures. While these environmental variables were represented with solid lines, unlike the depictions of squid populations, they were not presented as bounded territories but as disconnected waves that had starting and ending points that did not meet. Moreover, these waves overlaid the squid zones but did not disrupt or become entangled with them, thus emphasizing the purpose of the maps to identify and keep in view extractable squid natures.

In addition to maps that attempted to show correlations between areal concentrations of squid populations and ocean variables, Ganoza et al. (1997) provided the first maps of squid distribution in the water column to represent the three-dimensional nature of squid territories. This move represented a new level of detail in establishing not only the location of squid territories on an imagined, flat ocean surface, but also the location of vertical squid frontiers according to ocean depth. Ganoza et al. (1997, 49) provided four maps, one each for the waters (from north to south) off Puerto Pizarro, Cabo Blanco, Talara, and Paita. In each map, the water column was depicted by depth (from 0 to 250 meters) along the right side, by distance from the coast along the bottom (from 0 to 300 nautical miles), and by lines that crossed through the map indicating temperature zones. Squid appeared as dark hatch marks that could be found only after crossing over various frontiers—the water's surface and then the lines that indicated zones of the same temperature and salinity. The cross-section maps reduced the messy complexity of life in the eastern Pacific Ocean to a handful of variables that could be used to locate a single species and establish the likelihood of its presence amid specific ecological conditions.

The maps that IMARPE's scientists produced in their reports on jumbo squid populations reveal how marine science made squid populations visible to government regulators and fishers interested in squid extraction. Through precise abstractions that removed the complexities of life in the ocean, scientists' maps established when, where, and under what conditions squid life could be located. Initially, IMARPE scientists depicted squid as populations dispersed throughout Peru's "national" waters. However, once scientists determined where concentrations of the species could be found consistently, they represented squid populations as bounded territories with defined frontiers. When the basic parameters of squid availability were established, during the late 1990s and 2000s IMARPE's scientists focused more on studying fishers' engagements with squid populations. Maps in Mariátegui et al. (2000, 6) and Blaskovic, Alegre, and Tarfur (2008, 4) did not display squid populations in absentia, but where artisanal and industrial fishers stopped to jig for squid and what quantities they landed. These maps indicated the frontier areas in which squid life was being put to work and where new encounters were emerging along these watery frontiers.

UNDEREXPLOITED

While jumbo squid catches grew steadily between 1989 and 1994, they declined in the second half of the 1990s because oceanic conditions changed. In 1997 and 1998, the Pacific Ocean experienced a strong El Niño, which led to a precipitous drop in anchoveta landings as well as declining squid numbers. In 1996 most foreign jigging boats moved to Costa Rica "when the availability and abundance of jumbo squid decreased dramatically off Peru" (Arkhipkin 2015, 210). This shift had two important consequences. First, the jumbo squid fishery changed from one dominated by foreign boats to an increasingly domestic, artisanal fishery. Second, the rise and fall of jumbo squid numbers (as with anchoveta stocks decades before) revealed the difficulties of expanding an intensive fishery in an area prone to regular and dramatic fluctuations in ocean conditions. Jumbo squid landings plummeted between 1996 and 1998 as unusually cold La Niña waters gave way to a strong El Niño. In 1998, landings of the species dropped below one thousand metric tons for the first time in a decade.

Peruvian officials continued to emphasize that jumbo squid numbers were underexploited and represented an important resource for fisheries development. Much of this was a response to expanding global demand for squid meat and Peru's position in emerging commodity chains. In the early 1990s, Peru accounted for over 90 percent of the global trade in jumbo squid. IMARPE scientists continued to believe that jumbo squid preyed on anchoveta, whose numbers had rebounded in the mid-1990s, and so harvesting squid in greater numbers was an important means for promoting the revival of the anchoveta fishmeal industry (Arellano and Swartzman 2010, 142). Peruvian officials also stressed the need for and importance of more accurate scientific understandings of squid population dynamics to better estimate when and how squid stocks would fluctuate. They approached the desire to continue expanding the jumbo squid fishery amid dramatic ecological fluctuations as a technical problem that could be solved with better scientific knowledge.

In the second half of the 1990s, IMARPE scientists embarked on numerous survey expeditions aimed at better understanding squid migrations, population dynamics, and feeding patterns and the ways in which changing oceanic conditions affected them. In one such study on the growth and recruitment of juvenile squid, Juan Argüelles Torres (1996, 3–4) noted that "knowledge about the biological and population characteristics [of jumbo squid] is important for the establishment of adequate means for exploitation," but that "studies undertaken on this species are few." As Argüelles Torres and other IMARPE scientists pointed out in their studies, analyzing squid population dynamics was complicated by the fact that longitudinal data on the species was unavailable because it had been extracted for only a few years and because squid populations changed quickly with alterations in oceanic conditions. Jumbo squid live for one or two years and reproduced rapidly, which means that they can adapt on a population level much more quickly than species that have longer lives.

Another study, conducted during the cold-water conditions of the 1996 La Niña, documented highly dispersed and reduced squid numbers off Peru's north coast, leading the scientists who conducted it to remark that the "presence of giant squid is linked intimately to environmental conditions" (Ganoza et al. 1997, 36). An IMARPE survey conducted in March and April 1996 on squid populations from the central to northern regions of Peru's coast yielded similar results, with squid populations dispersed or not present throughout most of the areas sampled (Mariátegui et al. 1997). The authors remarked that the "situation of permanent fluctuation in the availability of the resource" required more advanced information about the "distribution and actual state [of squid] in relation to marine environmental conditions" (30). Echoing broader official concerns and mandates for the expansion of an industrial squid fishery, the scientists concluded that such information was critical for achieving the "optimal and rational exploitation of this resource" (30).

This preoccupation with the "optimal level of exploitation" was repeated verbatim in many of the studies that IMARPE scientists conducted on jumbo squid during the late 1990s.[15] These studies were conducted with the aim of better estimating squid populations to establish the overall biomass of squid more accurately in Peruvian waters from year to year so that sustainable quotas could be established for expanded squid fishing. This process mirrored IMARPE's efforts to estimate anchoveta populations to maintain a profitable industrial fishmeal sector and avoid the crashes that befell the species in preceding decades. It also reflected emerging fisheries management strategies in the 1980s and 1990s that relied on the establishment of vessel quotas. Such quotas emerged as a means of privatizing the extraction of fish, which required the scientific establishment of stock levels to decide how many tons of fish could be taken out each year and how much of that total each individual boat was allowed to catch.[16] The scientific-technical research that IMARPE conducted was aimed at establishing the most efficient and sustainable means for expanding the squid fishery by predicting where the squid would be in a given year (based on what was happening with oceanic conditions and water temperature) and what the maximum yield could be without causing a decline in squid populations (based on things such as sonar sampling). Furthermore, IMARPE studies reported detailed data on the "units of effort" required to extract a kilogram of squid in a particular place at a particular time (such as night versus day). The purpose of these data was to establish when, where, and what fishing methods would result in the greatest catches per unit of effort (generally measured in time), thus contributing to the efficiency and overall profitability of widescale squid extraction.

It was not a quota-regulated industrial fleet that generated a new boom in squid production following the 1997–98 El Niño but artisanal fishers who used what many officials considered inefficient, work-intensive means for landing growing quantities of the squid. In their recent evaluation of Peru's jumbo squid fishery, Carlos E. Paredes and Santiago de la Puente (2014, 14–16) list several important reasons for the boom in artisanal squid production. First, the 1997–98 El Niño depressed nearshore fisheries and encouraged artisanal fishers in many ports to venture farther out into the ocean in search of other species, such as squid. Second, jumbo squid became an especially important species when stocks of hake, a central target species for artisanal fish exports, faltered at the end of the twentieth century. Third, oceanic conditions in the early 2000s changed to favor the reproduction and rapid growth of jumbo squid, whose numbers increased dramatically (Argüelles et al. 2008). Fourth, because of diminished squid numbers between 1995 and 1999, foreign squid boats largely left Peruvian waters in search of better fishing. By 2002, artisanal boats were landing more squid than those of the industrial fleet. Two years later, landings of jumbo squid surpassed two hundred thousand metric tons for the first time. In the decade that followed, Peruvian fishers landed on average four hundred thousand metric tons of jumbo squid each year, with artisanal fishers accounting for roughly 90 percent of these landings.

ALLOWABLE CATCHES

As squid landings have become more lucrative and more important in Peru's export portfolio, there has been increased debate among Peru's fishers regarding who should have priority in the fishery's regulation. Artisanal fishers have asserted that they should have exclusive legal right to the fishery, given the industry's dominance of anchoveta catches. Peruvian officials have instituted an annual quota for jumbo squid catches and licensed artisanal boats to capture them. In theory, such a management strategy avoids stock depletion through up-to-date quotas that are based in scientific estimates of how many squid are swimming in Peruvian waters at a given time. One of the challenges to this management scheme is that scientists' knowledge of squid population biology continues to be limited. Furthermore, while a national-level approach to fisheries management is important for reinforcing the authority of state fisheries officials and regulatory schemes, it cannot account for what is happening to squid populations just outside of Peru's EEZ, where a large fleet of Chinese boats has targeted the species in international waters.[17] This situation reveals the limitations of state-sponsored fisheries regulations, even when based in the best science, to know and effectively monitor jumbo squid populations and avert future crises through management.

Within fisheries management policy, quotas have become the dominant means of regulating fisheries and are often touted as the only means of avoiding a "tragedy of the commons" in which an unlimited number of individual fishers are able to pursue a particular species and fish it until it is depleted.[18] However, a significant body of recent research has argued that such quota schemes privatize ocean resources, often for the benefit of larger corporations or fishing operations with more resources.[19] In 2008, the Ministerio de la Producción (Produce, Ministry of Production) instituted individual vessel quotas (IVQs) for the country's industrial anchoveta fleet. This meant that "based on the best years of landings since 2004," individual boats were awarded a portion of the total annual allowed catch of anchoveta (Aranda 2009, 149). While aimed at making the industrial fishery more accountable, the institution of IVQ's represented an enclosure of anchoveta stocks by the corporations represented by the Sociedad Nacional de Pesquería (SNP, National Fisheries Society). In the ensuing decade, these corporations accounted for 60 percent or more of Peru's annual anchoveta quota. The new regulations also officially excluded most small-scale industrial and artisanal boats from the lucrative fishmeal industry by making them ineligible for IVQs and thus preventing them from catching anchoveta for fishmeal.

Owners of some of the industrial boats that were excluded from the IVQ system sought to convert their anchoveta boats to squid boats. Amid this shift, artisanal fishers pressed the government to exclude industrial boats from the jumbo squid fishery and thus make it the legal preserve of artisanal fishers. If anchoveta was only for the industrial fleet, they asserted that squid should be only for artisanal fishers. In 2011, the government of center-left president Ollanta Humala (2011–16) did just that. Humala's administration sought to separate the fishmeal industry from direct influence in fisheries policy and promote the artisanal fishing sector. The government ended licensing for the industrial squid fishery, thus reserving jumbo squid for artisanal fishers. Produce's officials sought to balance market demands and ecological constraints with the social and political need to keep artisanal fishers employed at least at minimum levels.

Produce officials have worked to maintain the jumbo squid fishery as the domain of artisanal fishers in the face of pressure from the SNP. At the same time, Produce has subject artisanal fishers to an ever-expanding regime of regulations aimed at making them more visible to government regulators. Officials in Produce have expressed growing concern over the "informality" and "inefficiencies" of artisanal fishers. By law, artisanal fishers have been allowed to fish most species intended for direct human consumption (i.e., not fish for meal) without having to purchase specific licenses and accompanying quotas. Much of this has to do with the highly variable, localized, and dispersed nature of the tens of thousands of artisanal fishers who are active up and down Peru's coast. It also has to do with a long history of state neglect of these fishers given officials' focus on capturing the most lucrative commercial stocks for industrial producers to export (Viatori and Bombiella 2019).

In the past decade, Produce officials have drafted a series of decrees and regulations to address the "conditions of informality" in the squid fishery and establish the grounds necessary to subject squid fishers to a regulatory regime that would make it easier to track who is fishing for squid and how much of the species is being landed each year. The purpose of these regulations is to "optimize the exploitation and the equitable distribution of the economic and social benefits" of the squid fishery by establishing a formal registry of artisanal boats that are exploiting the squid fishery.[20] In 2017, Produce announced that it had taken the first steps toward obtaining a sustainability certification for the jumbo squid fishery from the Marine Stewardship Council, which conducts the largest consumer certification program for sustainable seafood in the world. These efforts have emerged in response to international pressure from importing countries, conservation organizations, and consumers who are concerned about Illegal, Unregulated, and Unreported (IUU) fishing in the region. IUU is a catchall term used by global monitoring bodies to identify and address fishing activities that undermine national and international legal norms and threaten the economic and ecological sustainability of fisheries. As Peru's jumbo squid fishery has become more important for global seafood markets, there has been increased international concern that significant portions of it are "illegal." Government regulations have been aimed at combating this label and the impact it could have on Peruvian squid exports.

Artisanal fishers largely have supported this formalization of the squid fishery with the hope that expanded government oversight would protect their legal right to squid catches from industrial boats. Artisanal fishers in Piura Region staged regular protests and marches between 2015 and 2018, pressing the government to recognize their official right to fish jumbo squid in addition to perico. Adopting government discourses of formality, these fishers argued that they were operating in a state of informality and needed formal fishing licenses to protect their catches from illegal fishing by industrial and foreign boats. The Comité de Pesca y Acuicultura de la Sociedad Nacional de Industrias (SNI, Committee on Fishing and Aquaculture of the National Society of Industries), which represents processing companies that have collaborated with artisanal fishers to export frozen squid, also publicly supported the exclusion of SNP (industry) boats from the squid fishery. The president of the committee argued that extracting an additional four hundred thousand metric tons of squid each year, as the SNP had proposed, could destroy Peru's jumbo squid stocks (*Gestión* 2016). In response to this pressure, and with help from a World Wildlife Fund (WWF 2018) project on sustainable fisheries, on June 30, 2018, Produce officials provided artisanal fishers in Paita, the capital of Piura Region, licenses for fishing jumbo squid. The five hundred fishers who received licenses accounted for approximately one-fifth of Peru's jumbo squid landings, and Produce officials claimed that licensing these fishers was a means of "formalizing their labor and advancing the sustainability of one of the principle economic activities of the country" (*La República* 2018a).

In response, the SNP pressured Produce to revoke these official permissions for artisanal squid fishers because protections for artisanal fisheries are unconstitutional exclusions. The SNP has used the same rationale for opposing a series of Produce regulations that have allowed limited small-scale and artisanal catches of anchoveta for processing and direct human consumption. Industry representatives have argued that the same regulations should be applied to all boats, whether they are artisanal or industrial, and that an individual boat quota system, which is used to regulate the industrial anchoveta fishery, is critical for accurately tracking who is extracting how much jumbo squid and combating "illegal" fishing (*Gestión* 2018).

Such assertions obscure the role that quotas have played in dispossessing large numbers of fishers from the anchoveta fishery and helping the members of the SNP to monopolize anchoveta stocks. Furthermore, it is not unregulated fishing by artisanal boats that has posed the greatest threat to Peru's marine ecologies but regulated industrial extraction of a very limited range of species. Since the fishmeal boom of the 1960s, industrial anchoveta fishing and fishmeal processing has distorted local fishing economies, reordered webs of marine species, and displaced artisanal fishers through the ecological degradation of once-productive coastal fisheries (Viatori and Bombiella

2019). Despite being subject to one of the most advanced, science-based regulatory regimes, Peru's anchoveta stocks have suffered from repeated boom-and-bust cycles since the 1970s because of overfishing and climatic fluctuations (Cushman 2013; Wintersteen 2021). While ENSO produces years of tremendous abundance, in the periods following warming phases it also results in (sometimes years of) very low stock numbers. These regular, but unpredictable, fluctuations create an unstable foundation for industrial production based on establishing continuous—and ever-growing—supplies of single marine species.

To avert a similar crisis in jumbo squid extraction, IMARPE scientists have sought new ways to measure squid biomass (they found that the acoustic sampling used to estimate anchoveta stocks is not as accurate for squid, which have a lower reflectivity) and new models for predicting squid populations from one year to the next. IMARPE studies conducted in the last decade have sought to understand how ocean temperatures and the abundance (or lack) of other species might be used to predict fluctuations in jumbo squid numbers (Blaskovic et al. 2008). This has been a challenging task given what the authors of a recent IMARPE report on jumbo squid population dynamics refer to as the species' "phenotypical plasticity" (Yamashiro, Soto, and Torres 2016, 17). Jumbo squid populations are "typically unstable and respond rapidly to changes in environmental conditions," which fluctuate considerably in the eastern Pacific Ocean (17). The authors of the report concluded that it was critical to take full advantage of squid populations when conditions were "favorable"—when ocean temperatures brought large concentrations close to shore. Doing so would maximize the "economic benefits for the country" by taking greater advantage of the total biomass of jumbo squid in Peruvian waters, which the authors estimated to be approximately two million metric tons (17).

During 2017, IMARPE undertook a research expedition to provide a new estimate of squid biomass, the data from which was used to establish the first global quota for jumbo squid catches in 2018. The institute's scientists used new methods to estimate that the maximum sustainable yield for the species was 135.4 million individual squid (IMARPE 2018). IMARPE scientists concluded that this new data confirmed that the species was "underexploited" in Peruvian waters, but that to ensure the resilience of the stock amid climatic fluctuations, no more than 96.7 million squid should be caught per year (IMARPE 2018). Produce set the maximum sustainable yield of jumbo squid to 609,000 metric tons for 2018.[21] This maximum allowed catch was a global quota that set a ceiling on total reported squid catches for the year. It was not divided into individual quotas that were assigned to boats, the way that the IVQ system functions for industrial anchoveta captures.

Artisanal fishers have harvested only about half of the maximum allowed catch in the strongest years, while landing a far smaller portion in weak years. Representatives of the SNP have highlighted the presumed disparity between estimates of maximum sustainable yields for jumbo squid and artisanal fishers' annual catches to assert that industrial boats should be granted access to the squid fishery. Fishmeal industry proponents argue that jumbo squid are "underexploited" in Peruvian waters and that the fishery could be expanded without negative ecological impacts. In recent years, as competition for Peru's dwindling fish stocks has increased, the SNP has decried the "informal" nature of artisanal fishing as a threat to the environmental sustainability of Peru's ocean ecosystems, given that artisanal fishers' catches are not regulated in the same way as those of the industrial fleet (Viatori and Bombiella 2019). In the case of the jumbo squid fishery, industry representatives have argued that the artisanal fishers do not have the capacity to exploit squid stocks to their full potential because artisanal boats are too small and inefficient. Furthermore, they have argued that artisanal fishers do not have the infrastructure to ensure a consistent, high-quality product. Most boats do not have insulated hulls and cannot keep squid as cold as possible during transport. Many artisanal docks in Peru also lack potable water and a steady supply of ice to maintain the freshness of the squid once it is landed. The SNP's representatives have argued that allowing industrial boats to participate in the squid fishery is necessary for extracting more rent from higher quality exports. Proponents of opening the squid fishery to industrial extraction have claimed that artisanal fishers do not pay for the right to fish squid, in the same way that industrial boats would, leading to additional lost revenues for the state.

In the past decade, the phrase "underexploited in jurisdictional waters" has become boilerplate language in Produce's regulations and IMARPE reports on the jumbo squid fishery. Some fisheries biologists in Peru and abroad have been more cautious about the promise of jumbo squid fisheries, noting that rapid fluctuations in populations can pose significant economic risks to fishers and cautioning that squid populations are "notoriously difficult to predict" and that many squid fisheries seem to have already reached peak catches (Doubleday et al. 2016, 407). Moreover, state management of jumbo squid populations is limited to legal catches by boats who are registering catches that count toward the national quota within Peruvian waters. While the Peruvian government has expanded the management and regulation of the squid fishery among Peruvian boats in its jurisdictional waters, an increasingly large fleet of primarily Chinese boats has targeted jumbo squid populations in the international waters just outside of Peru's EEZ, which ends two hundred nautical miles from the country's shore. The Chinese fleet's squid fishing is having an increasingly large impact on squid populations in the eastern Pacific. Smaller jigging boats are now present in these waters throughout the year, and from July to December larger boats from the southwest Atlantic shortfin squid fishery (which has experienced dramatic swings in recent years) move to open water just outside of Peru's jurisdiction to pursue jumbo squid. In recent years there have been more than four hundred Chinese boats operating in the area catching up to 350,000 metric tons, an amount that is close to what Peru's squid fleet catches in an average year (Li et al. 2019).

The emergence of China's long-distance squid fishery is the result of changes in the western Pacific Ocean that are like those that occurred in Peruvian fisheries and eastern Pacific Ocean lifeworlds since the 1970s. Chinese boats began to target squid populations in the high seas beginning in the late 1980s as traditional ground fish stocks and squid numbers declined in Chinese waters because of overfishing (Chen et al. 2008). Chinese squid boats, which now comprise "one of the largest fishing fleets for oceanic squid" active in the world, chase various squid species in the eastern Pacific, Atlantic, and Indian Oceans (Chen, Liu, and Chen 2008, 212). This squid fleet has been subsidized heavily by the Chinese state, which has provided fuel subsidies that have enabled China's long-distance fishing fleet to increase by roughly one-third since 2012. China's squid boats also receive up-to-date information from a network of research vessels and satellites that track squid populations in the high seas (Chen 2018). These measures have enabled Chinese boats to claim over half of the world's squid (including, but not limited to, jumbo squid) caught in international waters, giving the country tremendous influence over squid populations and markets around the world.

Catches of jumbo squid in international waters have not been closely regulated. The fishery is monitored each year by the South Pacific Regional Fisheries Management Organization (SPRFMO), a relatively new (founded in

2012) intergovernmental organization that has sought to foster cooperation among its member countries (which includes China) to manage the region's fisheries sustainably. At the organization's annual meeting, delegates from member countries report on their participation, for example, in the jumbo squid fishery. Chinese officials and scientists have asserted that squid populations are not susceptible to overfishing given their short life spans and rapid reproduction, and that Chinese fisheries science is sophisticated enough to respond to shifts in different squid populations (Hornby 2017). There are ongoing concerns among scientists and fisheries managers in Peru and other countries that Chinese officials are not being entirely transparent in their reporting on distant-water squid fisheries in the South Pacific and may be overestimating squid populations and underreporting their annual catches.

SQUID WORK

Peru's jumbo squid fishery exists in a tenuous moment in which booming squid populations and demand for them have been able to help sustain artisanal fishers. However, this shaky arrangement is threatened by ongoing climatic changes and industrial attempts to reconfigure ocean natures. A crash in squid populations would have a profoundly negative effect on these fishers, likely exacerbating existing inequalities and differences among industrial and artisanal fishing operations in the country. The center of Peru's squid fishery has been in the north, specifically in the port of Paita, where roughly half of the country's jumbo squid catch is unloaded in any given year. However, jumbo squid has become a significant part of artisanal fishing economies throughout the country, and at present artisanal fishers catch more jumbo squid (by weight) than any other single species. The jumbo squid fishery has impacted geographies of artisanal fishing in Peru as well as seasonal fishing schedules, markets, work, and economic differences among artisanal fishers. A change in existing jumbo squid world ecologies would reverberate throughout many artisanal fishing docks in Peru. This is true for Chorrillos, where I began this chapter. While jumbo squid has not been a significant source of catches in Chorrillos, unloading squid from boats has become an important source of income for fishers in the off season and has become a source of hope for future improvements in the dock's economy.

Elsewhere I have discussed in detail the economic, political, and ecological challenges that artisanal fishers in Chorrillos face.[22] A quick summary of these challenges is in order to provide context for thinking about how jumbo squid catches factor into artisanal fishers' livelihood strategies and aspirations. Fishers in Chorrillos have remained small-scale and nearshore in their focus. Most of the fishers ply local waters using wooden boats with hold capacities of one or two metric tons. Fishers in Chorrillos have a long history of providing fresh fish to Lima's residents, and their proximity to the city and its markets has meant that fishers have not had to develop the same kind of cooperative buying and transportation systems that fishers outside the city have created in recent decades. There is a fishers' association that manages the dock, collecting annual fees from members and vendors who sell fresh fish and prepared food. However, the local fishing economy is based primarily on individual connections that fishing families have with local consumers, restaurants, and other buyers. Rather than landing large quantities of fish for distant markets, fishers in Chorrillos have sustained themselves by landing small quantities of fish for sale in daily local markets. The fishing economy in Chorrillos has been rooted in the daily consistency of the local ecosystem and the ability of fishers to land a small amount of a wide variety of different fish species (depending on the season and water conditions) on a consistent basis.

The ability of the local ecology to support such activities has diminished in recent decades because of industrial overfishing by boats based in nearby Callao (one of the two largest fishing ports in Peru), pollution from the rapidly expanding population of Lima, and broader oceanic changes in weather and fish populations. Combined with increasing costs of living in Peru's capital city, this situation has exacerbated the precarity that artisanal fishers face in their efforts to make what they consider a decent life from fishing. For these fishers this means not just meeting the basic needs of their families, but also being able to live with some dignity by having enough money to meet cultural expectations, such as celebrating baptisms, participating in local religious festivals, or buying special food or clothes for their children. This has led fishers and their families to look for alternatives for generating more income while also maintaining the autonomy and dignity that comes from working on a fishing dock. While some fishers will work "on land," doing construction or other short-term jobs, they consider this a last resort because the work is low-paid and demeaning compared to the lives of fishers who make their own decisions about where, when, and how to work on any given day. Almost all the fishers who are in long-term relationships have partners who work on the dock as food vendors, which enables them to have their children around and helping with different aspects of work. During the summer months when beachgoers flock to the wharf, some fishers and their families give tourists boat rides.

Another potential option is to fish farther out and target species in the high seas, thus moving beyond the limitations of the nearshore fishery. This is an option that some artisanal fishers in the nearby ports of Ancón and Pucusana have pursued. However, given the limited scale of the local market, only a few fishers in Chorrillos have been able to amass the capital necessary (through savings and loans from family and other fishers) to build larger boats for fishing species such as bonito. These boats are still considerably smaller than those used by fishers form Paita to target and land large quantities of jumbo squid. High-seas fishing for species such as jumbo squid has not developed into a viable option for artisanal fishers in Chorrillos. Nonetheless, most years there is a good concentration of jumbo squid off Peru's central coast, attracting larger artisanal boats not only from Pucusana and Callao but also from Paita. The latter have been traveling south during the late winter months of August and September. These boats are artisanal boats, but they are at the upper end of what the government considers to be the legal-size limit for artisanal fishers and can make long voyages into high seas and land large quantities of squid.

Despite the size of their holds, they still need local ports where they can load up on ice and supplies before heading out and unload and sell their catches when they are done. Callao is an option, but given its reputation for crime and heavy boat traffic, squid captains from the north prefer Pucusana or Chorrillos for unloading their catches. Sometimes these boats will go to Pucusana, but often they can get a better price for their squid in Chorrillos, which does not have a Produce officer who monitors the prices at which squid are being bought or sold on a given day in other ports. This activity has provided a new source of work for fishers in Chorrillos at a time of the year when the local fishery is usually slow and income is hard to come by. Ten to fifteen fishers can earn a decent day's wage unloading squid from a boat and loading it into a refrigerated truck, which takes the squid to the large seafood market in Villa María or to a factory for processing. Usually there are a handful of boats that will unload each week in Chorrillos during the winter.

On a gray, cool day in September 2019, I sat with Enrique on a concrete bench on the dock in Chorrillos. There was a boat out in the harbor full of jumbo squid, and Enrique and a group of fishers were waiting to see if there would be work unloading the ship's cargo. Enrique was in his late twenties and had worked for a long time as an artisanal fisher in Chorrillos, fishing nearshore waters for the daily market and doing some stints on high-seas boats fishing for bonito. Recently, he had taken up work driving a moto-taxi back and forth from the dock in Chorrillos and the city above. However, a few months prior he had injured his lower back and could not stand the constant jarring and bouncing of the moto-taxi, which he gave up. The fishing in early September was poor. It was a time of year when the fishers said that the weather and water conditions were changing from winter to spring and there were few, if any, fish to be found in the bay. The cold-water fish were gone, and the warm-water fish had not yet entered. Occasionally unloading squid was Enrique's only option for income on the dock. He and the other fishers were all members of the local fishing association and were granted access to the unloading work by the fishing association's board. The squid boat captain would pay a fee to the association for the labor, which would then be divvied up among the workers.

It was not yet clear though that the boat would unload in Chorrillos. Most of the boat's crew were on the dock, sitting in the cantina drinking beers waiting to see when the squid would be unloaded. It was delayed by two things. One was that the refrigerated truck full of ice to transport the squid had not yet shown up. The other was that the boat's captain was debating whether to unload in Pucusana or Chorrillos. The price for squid was low and he was trying to figure out if he would get a better price in Pucusana, where he would be able to sell the squid and leave, or if it would be better in Chorrillos, where the squid would have to be transported to the market in Villa María and sold. The fishers and I sat and patiently waited as the hours passed. I had arrived around noon, and by the time it was three in the afternoon, Enrique and I and a couple of older fishers decided to go and sit in the cantina as well. Enrique ordered some chicken and rice, since he had not yet eaten lunch. Two older fishers and I sat with him and ordered a large bottle of Inka Kola to share. Afterward we mulled around the dock, waiting with the other fishers to see what would happen. Bundled in hats and sweatshirts to protect against the cold air coming in off the Pacific Ocean, the fishers stood around chatting and joking, poking fun at each other and complaining about the lack of fish to pass the time.

For a while I stood next to the president of the local fishing association, and we talked about the jumbo squid market and how he saw it as a path toward greater economic prosperity for the association's members. He pointed out that they had moved the food stalls from one part of the dock to another to make it easier for trucks to pass from the parking lot straight to the dock so that it would be easier to load squid directly on to the truck. He felt that squid was going to be an important part of the future of Peru's fishing industry and, given the diminishing quality of fishing in Chorrillos and the rapidly rising age of most of the association's fishers, that finding a way into the squid market would be important for guaranteeing future income for the association. He said that he and the association's other directors were talking to private investors about revamping the dock so that it would be easier for boats to disembark. The concrete dock in Chorrillos was last renovated and expanded in the 1990s and was designed for unloading small quantities of fish from small boats. The dock is not big enough and the bay not deep enough to unload larger boats directly. Fishers had to participate in a complicated, work-intensive relay using smaller boats to ferry ice, supplies, and squid to and from the larger boats. What he hoped for was sufficient investment to build a new concrete platform that extended farther into the bay so that larger artisanal boats could more easily unload their catches, thus making Chorrillos a more desirable port for squid boats to use. This hope was something that I heard often in the days that followed as I talked with other fishers and members of the association's administrative team. All of them saw improved infrastructure as an important step toward ensuring that fishers in Chorrillos could benefit from growing squid harvests even if they were not actively fishing the species. Such a move would allow association members to continue fishing when local fishing was good but also supplement their incomes unloading squid.

Finally, the boat captain decided to unload in Chorrillos, and the ice truck showed up around 5 p.m. The fishers started putting on their bright orange, waterproof overalls and rubber boots to keep them dry and warm. Enrique also put a black brace on to help protect his back when he lifted crates of squid. One of the fishers brought a boat with a blue awning and rows of several benches up alongside the dock. The boat had been converted from a fishing boat to a boat for tourist rides during the summer. Now it was being used to ferry workers and squid to and from the dock. The crew of fishers divided. Six got onto the boat and headed out to the squid boat where they loaded the squid into brightly colored plastic crates, with about forty kilos of squid into each crate. Then they transferred the full crates from the big boat to the smaller one and headed back to the dock. On the dock there were another five fishers waiting to pull the crates onto the dock and stack them up, while another group of four were rinsing the squid in big utility sinks that the association had installed the previous year and then hefted them into the ice truck (see figure 10). This process was repeated over and over as more and more squid went from the boat to the dock. When I left around 7 p.m., the fishers were still working to move the squid.

When I saw Enrique the next day, he said that it was about 10 p.m. by the time they finished. There was not as much squid as they had expected, only about seven or eight metric tons, which meant he was paid less than what he had hoped. That day the winds were up and coming from the north, which makes navigating the water in the bay dangerous. Fishers were staying put, no one was going out to see if there were any fish to be caught. Nor were there any squid to be unloaded. There were a few large boats sitting in the harbor, boats from Paita, but they were waiting to go out. The next day I showed up on the dock planning to meet Enrique. He was not there. I ran into the president of the association, and he said that a boat had arrived late the day before with a hold full of squid. A crew of fishers, including Enrique, had begun working to unload the boat around 9 p.m. They had not finished until 3 a.m., and most of them were still at home sleeping.

None of the fishers I spoke to mentioned the danger of unloading squid at night when the winds are up, but this was a difficult task that, like much work in artisanal fishing, involves a high risk of injury. This, combined with the relatively low pay that fishers receive for moving a load of squid, underscores the few options that they have to make a decent living by their standards. Fishers were content to have the work and often told me that they wished there was more of it. Even during the good months, though, there were not many squid boats unloading in Chorrillos. The association's president told me that in August and September there have been two or three boats per week and some weeks fewer. This has been enough to make an impact on the local economy, and the president's hope and the hope of many of his association's members is that a change in the dock's infrastructure could encourage more boats to bring their squid to Chorrillos. Even if this does

FIGURE 10 Artisanal fishers unload jumbo squid on the dock in Chorrillos. Photo by Maximilian Viatori.

happen, there is still likely to be significant precarity in work and pay for fishers in Chorrillos. Such a change will make them more dependent on the squid economy and more susceptible to vicissitudes in squid populations and market prices, not just from one port to another, but around Peru and in consumer markets around the world.

Furthermore, the impact of squid on the wharf economy in Chorrillos has been highly gendered. Given the precarity and devaluation of fishers' labor in Lima's urban economy, fishing families have engaged in "strategies of diversification" to sustain their livelihoods (Viatori and Bombiella 2019, 23, 29). These strategies followed gendered patterns that reflected widely circulating (but also slowly changing) ideas in Lima about what kinds of work are ideally linked to and reproduced in working-class men's and women's identities (23–24). Men work as fishers and when fishing is slow seek out manual labor work in the city, often in short-term construction or manufacturing contracts. Women work as vendors or fish cleaners on the wharf, and when the wharf economy is slow, seek out domestic service jobs or street vending jobs in city, in addition to being the primary caregivers for children and aging parents. Winter is a slow time for everyone on the dock, not just fishers. Luisa, who cleaned fish, once explained that she only has limited work on the dock during the winter months when certain buyers, usually from local restaurants, would come and buy a small crate of fish and want it cleaned and prepped to cook. "In summer, there are more sales, everyone goes to the beach, everyone eats fish," she said. "But in winter the situation is different." Ana, who had worked on the dock for more than a decade, said that when the water was rough in winter and there was no work on the dock, she would get packs of clothes hangers and go to some of the local markets to sell them or try to sell them on a street corner in Lima. These kinds of arrangements were not unusual—they were common strategies that women employed to help their families get by economically when things on the dock were slow. While the activity of unloading squid provides much-needed income for fishing families during these slow periods, it does so in a way that largely bypasses the wharf economy and the women who work in it because the squid is not sold or cleaned in market, which is staffed primarily by women. The limited benefits of manual labor of unloading squid catches go exclusively to men.

The precarities that undergird the squid economy reveal some significant ways in which changing world ecologies reinforce, rework, and deepen existing inequalities, not only between humans and nonhumans but among workers positioned differently in various sectors of Peru's fishing economy. The situation of fishers in Chorrillos is closely linked to the historical development of Peru's industrial fisheries.[23] For example, fishers in Chorrillos participated in the first industrial fishery in the 1930s and 1940s for the export of bonito, unloading catches in Callao. During the anchoveta boom, the fishery in Chorrillos was impacted by industrial boats that swept through the bay when they needed to top off holds before heading to Callao. As older fishers have noted, there used to be anchoveta off the coast of Chorrillos before it was fished out by industrial boats. After the collapse of anchoveta stocks in the 1970s, Chorrillos and other artisanal ports absorbed surplus labor as fishers looked for work. In the decades that followed, the growing numbers of fishers and decreased productivity of the local fishery combined with financial and political crises in Peru in the 1980s and 1990s, which negatively impacted industrial and artisanal fisheries, contributed to growing precarity in the local fishing economy. This created some of the conditions for fishers' inclusion in (albeit on the margins of) the emergent squid world ecology. Fishers' participation in the jumbo squid economy is possible because of a surplus of labor on the dock in Chorrillos—local fishers without enough work who have flexibility and willingness to unload squid when and if it shows up and for a small fee. Everything about these potential exchanges is in flux—the pay, the hours, the timing, and the quantities of squid that arrive. Fishers have been willing to accept this because it fits within their existing work dynamics and enables them to pick up extra work without having to leave the dock. It also reinforces their marginality not only within the squid economy but also among artisanal fishers as individuals who do not have the capital to participate in the work of pursuing and catching squid and, therefore, extracting greater value from their labor.

(DE)VALUED

Global demand for jumbo squid continues to increase. In 2018, Peruvian exports of jumbo squid exceeded projections for the year, totaling $624 million, which set a record for the country. While the per-kilo price for frozen squid remains low compared to other more sought-after seafood, squid prices have increased in recent years in response to low production years in 2015 and 2016. Furthermore, a growing market has emerged for meal made from jumbo squid, which fetches a higher price given its value-added processing. In the last decade, Peruvian exports of squid meal have grown steadily with over twenty-five companies now producing meal from squid catches. In the early 2000s, food scientists in Peru first lauded jumbo squid meal as a cheap form of easily digested protein that could be incorporated into other processed foods, such as instant soup or pasta. A high percentage of squid meal is protein, significantly higher than other fish meals, making it ideal for such applications. Advances in processing have also made it possible to remove the "fishy" taste and smell from the meal. In recent years, a market for squid meal as feed also has emerged for farmed shrimp in places such as Ecuador and Indonesia, as well as lobster and some species of farmed fish.

Squid meal exports have remained only a fraction of the Peruvian exports of frozen squid for human consumption and represent an even smaller fraction of the quantities of anchoveta fishmeal the country exports. However, the processing of squid for meal represents a step toward extracting greater value from jumbo squid catches through processing.[24] It also represents a potential means through which squid life is devalued, given the large number of fresh squid that is needed to produce a small quantity of dried fishmeal.

Amid this interest in expanding squid markets, there are indications that the tenuous world-ecology that has sustained Peru's jumbo squid catches is already beginning to come undone (Ryan 2021). Climate change is having a profound effect on squid populations and other sea creatures, which are increasingly migrating toward the poles as equatorial waters warm (Brito-Morales et al. 2020; Lenoir et al. 2020). One likely impact of this is that overfishing will occur because local-based fleets cannot move with species and so will continue to fish what they can in their restricted zones, while international fleets that skirt national regulations will continue to move and extract species at unsustainable levels (Young et al. 2019). This dynamic highlights the ongoing issue of how difficult it is to coordinate catches across national and international jurisdictions. In 2021, the SPRFMO implemented mandatory reporting of squid catches, but it has not established a catch quota, and enforcement remains weak for an organization that relies on the voluntary cooperation of its members. To comply with these regulations, Peruvian artisanal squid boats are required to formalize and license to enter international waters to fish squid. This is a process that is economically and legally difficult for many artisanal fishers to comply with and may function as a means through which they are slowly dispossessed from the squid fishery as larger, international industrial boats extract as much value from squid life for as long as they can.

Such relationships and considerations are largely absent from dominant approaches to understanding and managing Peru's squid fishery. In Peru (and around the world), fisheries science and management policies have focused on the identification and regulation of specific forms of life for commodification, thus ignoring the broader ecological, social, and political relationships that make the production (and imperilment) of life possible. It is this separation of a specific life from the myriad unequal relationships that constitute it that enables entwined processes of accumulation, displacement, and environmental degradation. Making these relationships visible is tantamount for analyzing and making sense of the contemporary politics of life. What is required is a careful, historically rooted reading of how different humans are connected to nonhumans in various and unequal ways and the central role that these inequalities play in producing contemporary capitalist world ecologies.

The development of Peru's jumbo squid fishery underscores the importance of historically attuned anthropological studies that keep in focus the ever-changing role that science, capital, and politics play in reshaping oceanscapes and how different species gather to make—at least momentarily—new, tentative modes of being. Reorganizations of ocean life to facilitate the industrial capture of marine species and the use of the ocean as a carbon sink created the conditions for the proliferation of jumbo squid in the eastern Pacific Ocean. Marine scientists played a critical role in identifying squid as a form of life that could be classified, mapped, and turned into a viable commodity. A series of earlier displacements led impoverished artisanal fishers to engage in new relationships of ecological knowledge, predation, and capture with squid. These processes and conditions created a tenuous link between squid and artisanal fishers that is now imperiled by climatic fluctuations, unstable markets, and renewed threats of industrial dispossession.

EPILOGUE

WHEN crude oil mixes with moving seawater it produces a chocolatey-colored foam that floats along the surface of the ocean. Swaths of brownish bubbles and dark stains in the ocean were visible in a smartphone video that artisanal fishers from Ancón, a small city just north of Lima, shared on February 18, 2022 (Cárdenas 2022a). A fisher narrated the images, commenting that "the signs of petroleum are still visible and yet the company wants to say that there is no petroleum." Days later, the Spanish-based multinational oil company Repsol announced that it had cleaned up 98 percent of the oil that had been spilled the month before at La Pampilla refinery, which Repsol has managed since 1996 (and which is different from Playa La Pampilla discussed in chapter 1).[1] Not only did artisanal fishers refute this claim and provide evidence against it, but so too did state officials and environmentalists. The minister of environment, Modesto Montoya, said that Repsol could not claim that it had cleaned up 98 percent of the oil because there were beaches north of Ancón that were still contaminated, and a significant portion of the oil had been dispersed into the ocean and was unrecoverable (*Caretas* 2022). Juan Carlos Riveros, a biologist and scientific director for Oceana Perú, said that what artisanal fishers showed in their videos was "without a doubt" petroleum. He added that nowhere "in the world would more than 25 percent of an oil spill be recovered, generally it is

10 to 12 percent" while adding that "half of the oil spilled in the sea more or less remains there" (Cárdenas 2022a).

The oil circulating off Peru's central coast was from an incident that occurred on January 15, 2022. An Italian-flagged tanker ship was in the routine process of discharging its cargo of Brazilian crude oil into a loading buoy that was connected by an underwater pipeline to La Pampilla refinery in Ventanilla, a district of Callao. It instead dumped 11,900 barrels of oil directly into the ocean. As the inky liquid poured into the water, prevailing currents pushed it north along the coast. It was not long until foamy, dark slicks appeared off the shores of Ventanilla as well as the districts of Ancón, Chancay, Aucallama, and Santa Rosa. Tarry black balls washed ashore, and oil covered the rocks at Playa Cavero in Ventanilla and more than twenty other beaches in the area. Dead fish, sea birds, and marine mammals littered the shore. Walter de la Cruz, a local artisanal fisher, told reporters days after the spill that the area smelled "like death" (*Reuters* 2022). Peruvian president Pedro Castillo visited Playa Cavero on January 20 to announce measures to hold Repsol responsible for the "ecocide" that had occurred.[2] The government suspended operations at the refinery, instituted a judicial order preventing Repsol executives from leaving the country, and levied fines. The government also requested assistance from the UN Environment Programme (UNEP) and the UN Office for the Coordination of Humanitarian Affairs (OCHA), which through the Joint Environment Unit (JEU) deployed a team of experts to assess the scope and impact of the spill. The team issued a report on February 24 that outlined the extent of the spill and its damage: it spanned 80 kilometers of coast, covered 1,400 hectares of ocean, affected an ecologically diverse and sensitive zone that included three protected coastal areas, and put 3,000 fishing families out of work.[3] According to the report, the incident was "one of the worst ecological disasters in Peru's recent history."

Repsol's representatives denied any responsibility for the spill and launched an aggressive public relations campaign to defend their position. Government officials claimed that the company waited twenty-four hours to initiate a contingency plan, which allowed the spill to spread and affect a greater area than if it had been quickly contained. Repsol's representatives denied this and claimed that a contingency plan was put into effect the night of the spill (*El Comercio* 2022a).[4] Government officials also asserted that the company grossly misrepresented the extent of the spill. The company initially reported that the spill was less than *seven gallons*, before later updating the figure to 10,396 barrels, following government estimates that 11,900 barrels were spilled.[5] Repsol representatives claimed that "the oil spill was caused by a maritime phenomenon [that was] unpredictable by the company, [and which was] caused by the volcanic eruption in Tonga."[6] The statement referred to the eruption of the volcano Hunga Tonga-Hunga Ha'apai on the island nation of Tonga on January 15, which sent shock waves around the globe and triggered tsunami warnings throughout the Pacific Basin. Unlike in neighboring Chile and Ecuador, no tsunami alerts were issued for the Peruvian coast. High waves were recorded in northern Peru, where two people drowned. However, both the captain of the *Mare Doricum* tanker and witnesses who were in the area at the time of the spill reported calm seas (*La Mula* 2022a; León 2022).

On January 19, Lima-based RPP news broadcast the first interview with a Repsol official following the spill. Program host Omar Mariluz questioned Tine Van Den Wall Bake, the director of communications and institutional relations for Repsol Perú, who repeatedly denied responsibility for the event.[7] According to Van Den Wall Bake, a wave "threw the ship against our installation." When Mariluz questioned why Repsol had delayed in reporting the incident and why they had initially reported only seven gallons spilled, she replied that by law Repsol had twelve hours to report the spill and had to specify an amount, but at that point was not aware of the extent of the spill. Mariluz asked why the company's personnel could not distinguish between seven gallons and six thousand barrels (which was at the time the amount the government believed had been spilled). Van Den Wall Bake replied that "this lamentable meteorological incident or, I mean, anomalous wave" picked up the spill and "transported it very far away" so that it was not until the following afternoon that patrol boats discovered how far the oil had traveled. Mariluz pointedly asked Van Den Wall Bake, "Do you consider yourselves responsible for the ecological disaster that occurred?" to which she responded, "No." He quickly followed asking, "No? Who is responsible?" Van Den Wall Bake asserted that "we did not cause the ecological disaster and I cannot say who is responsible." In the ensuing weeks, Repsol's representatives blamed the ship captain for shifting the boat during discharge. In turn, the captain accused the company of numerous irregularities (La Mula 2022a).[8]

Peruvian government officials maintained that Repsol was legally responsible for the spill and its cleanup. It also seized the *Mare Doricum* and requested the extradition of the ship's captain. In February and March, the government levied multiple fines against Repsol. On May 13, Julián Palacín Gutiérrez, the executive president of Peru's Instituto Nacional de Defensa de la Competencia y de la Protección de la Propiedad Intelectual (INDECOPI, National Institute for the Defense of Competition and Protection of Intellectual Property) announced that a $4.5 billion lawsuit had been filed in a Lima civil court against Repsol and five other companies involved in the spill (including the owner of the tanker) for damages related to the environmental disaster. Palacín Gutiérrez commented that the suit indicated that anyone who "operates a risky asset or engages in a risky activity and causes damage to another is obligated to provide compensation" (*El Comercio* 2022b).

Analysts in Peru and around the world have expressed skepticism that the Peruvian government will be able to hold Repsol accountable for the spill and its long-term impacts (Collyns 2022). Repsol was responsible for a previous, albeit much smaller, spill in 2013 and received only a small fine. Moreover, there is a long and an ongoing history of corporations acting with impunity regarding oil spills and wastewater dumping in Peru's Amazonian provinces (Fraser 2018). For decades Peru's governments have prioritized mineral extraction and private enterprise over environmental and social regulation, given the country's economic dependence on extractive industries. The result is that Peru's relatively weak regulatory system will make it difficult for the government or groups of citizens, such as the artisanal fishing associations impacted by the spill, to hold Repsol accountable (Tegell 2022).

While Repsol, the tanker ship company, and the Peruvian government have blamed each other for the disaster, artisanal fishers along the coast north of Lima have been left to deal with the impacts of the contamination. The spill put several thousand fishers in Ancón, Chancay, Aucallama, and Santa Rosa out of work. Artisanal fishing livelihoods are already precarious—most artisanal fishers rely on daily income they get from catching and selling fish and have little to no safety net. Moreover, artisanal fishers were coming off two difficult years because of the COVID-19 pandemic, which devastated Peru and depressed fishing economies. The country recorded one of the highest per capita death tolls in the world, and for months in 2020 artisanal fishing docks were closed as part of state measures to slow the spread of the disease. Fishing activity around the country was down by 80 percent in the first half of 2020 and had only slowly recovered in the months that followed.

Support for fishers from Repsol was slow and patchy. In the days following the spill, Repsol delayed hiring international experts to direct the oil cleanup.

Instead, they recruited unemployed fishers to begin the work, but the company did not provide them with adequate wages to cover their lost income or give them proper protective equipment. In an interview published in *La República* (Cárdenas and Espíritu 2022), Felipe Trillo Piedra, a fisher from Ancón, summed up the situation:

> We live day-to-day from fishing. All of us fishers go out, we do not wait for someone to come and support us, because we know how to work. Right now we are not working, that is the problem. Repsol supports us through [work] cleaning the sea. [Repsol] takes us to the sea to collect the oil. They pay us 700 soles for each boat, but there are three fishers in each one. In the end, each one receives 150 soles, approximately, because we pay for the fuel. Also, it was only three weeks ago that they began to give us all the tools, before that we went out with nothing. Before I used to earn up to 600 soles a day. I have five children, two of them in college. I go out to clean the sea, but it is not enough. I have to look for another job, even if it is construction because I have to feed my children, among them there are little ones. Where do I get the money? 200 soles are not enough for the week. What Repsol gives us is not enough for us. Now that [the cost of] everything is going up, that money only lasts for two or three days.

Fishers were not the only ones who were negatively affected by the spill. A whole web of fishing- and tourism-based livelihoods suffered. Fish vendors, fish cleaners, food stall operators, and other people who relied on local dock economies were suddenly left with little or no work.

Angélica Sánchez Valderrama, who operated a food stall on the dock in Ancón, told *La República*:

> Diners no longer come. Now I only serve one little table. Before, we sold every day [, even] on Saturdays and Sundays. Now we barely sell 50 soles. Before each day we made 800 soles to 1,000 soles, and on the weekends it was triple. Now at the end of the week we only reach 300 soles. We have had to lay off staff. Five-to-six people worked here. Now I bring my daughter and I have an assistant. We bring fish from the deep sea because there is nothing from the beach. Basically, we cook with bonito and perico. But people are afraid, they ask [about the fish]. We do not sell

any fish or shellfish unless they are frozen and not from here. We come every day, even if we only sell one dish, because from this our children eat. What can we do? We depend on this.

In the face of government pressure and mounting protests from fishing associations, the company agreed to pay stipends to fishers and their families. However, Repsol did not begin paying the stipends until March, and the amount was not enough for them to cover fishers' lost income (Cárdenas 2022b). Fishing families had to pool their resources in *ollas comunes* ("communal pots" or community-organized soup kitchens) to survive (La Mula 2022b).

Oceana Perú assessed the economic impact of the oil spill on artisanal fishing in Ancón and Chancay, utilizing existing government data on annual landings and the average price of different fish from these two areas that were most affected by the spill (Oceana Perú 2022). Oceana Perú cautioned that such data could not account for the total damage of the spill on artisanal fishers or the coastal ecosystem, but it did provide a baseline for establishing financial compensation for the dramatic impact the environmental disaster has had on coastal communities. Since 2016, nearshore artisanal fishing in Ancón and Chancay has generated on average $2.5 million per year. The spill occurred in January, during Peru's austral summer and the high point for artisanal fishing, when a significant portion of that revenue was being produced.

Estimating the economic losses to artisanal fishers from the spill was an important step in seeking financial compensation from the government or Repsol. However, lost revenue was just the tip of the iceberg in terms of conceptualizing the damage the spill had (and will have) on the coastal ecologies that made fishing livelihoods possible. People do not just fish to make money, as artisanal fishers throughout Peru have reminded me for years. Artisanal fishing provides people with a livelihood that offers them more autonomy and dignity than other forms of labor that are available to people with limited social capital in coastal Peru. The economic, social, and cultural relationships that underpin artisanal fishing are made possible by fishers' knowledge about and commitments to coastal ecologies. The spill upended these webs of relationships in ways that will force artisanal fishers, vendors, food stall operators, and other people intimately engaged with coastal ecologies to consider if and how they can continue to forge livelihoods amid the detritus of this environmental disaster. Roberto Zamora, an artisanal fisher from Ventanilla, indicated the extent of damage on multiple scales when he told a reporter that the oil spill had "poisoned the sea" and Repsol showed "a lack of respect for our ocean. It has not just affected me. It has not just affected fellow fishermen. It's an offense to the whole world" (Taj 2022a).

Echoing these sentiments, environmental scientists who surveyed the damage emphasized the long-term impacts of the contamination on coastal ecologies. Yuri Hooker, the Coordinator of the Marine Biology Lab at Cayetano Heredia University, informed *La República* that "when damage is caused to the environment, it cannot be repaired even with all the money in the world or, as has been suggested, 'clean it up and that is it'" (Gallegos 2022). He elaborated,

The consequences of contamination, especially with polycyclic aromatic hydrocarbons [that are found in crude oil], occur over the course of years. Physiological failures will be generated in the functioning of organisms and genetic alterations of DNA, which lead to tumors and cancer, both for aquatic organisms and for those who eat these shellfish or fish, such as humans. Everything seems fine, but the contaminant is there, and these hydrocarbons are resistant and remain in the environment for years.

Christel Scheske, an environmental specialist for the Sociedad Peruana de Derecho Ambiental (SPDA, Peruvian Society for Environmental Law) told the *Guardian* that "heavy metals from the crude oil will remain in the ecosystem for many years, rendering fish, mollusks and other marine species dangerous for human consumption, and affecting the entire marine food web" (Collyns 2022).

Widely circulating representations of the oil spill demonstrate the importance of analyzing how different actors define an environmental event at different scales (both in time and space) and what components of the event actors scale up or down in their knowledge production about it. Such analyses are crucial for understanding how certain forms of environmental and climatic knowledge become authorized ways of representing particular events while others are marginalized, and the role this process plays in shaping how people experience environmental and climatic events unequally. All knowledge is produced in and made meaningful by specific cultural, social, and political contexts and relationships—it is "situated" (Haraway 1988). However, certain forms of knowledge appear to be "standard" or "universal" or "global" because they dovetail with dominant governance projects and are wielded by actors with institutional or social capital. Other forms of knowledge that are not aligned with governance regimes or are associated with marginalized actors are excluded or only partially integrated into broader discussions of environmental issues. In their debates about who bore responsibility for the spill, Repsol and state officials channeled internationally circulating languages of corporate responsibility, disaster remediation, or environmental regulation in attempts to establish their framings as authoritative understandings of the spill. In contrast, the knowledge and experiences of artisanal fishers and vendors were only partially included in these broader debates and often were limited to accounting for the impacts of lost income on fishing communities.

Repsol's representatives engaged in a concerted public relations push through, for example, a website dedicated to providing regular press releases and video updates on the progress they made in the cleanup and community support for artisanal fishers (https://compromisorepsol.pe). They framed the spill as a single event with a clear (and short) time duration that could be measured in months and had a specific end. While denying any responsibility for the spill, Repsol's agents repeatedly announced that they were following globally recognized industry procedures, using state-of-the-art technologies, and relying on the knowledge of international experts in oil-spill remediation to quickly contain and clean up the areas of the ocean and coasts that were most impacted. Similarly, they treated the losses suffered by artisanal fishing communities as one-time events that could be resolved through employing fishers to do cleanup work and paying them vouchers and stipends for lost income.

State officials rejected Repsol's denial of responsibility for the spill and framed the oil spill as an exceptional event that had no historical parallel. By asserting that the oil spill was an ecocide and the worst disaster in recent Peruvian history, state officials argued that the event was a disaster that represented a break with the normal functioning of time, economics, and the environment, and thus required unusual measures to restore things as they were. Officials' claims were reinforced by and rooted in widely circulating images of oil-covered sea birds, stained patches of ocean, and tarry beaches—images of the damage caused by the spill that could be scaled as "globally" understood indicators of the environmental harms of oil spills worldwide that were recognized by international bodies such as the UN.

While Repsol and state agents defined the scope and scale of the oil spill in contrasting ways, they both framed the spill and appropriate responses to it in narrow technical and economic terms—how much oil could be recovered and how soon, how much was reasonable to pay fishers for lost work, or how much full remediation would really cost. This obscured the myriad cultural, social, and ecological impacts of the spill on coastal lifeworlds. This erasure was compounded by Repsol's and the state's (as well as the UN's) representation of the spill as a discrete event, which marginalized ongoing histories of oceanic contamination and their unequal impacts on different people and species. A pair of editorials published in *La Mula* rejected the idea that the spill represented a departure from the environmental and political "norm" in Peru. The writer Jorge Frisancho (2022) retorted that "the extraction and processing of hydrocarbons causes continuous and irreparable damage," and that "damage and impunity are not the exception but the rule of extractive operations: this is how the system works." Enrique Ortiz Tejada (2022), the president and founder of the environmental organization Conservación Amazónica, rhetorically questioned if the spill was the worst ecological disaster in Peru's history or even in the country's maritime history. Equally devastating or worse disasters have occurred such as the "anchoveta debacle during the government of General Velasco—from which we have not yet recovered—the more than 200,000 hectares deforested in the Amazon in 2020, or the illegal mining that poisons the rivers" (Ortiz Tejada 2022).

As this book demonstrates, the January 15 spill is part of an ongoing history of "cheapening" (Moore and Patel 2017) the Pacific Ocean's ecologies to enable intertwined processes of production, capital accumulation, and waste disposal that are at the heart of local, regional, and transnational political economies. Modern carbon capitalism has treated the ocean as an open, stable plane for the transportation of raw materials and commodities, such as unrefined crude, as well as a sink for making the detritus of capitalism disappear (at least momentarily) for free. Oil leaks and spills have been a regular aspect of carbon capitalism—on average there is at least one major tanker spill each year, in addition to millions of barrels of waste oil that are released into the ocean in smaller spills and discharges. Less than two weeks after the spill in Ventanilla, Peru's navy confirmed a spill from an offshore oil rig operated by the Savia company in northern Peru near Cabo

Blanco. On April 28, another of the company's aging rigs collapsed into the Pacific Ocean, spilling oil and leaking gas into the sea. In 2021 and 2022, the company reported forty-six spills from its operations (Carrere 2022). These were small spills, especially compared to the January 15 event, and as such were not scalable to the level of "international" or even "national" concern. However, fishers repeatedly expressed concern over the "incessant" nature of these small spills and the impact that aging and malfunctioning petroleum infrastructure has had on local ecosystems (Carrere 2022).

Governments and corporations have constructed a vast network of oceanic and coastal infrastructure to facilitate the global flow of oil (among other resources and commodities) from points of extraction to consumption, transporting crude oil from Brazil via an Italian-flagged tanker ship to Peru for processing and distribution. This infrastructure, as with coastal development in general, has sought to fix coasts in Peru and around the world to make the ocean into a stable backdrop for the unfolding of economies. But the ocean is fundamentally unstable—it is always moving, always changing, and constantly wearing away at and undermining fixed infrastructure. In the wake of the January 15 spill, pictures emerged of corroded, aging pipelines that connected loading buoys to La Pampilla refinery (Taj 2022b). It may not have been a single, unpredictable wave that produced the spill, but years of constantly moving saltwater working away at the static lines that refinery operators neglected, taking the stability of the underwater pipeline for granted. Such failures will only increase in frequency and scale as creaking infrastructure confronts increasingly unstable oceans that have been transformed by carbon emissions.

Widely circulating representations of such failures repeatedly erase the unequal burden that racialized and socially marginalized people, such as artisanal fishers, face in dealing with environmental crises and the work they must do to forge new ecological commitments in the aftermath of (slowly or abruptly) unfolding oceanic disasters. Framing the January 15 oil spill as a finite event, as Repsol and state officials did (albeit to different ends), belies the reality that petroleum contamination stays in the environment for years and decades and thus also erases the ongoing work that people will have to undertake to live with this contamination. Over the course of time, the ocean makes the contamination less visible as the oil is dispersed to different parts of the coast and a significant portion of it sinks. After the short-term stipends and compensation are paid, fishers, vendors, and other people reliant on coastal economies likely will be left to deal with the unfolding effects of a further-compromised ecology in addition to fish, birds, marine mammals, and a host of other species that will confront a reordered ecology.

As these developments underscore, the dynamics I have examined in this book continue to develop in complex, unexpected, and sometimes startling ways that resist neat conclusions. However, the analyses I offer in this book of life and inequality in the eastern Pacific Ocean reveal the importance of studying the semiotic work that undergirds different representations of environmental crises for understanding how and why different people experience these crises and their effects in unequal ways. Dominant interpretations of oceanic issues rely upon the decontextualization of specific facts and their selective translation from one scale to another to produce erasures of the racialized systemic inequalities, histories of uneven development, and extractive violence that have made modern ocean ecologies possible. Such readings not only attempt to erase these inequalities but also work to discredit the profound knowledge that socially marginalized groups of people have of the inequalities at the heart of capitalist ecologies and the crises they have produced. These erasures underscore the importance of constructing alternative representations of the ocean, which draw on knowledge and experiences that have been submerged by dominant interpretations of coastal nature, marine pollution, extreme weather, and overfishing. The analyses I have produced in this book forefront the engagements and commitments that make oceanic ecologies possible, as well as the material relationships and unequal positions of different actors and species within them.

How we represent the ocean in discussions about environmental and climate crises matters. This book underscores the necessity of understanding ocean ecologies as contingent, precarious constellations of unequal climatic, economic, and social relationships that create the potential for future unruly and messy changes. Understanding rapidly changing Pacific Ocean worlds is only possible by keeping in sight the ways in which processes of violence, displacement, and capital have organized ocean natures and lives to enable profoundly uneven accumulations of value and harm. The struggles of artisanal fishers, the booms and busts in different fish and cephalopod species, extreme weather events and people's unequal experiences of their impacts, the circulation of ocean waste and contamination, and the materiality of coastal development must be analyzed alongside each other because they are products and producers of the same oceanic ecologies. Making the connections among these dynamics visible is critical for articulating environmentally and socially just futures precisely because dominant representations of the ocean obscure key economic, ecological, and historical relationships in ways that perpetuate multispecies inequalities.

ACKNOWLEDGMENTS

THIS book never would have happened were it not for the unbelievable support, kindness, and love of so many different people. Since 2012, numerous fishers, vendors, surfers, scientists, activists, and government officials in Peru have made this work possible by generously sharing their time and knowledge about Peru's coast and the Pacific Ocean. To preserve their anonymity, I cannot thank them by name, but I value every one of their contributions. I am especially grateful to the fishers and vendors in Chorrillos who have shared their lives and knowledge about the Pacific Ocean with me.

At Iowa State University I have received ongoing intellectual and financial support that has been critical for the success of this project. In the fall semester of 2019, I received a Faculty Professional Development Assignment, which provided me with the time I needed to write the first draft of this manuscript. Funds from the Department of World Languages and Cultures enabled me to make regular research trips to Lima. Most important, I have benefited from the best group of colleagues that I could hope for. I am particularly grateful to Amanda Runyan and Chad Gasta for their regular help, support, and counsel. I owe special thanks to Megan Myers for her willingness to cover my course on short notice in the spring of 2019. Grant Arndt was kind enough to read and provide insightful feedback on earlier drafts of each of the book's chapters. Brian Behnken was generous with his support and encouragement at key points in this project's development. Particularly during the spring 2019 semester, my colleagues in the Department of World Languages and Cultures demonstrated an exceptional level of kindness and care for my family and me.

I presented earlier drafts of this book's chapters at the American Anthropological Association meetings in 2021, the International Congress of the Latin American Studies Association in 2019 and 2021, and the Biennial Meeting for the Society of Cultural Anthropology in 2018. I am grateful to all those who provided helpful feedback at these events. A portion (roughly half) of chapter 1 was published in the *Journal of Latin American and Caribbean Anthropology* 25 (1): 84–103 as "Saving the Costa Verde's Waves: Surfing and Discourses of Race–Class in the Enactment of Lima's Coastal Infrastructure." I am grateful to my co-author, Brandon Scheuring, for agreeing to allow that material to appear in this book. Héctor Bombiella helped me with the research for several of the chapters in this book, particularly the one on El Niño. Many thanks also to Yibo Fan for his help with the maps.

It has been a true pleasure to work with everyone at the University of Arizona Press. I am especially grateful to Allyson Carter for her support of this project. Thanks go to the two external reviewers who took the time to provide helpful and thoughtful comments on an earlier draft of this book, which helped to strengthen the final product.

I owe my greatest thanks to my good friends and family, whose support and care sustained me through the challenges that surrounded this project. Thanks to Mark Looney for being a loyal friend through it all. Thank you to my sister, Melissa, for making sure I got the right care and for making that 2019 trip. Thank you to my brother, Ben, for always being there and willing to talk. Thank you to my parents, Max and Anne, who have always gone above and beyond to do whatever was needed. And to my family—Anneke, Elio, and Nico—the greatest thanks of all. Without you none of this would have been possible and none of it would have mattered. I am forever grateful for you.

NOTES

INTRODUCTION

1. On the practice and politics of how different actors use different scales to frame environmental or climatic information, see Barnes (2015), Broad and Orlove (2007), Hulme (2010), and Sayre (2017).

2. Editorials published in *La República*, the center-left newspaper of note, did not comment directly on the IPCC report, but rather focused on the words and activism of Greta Thunberg at the UN Climate Summit and denounced governments around the world, including Peru's, for not acting more decisively to reduce emissions and avert the most catastrophic effects of climate change (Miranda 2019; Silva Santisteban 2019).

3. See, for example, *La República* (2020).

4. The pioneering work on this is Matos Mar (1984). See also Blondet (1991).

5. In addition to the studies cited in the text, see Teves et al. (1996).

6. The concept of vulnerability has become a cornerstone of scientific and social scientific analyses of climate change and generally is used to refer to whether people can access the (political, economic, material, etc.) resources they need to adapt to climatic or environmental changes. Numerous anthropological works have critiqued and expanded the idea of vulnerability, demonstrating that existing inequalities shape differences in the degrees to which people can adapt, and in turn climate change multiples the effects of these existing inequalities (O'Reilly et al. 2020, 19). For examples of anthropological approaches to vulnerability, see, among others, Colten (2006), Han (2018), Hughes (2013), and Vásquez-Léon (2009).

7. See Malm and Esmailian (2012) for an analysis of the political and economic inequalities that have exposed impoverished Egyptian farmers to greater vulnerability from rapid salinization of their fields caused by rising sea levels and Ley (2021) for an analysis of the lived experiences of sea level rise in Semarang.

8. There is a long and well-documented history of powerful institutions establishing the authority of official forms of knowledge—scientific, bureaucratic, regulatory—through their opposition to "folk," Indigenous, or local knowledges, which powerful actors routinely have denigrated as supposedly imprecise and unable to be separated from their immediate contexts (see Arndt 2022).

9. Atmospheric chemist Paul Crutzen and biologist Eugene Stoermer (2000, 18) used the term "Anthropocene" to emphasize the outsized role that humans had come to play in shaping the current geological epoch. Numerous scholars have commented on the importance of the concept for highlighting humans' role in driving climate change but have argued that it ignores the role that colonialism, imperialism, and capitalism have played in driving climate change by attributing it to a socially and historically generic "Anthropos." In its place, they have proposed terms such as "Capitalocene" (Moore 2016), "Plantationocene" (Haraway 2015) and "Anthropo-not-seen" (de la Cadena 2015b). While recognizing and keeping in mind its many limitations, I have chosen to use Anthropocene here in the spirit of "critical and curious engagement rather than celebration or rejection" (Tsing, Mathews, and Bubandt 2019, S187).

10. See https://www.oceandecade.org/about.

11. An example of this vulnerability is the fact that most of the world's tropical glaciers are found in Peru and provide water not only for people living in the Andes, but also for coastal cities, such as Lima, which relies on glacial runoff to feed the rivers that comprise the city's sources of water. The tropical glaciers have receded substantially in recent decades, thus threatening the water source for the majority of Peru's population.

12. Despite this, sea level rise is barely mentioned in the climate change plan for Lima Province, which was adopted in April 2021. The 391-page document outlines the climate risks that the city and surrounding province face in the next decades and the steps that need to be taken to mitigate them. While the plan acknowledges that "sea level rise is one of the dangers that Lima Province faces" it is not identified as one of the primary threats confronting the province (which are landslides, floods, heat waves, and drought) and is discussed only in footnotes. The document can be accessed at https://smia.munlima.gob.pe/documentos-publicacion/detalle/565.

13. See, for example, Broad and Orlove (2007), de la Cadena (2015a), García (2021), Ojani (2021), and Stensrud (2021).

CHAPTER 1

1. On science and technology studies and anthropological approaches to infrastructure, see, among others, Harvey (2014), Harvey and Knox (2015), Larkin (2013), Star (1999), and Zeiderman (2016). See Hetherington and Campbell (2014) for an overview of the changing role of infrastructure projects in governance in Latin America.

2. In addition to the works cited in the text, see, for example, Dietz (1998), Driant (1991), and Matos Mar (1984).

3. I am grateful to one of the external reviewers for suggesting this point and its expression in Finnegan's work.

4. In attempts to ameliorate these erosive disruptions, municipalities have invested in extensive net and anchor systems to fix the cliffs in place. A recent study commissioned by the APCV indicated that 30 percent of the zone's cliffs present a high risk for dangerous slides, while an additional 40 percent pose a moderate risk that would intensify with expanded construction along the cliff tops (León 2015).

5. Kahanamoku was an Olympic gold medalist in swimming and played a central role in popularizing surfing around the world through his extensive travels to Australia and the United States in the early twentieth century. However, as I. H. Walker (2011, 14, 32, 59) argues, within dominant surfing narratives Kahanamoku is often credited with introducing surfing as a recreational pursuit in a manner that occludes the ongoing practice and development of the sport not only by Kahanamoku, but other Hawai'ians throughout the twentieth and twenty-first centuries.

6. In 1965, Pomar made surfing history by becoming the first Latin American to win the World Surfing Championship, when he won the competition in Lima. For a discussion of Pomar's claims, see Warshaw (2010, 19–22). Summarizing the argument against Pomar, Warshaw notes that "none of the evidence proves that wave-riding in ancient Peru developed into an established, widespread form of recreation." "Unlike ancient Peru," Warshaw (23) argues, "where wave-riding was a byproduct of work and probably limited to fishermen, surfing in Hawaii was both recreational and universal." In their global history of the development of surfing, Westwick and Neushul (2013, 7) put it in these terms: "Polynesians surfed; in Peru, fishing villagers rode waves on reed boats called caballitos; in West Africa, young kids surfed on wooden planks. One can debate, as some do, which one of these places was first, but there is no disputing that modern surfing, the sport we know today, came out of Hawaii."

7. See https://hazlaportuola.pe/es; the campaign can also be followed on Twitter via #HAZlaportuOla.

8. Information on the film can be found at www.alamar.pe.

9. The historical contexts of surfing in Hawai'i and Peru are different in significant ways, making direct comparisons between the two difficult, if not impossible. However, I. H. Walker's (2008, 2011) examination of the Waikiki Beachboys, famed Native Hawai'ian watermen, has some similarities to surf instructors in Lima. Although the Beachboys made their livings by teaching and entertaining white tourists, they did so in a manner that asserted their dominance in the surf, resisted colonial social categories, and asserted their right to Hawai'i's seascape.

CHAPTER 2

1. See Viatori and Bombiella (2019, 132).
2. See, for example, West (2016) and Tsing (2013).
3. A summary of these numbers and a discussion of the magnitude of this issue can be found at https://www.nationalgeographic.org/encyclopedia/great -pacific-garbage-patch.
4. An informative overview of the different kinds of ocean currents can be found at https://ocean.si.edu/planet-ocean/tides-currents/currents-waves-and-tides.
5. These specific numbers are taken from https://ourworldindata.org/plastic -pollution, but are widely available in numerous other sources.
6. Such currents can be generated by different forces, such as the movement of ocean waves, differences in salinity where rivers empty into the ocean, and prevailing winds, which can create surface currents or contribute to coastal upwelling or downwelling (Gelfenbaum 2005, 259–60). Rising and falling tides also create currents along the shore, particularly in bays and at river mouths. At high tide a flood current moves water toward shore, whereas a low tide creates an ebb current that moves water away from shore.
7. The South Pacific Ocean's eastern boundary current, the Peru Current, is comprised of four currents. In their overview of the current, Karstensen and Ulloa (2019, 387) detail these four currents: (1) the Pacific Ocean Current, which flows offshore, carrying cold surface water toward the equator; (2) the Peru Coastal Current, which flows near-shore, carrying cold surface water toward the equator; (3) the Peru-Chile Countercurrent, which flows toward the South Pole, carrying warm surface water; and (4) the Peru-Chile Undercurrent, which flows toward the South Pole, carrying warm subsurface water toward the South Pole.
8. See also Alley (2002), Bauman (2004), and Checker (2005).
9. This point is developed in detail by Gershon (2019) and Star and Griesemer (1989).
10. On the work required to translate a fact from one sociohistorical context to another to keep its meaning stable or establish its authority, see Mathews (2014). On the importance of studying how facts are translated across social assemblages and the importance of this process for imagining and maintaining social boundaries, see Gershon (2019). Gal (2015, 22) defines translation as a "set of semiotic processes that purport to change the form, the social place, or

the meaning of a text, object, person, or practice while simultaneously seeming to keep something about it the same." For Gal translations are moments of inequality making—they are not just about navigating overlapping social assemblages, but about producing and reproducing hierarchy between them.

11. These reports can be found at https://oceanconservancy.org/trash-free-seas/international-coastal-cleanup/.

12. For anthropological analyses of the "green economy," see, for example, Büscher, Dressler, and Fletcher (2014).

13. These quotes come from https://www.actualidadambiental.pe/municipalidad-de-lima-organiza-la-carrera-lima-corre-sin-plastico/.

14. See http://loop.pe/oceanos-limpieza-playa-nestle/.

15. A clip of this broadcast can be viewed at https://www.youtube.com/watch?v=Q3zg8JsUtYM.

16. The interview is available at https://www.youtube.com/watch?v=PgdzRIg-emg.

17. This can be viewed at https://www.youtube.com/watch?v=OO5tqhIMrrI.

18. The episode can be seen at https://www.youtube.com/watch?v=SgUauPWCZyA.

19. See http://veranosaludable.minsa.gob.pe.

20. The DIGESA testing data can be found at https://sinia.minam.gob.pe/documentos/calificacion-sanitaria-las-playas-departamento-lima-1986-2007.

21. *E. coli* is the most common thermotolerant coliform bacteria and, depending on the strain, can cause a range of infections that can result in diarrhea and abdominal pain for several days.

22. See http://veranosaludable.minsa.gob.pe.

23. This broadcast is available at https://www.youtube.com/watch?v=BTzZAL2RnKo.

24. For a more in-depth discussion of these dynamics, see Viatori and Bombiella (2019).

25. See Bresnihan (2016) and Viatori and Bombiella (2019).

26. This point is developed in detail in Viatori and Bombiella (2019, 151–86).

27. See Viatori and Bombiella (2019, 8–9).

28. On the semiotics and politics of risk interpretation, see Orsini (2020).

29. See Viatori and Bombiella (2019, 127–35).

30. Recently, a $20 million Ocean Cleanup project attempted—and failed—to launch a floating barrier that would collect plastic in the Great Pacific Garbage Patch (Summers 2018). Even if such surface cleanup projects were feasible on a large scale, scientists point out that they would miss most of the plastic waste in the ocean, which breaks into tiny pieces that would pass through collection nets and which eventually sinks to the sea floor.

31. The COVID-19 pandemic resulted in a massive increase in Peru and around the world of single- or limited-use plastics, especially personal protective equipment such as disposable masks, most of which were made from plastic polymers that break down into microplastics in the ocean. Many reusable products, such as cloth shopping bags, were discouraged, and in some places,

bans or limits on single-use items, such as plastic bags and disposable cups and bottles, were put on hold. Moreover, at the same time, the global price of oil dropped because of a rapid decline in travel and transportation, making the production of plastics cheaper than it had been in years. It was not long before masks washed up on beaches. In Lima, the distribution and accumulation of COVID trash followed existing trends, with the greatest concentrations showing up on the most frequented recreational beaches in the southern portion of the bay, such as Agua Dulce and Las Sombrillas (De la Torre et al. 2021). In keeping with existing approaches to oceanic waste, government officials and NGO representatives urged individual Peruvians to dispose of masks and other personal protective equipment "responsibly" by not throwing them in the street or the ocean, but by properly bagging them and putting them out for trash pickup.

CHAPTER 3

1.   See Peterson and Broad (2008) and Strauss and Orlove (2003).
2.   An extensive literature in anthropology, linguistics, and science and technology studies examines this dynamic. See, for example, Baake (2003), Jasanoff (2004), Kövecses (2010), and Lakoff and Johnson (1980).
3.   See Glantz (2001, 15), Carrillo (1892), and Pezet (1896).
4.   The term El Niño is often used as a shorthand to refer to the warming phase of a the El Niño–Southern Oscillation. However, there are three phases, each of which is characterized by distinct oceanic and atmospheric conditions: neutral ENSO, El Niño, and La Niña. Sarachik and Crane (2010) provide an in-depth overview of these three phases and the impacts on regional and global weather patterns. Less attention has been paid to the La Niña cycle both by scientists and among the larger public, in part because its effects appear to be less dramatically different from normal than El Niño and because there have been twice as many El Niño events as La Niñas since the 1970s (Glantz 2001, 72).
5.   In his intellectual history of El Niño research in Peru and the southern Pacific, Gregory T. Cushman (2004b) shows that hemispheric inequalities shaped the articulation and dissemination of the concept of "El Niño," which emerged as an international object of scientific inquiry through foreign colonial and imperial networks. The relationships that comprised these networks were not equal and rested upon particular networks for the exchange and the production of knowledge about the southern Pacific's climate that privileged U.S. geopolitical, scientific, and commercial interests (Cushman 2004a). This has been (and continues to be) an issue in the production of research on and forecasting systems for El Niño systems.
6.   Following the advent of the modern nation-state in Latin America and around the world, weather forecasting became a means of practicing and performing not only the authority of the state, but also new concepts of citizenship, plan-

ning, and risk (Orlove et al. 2011). Beginning in the late nineteenth century, Latin American governments created national meteorological and hydrological services, charged with providing scientific weather forecasts for public consumption and guiding state planning. This was part of a broader global trend in efforts to mitigate risk in a range of economic and social endeavors through state planning that was based on the scientific assessment of the probability that a range of different outcomes could occur (Beck 1992). Sociologists of risk, such as Ulrich Beck (2009, 293), have argued that this was a means by which state actors sought to reduce future uncertainty by making it part of an "extended present." In his study of government forecasters in the United States, Gary Alan Fine (2007, 14) states that the job of weather forecasters is to "predict what will happen in the future, establishing and drawing on the past, and then to communicate with a public so that others can act on these predictions." Such predictions, however, are complicated by the reality that "weather is a chaotic system that is unlikely to be perfectly modelled" (8). Thus, "forecasting is a social process" that relies upon the public performance of meteorological authority and "institutional legitimation" to present "uncertainty as confident knowledge" (100–101, 103).

7.   In 1984, the NOAA's Tropical Ocean Global Atmosphere (TOGA) program began the creation of the Tropical Atmosphere Ocean (TAO) array, a system of seventy moored weather buoys located along the equator approximately from Papua New Guinea to the Galapagos Islands. Upon the array's completion in 1994, researchers had access to reliable, real-time data on "surface winds, sea surface temperature, upper ocean heat content, near-surface currents, and sea-level in the tropical Pacific" (McPhaden 1993, 36). More than twenty years after its completion, data from the array remains the most important source of data for tracking, researching, and forecasting ENSO events. For a summary and analysis of the development of ENSO modeling and forecasting, see Sarachik and Cane (2010); on the complexities and problems with these predictions, see, for example, Glantz (2001) and Guilyardi (2015).

8.   In their book on the role of El Niño in world history, Richard Grove and George Adamson (2018, 204) note that these El Niño zones "were actually defined somewhat arbitrarily, the results of a pencil sketch by the meteorologist Gene Rasmusson during a radio interview in 1982–1983." In 1997, "Anthony Barnston and colleagues added the Niño 3.4 region" as "an area particularly sensitive to El Niño located between Niño 3 and Niño 4" (204). Grove and Adamson (2018) point out the arbitrary nature of these divisions to underscore the point that scientists, government officials, and citizens come to know ENSO through statistical indices that highlight key aspects of ENSO. They argue that such "indices obscure uncertainty and create the illusion of a simple and predictable climate" (202). The problem with this is that indices, such as sea surface temperatures in zone 3.4, are better at highlighting and predicting some aspects of ENSO than others, which is one reason why predictions are not always accurate. Further-

more, in the past twenty years, scientists have continued to debate what, exactly, defines ENSO and whether there are multiple types of El Niño warming events, which would require different models for predicting.

9.   The impacts of ENSO extend beyond the southern Pacific Basin and, especially during big events, shape weather patterns around the world. As the largest of the world's oceans, the Pacific plays an outsized role in global climate patterns. In El Niño years, there are typically fewer hurricanes in the Atlantic Ocean, while La Niña years have the opposite effect. In addition to flooding in Peru, El Niño events can generate warmer than usual winter temperatures in southern Alaska and western Canada, increased precipitation in the southern United States, and droughts in northeastern Brazil, southern Africa, and India. Meteorologists refer to these long-range (both in terms of distance and time) impacts as "teleconnections."

10. See, for example, Barrios (2017) and Pulwarty, Broad, and Finan (2004).

11. Weather forecasting is not only a social process in that it requires the performance of meteorological facts that publics are willing to accept as authoritative, but also in the unequal provision of such information and its consumption by different sectors of society. See Orlove et al.'s (2011, 120) analysis of "weather citizenships" versus "climate citizenships" in Latin America.

12. Crisis as a permanent state represents one means of justifying the withdrawal of state services, privatization, and the institution of displacements. For example, post-Katrina reconstruction became a slow process whereby many "residents of New Orleans" came to realize that life "as they knew it is gone and that living in a state of quasi-emergency, of 'responding' to ongoing trauma, is 'the norm'" (Adams, Van Hattum, and English 2009, 632). See also Browne (2015).

13. The country sits on the "ring of fire"—a belt of seismic and volcanic activity that encircles much of the Pacific Ocean and produces most of the world's earthquakes and volcanic eruptions. The Nazca and South American tectonic plates, which comprise part of this ring, meet just off the coast of Lima. The ongoing movement of the Nazca plate under the South American plate has, in addition to creating the Andes Mountains, led to dozens of major earthquakes through Peru's history.

14. See Carey (2008) and Oliver-Smith (1986). Broad and Orlove's (2007) analysis of the state's response to the 1997–98 El Niño shows how natural disaster preparation can function to bolster state authority. In the run-up to the widely forecasted El Niño, different actors selectively drew upon globally circulating images of the oceanic and atmospheric event and reworked them to advance their political authority in specific local contexts.

15. The investigation resumed in May, and ultimately the opposition lawmakers compelled Vizcarra to resign—at that point he was the third minister that congress had forced out. Political tensions between congress and the president intensified throughout the remainder of the year. On December 15, 2017, the congress began impeachment proceedings against Kuczynski, who admitted

that he had accepted money from the Brazilian construction giant Odebrecht, after previously denying that he took bribes. These payments were part of a vast network across the continent that funneled roughly three quarters of a billion dollars in bribes from Odebrecht to politicians in return for construction contracts. Kuczynski narrowly survived the impeachment vote and days later issued a "Christmas pardon" for imprisoned former president Alberto Fujimori, the father of Keiko and Kenji Fujimori, both of whom were serving in congress at the time. The pardon led to widespread public protests and accusations that Kuczynski had cut a deal with Kenji Fujimori to stay in office. Kuczynski's actions also were denounced by international human rights organizations and, ultimately, the pardon was overturned by Peru's Supreme Court in 2018. Furthermore, numerous officials in Kuczynski's government resigned in protest. In March 2018, the congress resumed impeachment hearings amid ongoing accusations of corruption against Kuczynski. While he initially promised to fight impeachment, he decided to resign on March 21, 2018, after videos surfaced of Kenji Fujimori attempting to buy votes against the December 2017 impeachment vote. Two days later, Martín Vizcarra, who had become Kuczynski's first vice president, took over the office of president.

16. A video of this interview can be viewed at https://www.youtube.com/watch?v=nCvYYnJJ-Do.

17. Most of the public reporting and discussion about the coastal El Niño and Peru's fishing sector focused on what effects (if any) the climate event would have on the industrial anchoveta fishery. During El Niño years the higher-than-average water temperatures in the eastern Pacific interfere with anchoveta reproduction and growth, causing a significant decline in stocks. Pressure and overfishing by the industrial fleet have led to historic collapses in anchoveta numbers, the most traumatic of which occurred after the 1972–73 El Niño. The development of coastal warming in early 2017 raised concerns that the fishmeal industry could face yet another setback. Indeed, in the first quarter, anchoveta landings were down. However, by March state officials and government scientists reported that anchoveta recruitment looked to be strong enough to proceed with the normal anchoveta season (Gestión 2017a).

18. The situation for artisanal fishers in the north could not have been more different. The mariculture sector was especially hard hit, with production of scallops dropping by 80 percent in 2017 (Gestión 2017b). In their overview of the impact of the coastal El Niño on artisanal fisheries and mariculture in northern Peru, Lotta Clara Kruger et al. (2018, 5–6) report that there was a "complete scallop die off in the bay of Sechura" because of increased ocean water temperatures and decreased salinity due to the torrential rains. Such disasters increased economic precarity in the short term and the long-term potential for dispossession as many artisanal scallop farmers lacked capital to restart their operations, opening the possibility for outside companies with capital to take over in the area (Kruger et al. 2018). Artisanal fishers were unable to fish during the months

of February and March as heavy rains flooded their communities and blocked roads. Once the rains abated, they faced numerous challenges. The destruction of transportation infrastructure hurt fishers in the north, which is the most important zone in Peru for the production and export of fish for direct human consumption. Because of flooded roads and damaged bridges, fishers were not able to get their products to Paita, the main port in the region. Furthermore, many fishers delayed their return to fishing because of damage to their boats, equipment, and ports. Amid such challenges state aid was "non-existent," forcing small-scale fishers to deal with their problems on their own (6). Moreover, as Kruger et al. (2018, 8) note, the destruction of mariculture operations placed increased pressure on capture fisheries as scallop farmers looked for other sources of income. All of this contributed to greater economic precarity for the region's artisanal fishers.

19. I have written about the factors that contribute to ongoing precarity among artisanal fishers in Lima in detail elsewhere. See Viatori and Bombiella (2019, 22–24, 119, 173–76).

20. See Viatori and Bombiella (2019, 37).

21. See, for example, Cai et al. (2018).

CHAPTER 4

1. The class *Cephalopoda* includes octopus, cuttlefish, nautilus, and squid—species that are very adaptable ecologically and often regarded as the most intelligent invertebrates (Godfrey-Smith 2016; Montgomery 2015; Williams 2010).

2. Interactions between humans and nonhumans have emerged at the forefront of cultural inquiry in recent years as anthropologists, historians, and scholars active in science and technology studies theorize how humans and animals "become with" one another (Haraway 2008, 3) and how life is produced and imperiled amid contemporary climate change and ecological degradation (Blanchette 2020; Boyd 2017; Cassidy 2012; Ingold 2013; Kirksey and Helmreich 2010; Kohn 2013; Nadasdy 2007; Sodikoff 2012; Seshia Galvin 2018; Weston 2017). Anthropologists Lieba Faier and Lisa Rofel (2014, 362) argue that "ethnographies of encounter" reveal "how meanings, identities, objects, and subjectivities emerge through unequal relationships involving people and things." It is through such relationships that "beings, species, and categories of nature/culture get made" and come to constitute broader economic, cultural, and environmental processes (373). An important body of work in Latin American history has studied the importance of "the nonhuman actor" in the development of "colonial and postcolonial Latin American societies" (Few and Totorici 2013, 3, 5; see also Asúa and French 2005; Crosby 1973; and Melville 1994).

3. See, for example, Haraway (1989), Latour (1987), Mitchell (2022), and Ross (2017).

4. Sayre (2017, 2) suggests, but does not develop, the parallel between rangeland and fisheries science, noting that "the closest analogue to rangelands is neither croplands nor forests, but the open oceans and, indeed, fisheries science and range science have more in common than one might expect."

5. For a more extensive theorization of this point, see Steinberg (2001, 2009).

6. See Mariátegui, Rojas, and Ladrón (2000, 3), and Blaskovic, Alegre, and Tarfur (2008, 6).

7. See Seibel (2015, 2016).

8. Throughout much of the twentieth century, scientists spent more time using squid specimens as proxies for understanding human neuroscience than they did researching squid life histories. Although squid have decentralized brains that are unlike those of humans, they share the same basic building block—the neuron. And squid possess the "largest nerve cells on earth," which made them ideal subjects for early neurological research (Staaf 2017, 5). As Wendy Williams (2010, 11) remarks in her history of squid research, without these cephalopods "neurosurgeons would be a little less well trained, obstetricians a little less well informed, and geriatricians much less knowledgeable about the aging process."

9. The jumbo squid is a member of the family *Ommastrephidae* of flying squid.

10. For an extended discussion of this process and the politics that informed it, see Viatori and Bombiella (2019, 39–63).

11. Benites and Valdivieso (1986, 120) report that in 1980 there were fifteen Japanese squid boats licensed to fish in Peruvian waters for *calamar*, smaller squids from the families *Loliginidae* and *Ommastrephidae*.

12. See, for example, Rubio and Salazar (1992, 24) and Mariátegui and Taipe (1996, 16).

13. Moore (2015, 63) argues that "frontier-making" is central to capitalism because the production of new frontiers enables ongoing accumulation through "the commodity-oriented appropriation of unpaid work/energy." As Moore and Patel (2017, 19) put it, "Through frontiers, states and empires use violence, culture, and knowledge to mobilize natures at low cost."

14. The ocean was, to use Steinberg's (2009, 488) words, depicted as an "external surface for movement."

15. See, for example, Mariátegui et al. (1998, 28) and Mariátegui et al. (2000, 4).

16. See McCormack (2017) on the role that IVQs have played in privatizing ocean commons for large corporations.

17. Additionally, there have been reports of Japanese boats continuing to harvest jumbo squid without permission in Peru's EEZ. Such actions complicate Peruvian state attempts to regulate the squid fishery, since boats can travel through Peruvian waters as long as they fly a national flag, and tracking unreported catches in Peru's large expanse of Pacific Ocean largely exceeds the ability of Peruvian officials to enforce state fisheries authority.

18. See, for example, Hardin (1968) on the "tragedy of the commons."

19. See, for example, Longo, Clausen, and Clark (2015), McCormack (2017), and Pálsson and Durrenberger (1990), among others.

20. The regulation governing this is DEC-100-291-2013-PRODUCE.

21. The quota was established in No.115–2018-PRODUCE.

22. See Viatori and Bombiella (2019), especially chapters 4 and 5.

23. This is a history I have discussed and analyzed in greater detail elsewhere. See Viatori and Bombiella (2019, 64–87).

24. See Ezquerra-Brauer, Marina, and Aubourg (2019).

EPILOGUE

1. The video announcement can be viewed at https://www.youtube.com/watch?v=h3Rz5i2tq-Q and is linked on the Repsol webpage https://compromisorepsol.pe/avances-en-remediacion/; La Pampilla refinery supplies about 40 percent of Peru's fuel and processes around 120,000 barrels of oil each day.

2. A portion of his speech can be seen at https://www.youtube.com/watch?v=BnjoYGD4000.

3. The report can be found at https://eecentre.org/wp-content/uploads/2022/03/2022-02-24-PE-Oil-Spill-After-The-Spill-ENG.pdf.

4. On January 20, Repsol issued a press communication in which it stated that it had activated a contingency plan and that "we regret not having adequately communicated all our commitments and actions carried out and assumed to address the impact generated by the oil spill in Ventanilla." The communication can be found at https://compromisorepsol.pe/repsol-plan-de-contingencia-activado/. The company announced on January 21 that it had submitted a timeline of events to government officials; see the press communication at https://www.repsol.pe/es/sala-prensa/notas-prensa/nuevo-comunicado.cshtml.

5. See the January 28 press release at https://compromisorepsol.pe/repsol-cantidad-barriles-derramados/.

6. This quote is from the January 20 Repsol press communication at https://compromisorepsol.pe/repsol-plan-de-contingencia-activado/.

7. The interview can be viewed at https://www.youtube.com/watch?v=yCZvB-5Nss8.

8. See https://insurancemarinenews.com/insurance-marine-news/mare-doricum-captain-sends-letter-of-protest-to-peruvian-administration/.

REFERENCES

Adams, Vincanne, Taslim van Hattum, and Diana English. 2009. "Chronic Disaster Syndrome: Displacement, Disaster, Capitalism, and the Eviction of the Poor from New Orleans." *American Ethnologist* 36, no. 4: 615–36.

Alegre, Ana, Frédéric Ménard, Ricardo Tafur, Pepe Espinoza, Juan Argüelles, Víctor Maehara, Oswaldo Flores, Monique Simier, and Arnaud Bertrand. 2014. "Comprehensive Model of Jumbo Squid *Dosidicus gigas* Trophic Ecology in the Northern Humboldt Current System." *PLoS One* 9, no. 1: 1–11.

Alexander, Catherine, and Joshua Reno, eds. 2012. *Economies of Recycling: The Global Transformations of Materials, Values and Social Relations.* London: Zed Books.

Alfaro Medina, Arturo E. 2007. "Problemática de la Basura Marine en el Perú." Plan de Acción para la Protección del Medio Marino y Áreas Costeras del Pacífico Sudeste Comisión Permanente del Pacífico Sur, Secretaría Ejecutiva del Plan de Acción del Pacífico Sudeste.

Alley, Kelley D. 2002. *On the Banks of the Ganga: When Wastewater Meets a Sacred River.* Ann Arbor: University of Michigan Press.

Appel, Hannah, Nikhil Anand, and Akhil Gupta. 2018. "Introduction: Temporality, Politics, and the Promise of Infrastructure." In *The Promise of Infrastructure*, edited by Nikhil Anand, Akhil Gupta, and Hannah Appel, 1–38. Durham, N.C.: Duke University Press.

Aranda, Martin. 2009. "Evolution and State of the Art of Fishing Capacity Management in Peru: The Case of the Anchoveta Fishery." *Pan-American Journal of Aquatic Sciences* 4, no. 2: 146–53.

Arellano, Carlota Estrella, and Gordon Swartzman. 2010. "The Peruvian Artisanal Fishery: Changes in Patterns and Distribution over Time." *Fisheries Research* 101:133–45.

Argüelles Torres, Juan. 1996. "Crecimiento y reclutamiento del calamar gigante *Dosidicus gigas* en el Perú (1991 a 1994)." *IMARPE Informe Progresivo* 23:3–14.

Argüelles, Juan, Ricardo Tarfur, Anatolio Taipe, Piero Villegas, Friedeman Keyl, Noel Dominguez, and Martín Salazar. 2008. "Size Increment of Jumbo Flying Squid *Dosidicus gigas* Mature Females in Peruvian Waters 1989–2004." *Progress in Oceanography* 79:308–12.

Arkhipkin, Alexander. 2016. "Octopus and Squid Populations Are Booming—Here's Why." The Conversation. May 24, 2016. http://theconversation.com/octopus-and-squid-populations-are-booming-heres-why-59830.

Arkhipkin, Alexander I., Paul G. K. Rodhouse, Graham J. Pierce, Warwick Sauer, Mitsuo Sakai, Louise Allcock, Juan Arguelles, John R. Bower, Gladis Castillo, Luca Ceriola et al. 2015. "World Squid Fisheries." *Reviews in Fisheries Science and Aquaculture* 23, no. 2: 92–252.

Arndt, Grant. 2022. "The Indian's White Man: Indigenous Knowledge, Mutual Understanding, and the Politics of Indigenous Reason." *Current Anthropology* 63, no. 1: 10–30.

Asúa, Miguel de, and Roger French. 2005. *A New World of Animals: Early Modern Europeans on the Creatures of Iberian America*. Burlington: Ashgate.

Autoridad del Proyecto Costa Verde (APCV). 1995. "Plan maestro de desarrollo de la Costa Verde." Municipalidad de Lima. http://www.apcvperu.gob.pe/index.php/plan-maestro.

Baake, Ken. 2003. *Metaphor and Knowledge: The Challenges of Writing Science*. Albany: State University of New York Press.

Bailey, Connor. 1985. "The Blue Revolution: The Impact of Technological Innovation on Third-World Fisheries." *Rural Sociologist* 5, no. 4: 259–66.

Barandiarán, Gonzalo. 2004. *Olas peruanas*. Lima: BankBoston.

Barnes, Jessica. 2015. "Scale and Agency: Climate Change and the Future of Egypt's Water." In *Climate Cultures: Anthropological Perspectives on Climate Change*, edited by Jessica Barnes and Michael Dove, 127–45. New Haven: Yale University Press.

Barrios, Roberto E. 2017. "What Does Catastrophe Reveal for Whom? The Anthropology of Crises and Disasters and the Onset of the Anthropocene." *Annual Review of Anthropology* 46:151–66.

Bauman, Zygmunt. 2004. *Wasted Lives: Modernity and Its Outcasts*. Oxford: Polity.

Beck, Ulrich. 1992. *Risk Society: Towards a New Modernity*. London: SAGE.

Beck, Ulrich. 2009. "World Risk Society and Manufactured Uncertainties." *Iris* 1, no. 2: 291–99.

Benites, Carlos, and Violeta Valdivieso. 1986. "Resultados de la pesca exploratoria de 1979/80 y desembarque de cefalopodos pelagicos en el litroal Peruano." *Boletín del Instituto del Mar del Perú* 5:107–39.

Bergmann, J., K. Vinke, C.A. Fernández Palomino, C. Gornott, S. Gleixner, R. Laudien, A. Lobanova, J. Ludescher and H. J. Schellnhuber. 2021. *Assessing the Evidence: Climate Change and Migration in Peru*. Potsdam and Geneva: Potsdam Institute for Climate Impact Research and International Organization for Migration.

Berry, S. Stillman. 1912. "Review of the Cephalopods of Western North America." *Bulletin of the Bureau of Fisheries* 30:267–366.

Blanchette, Alex. 2020. *Porkopolis: American Animality, Standardized Life, and the Factory Farm*. Durham, N.C.: Duke University Press.

Blaskovic, Verónica, Ana Alegre, and Ricardo Tarfur. 2008. "Depredación del calamar gigante (*Dosidicus gigas*) sobre los principals recursos pesqueros en el litoral Peruano durante el 2007." *IMARPE Informe Técnico*. https://www.researchgate.net/publication/305499082_Depredacion_del_calamar_gigante_Dosidicus_gigas_sobre_los_principales_recursos_pesqueros_en_el_litoral_peruano_durante_el_2007/link/5792290808ae33e89f750440/download.

Blondet, Cecilia. 1991. *Las mujeres y el poder: Una historia de Villa El Salvador*. Lima: Instituto de Estudios Peruanos.

Boyd, Brian. 2017. "Archaeology and Human-Animal Relations: Thinking through Anthropocentrism." *Annual Review of Anthropology* 46:299–316.

Bresnihan, Patrick. 2016. *Transforming the Fisheries: Neoliberalism, Nature, and the Commons* Lincoln: University of Nebraska Press.

Brito-Morales, Isaac, David S. Schoeman, Jorge García Molinos, Michael T. Burrows, Carissa J. Klein, Nur Arafeh-Dalmau, Kristin Kaschner, Cristina Garilao, Kathleen Kesner-Reyes, and Anthony J. Richardson. 2020. "Climate Velocity Reveals Increasing Exposure of Deep-Ocean Biodiversity to Future Warming." *Nature Climate Change* 10:576–81.

Broad, Kenneth, and Ben Orlove. 2007. "Channeling Globality: The 1997–1998 El Niño Climate Event in Peru." *American Ethnologist* 34, no. 2: 285–302.

Browne, Katherine E. 2015. *Standing in the Need: Culture, Comfort, and Coming Home after Katrina*. Austin: University of Texas Press.

Buesseler, Ken, Di Jin, Melina Kourantidou, David Levin, Kilaparti Ramakrishna, Philip Renaud 2022. *The Ocean Twilight Zone's Role in Climate Change*. Woods Hole Oceanographic Institution Report. https://twilightzone.whoi.edu/wp-content/uploads/2022/02/The-Ocean-Twilight-Zones-Role-in-Climate-Change.pdf.

Büscher, Bram, Wolfram Heinz Dressler, and Robert Fletcher, eds. 2014. *Nature, Inc.: Environmental Conservation in the Neoliberal Age*. Tucson: University of Arizona Press.

Butt, Tony, Paul Russell, and Rick Grigg. 2004. *Surf Science: An Introduction to Waves for Surfing*. Honolulu: University of Hawai'i Press.

Cai, Wenju, Guojian Wang, Boris Dewitte, Lixin Wu, Augus Santoso, Ken Takahashi, Yun Yang, Aude Carréric, and Michael J. McFaden. 2018. "Increased Variability of Eastern Pacific El Niño under Greenhouse Warming." *Nature* 564:201–6.

Caramanica, Ari. 2017. "Desastres Artificiales." *El Comercio*. April 6, 2017.

Caravedo Molinari, Baltazar. 1977. "The State and the Bourgeoisie in the Peruvian Fishmeal Industry." *Latin American Perspectives* 4, no. 3: 103–23.

Cárdenas, Abel. 2022a. "Pescadores comparten videos que desmienten a Repsol sobre limpieza del mar." *La República*. February 24, 2022.

Cárdenas, Abel. 2022b. "Repsol paga bono en medio de protestas." *La República*. March 16, 2022.

Cárdenas, Abel, and Piero Espíritu. 2022. "Pescadores: 'No nos alcanzan los 200 soles que nos entrega Repsol.'" *La República*. February 20, 2022.

Caretas. 2022. "Ministro del Ambiente: Abren cuarto proceso sancionador contra Repsol por incumplir responsabilidades." February 21, 2022.

Carey, Mark. 2008. "The Politics of Place: Inhabiting and Defending Glacier Hazard Zones in Peru's Cordillera Blanca." In *Darkening Peaks: Glacier Retreat, Science, and Society*, edited by Ben Orlove, Ellen Wiegandt, and Brian H. Luckman, 229–40. Berkeley: University of California Press.

Carr, E. Summerson, and Michael Lempert. 2016. "Introduction: Pragmatics of Scale." In *Scale: Discourse and Dimensions of Social Life*, edited by E. Summerson Carr and Michael Lempert, 1–21. Berkeley: University of California Press.

Carrere, Michelle. 2022. "Las razones detrás del hundimiento de la plataforma petrolera y los incesantes derrames en la costa norte de Perú." *Mongabay*. May 18, 2022.

Carrillo, Camillo N. 1892. "Estudios sobre las Corrientes oceánicas y especialmente de la corriente Humboldt." *Boletín de la Sociedad Geográfico Lima* 2:72–110.

Carse, Ashley. 2012. "Nature as Infrastructure: Making and Managing the Panama Canal Watershed." *Social Studies of Science* 42, no. 4: 539–63.

Carse, Ashley, and Joshua A. Lewis. 2017. "Toward a Political Ecology of Infrastructure Standards: Or, How to Think about Ships, Waterways, Sediment, and Communities Together." *Environment and Planning A* 49, no. 1: 9–28.

Cassidy, Rebecca. 2012. "Lives with Others: Climate Change and Human-Animal Relations." *Annual Review of Anthropology* 41:21–36.

Checker, Melissa. 2005. *Polluted Promises: Environmental Racism and the Search for Justice in a Southern Town*. New York: New York University Press.

Chen, Stephen. 2018. "How China's Squid Fishing Programme Is Squeezing Its Neighbours and Creating Global Sea Change." *South China Morning Post*. June 17, 2018.

Chen, Xinjun, Bilin Liu, and Yong Chen. 2008. "A Review of the Development of Chinese Distant-Water Squid Jigging Fisheries." *Fisheries Research* 89:211–21.

Choy, Tim. 2011. *Ecologies of Comparison: An Ethnography of Endangerment in Hong Kong*. Durham: Duke University Press.

Claus, Anne E. 2020. *Drawing the Sea Near: Satoumi and Coral Reef Conservation in Okinawa*. Minneapolis: University of Minnesota Press.

Collyns, Dan. 2022. "Peru Demands Compensation for Disastrous Oil Spill Caused by Tonga Volcano." *Guardian*. January 19, 2022.

Colten, Craig E. 2006. "Vulnerability and Place: Flat Land and Uneven Risk in New Orleans." *American Anthropologist* 108, no. 4: 731–34.

Comisión de la Verdad y Reconciliación del Perú (CVR). 2003. *Informe Final*. Lima: CVR.

Correa, David, Jorge Tam, José Pasapera, Miguel Saavedra, and Augusto Ingunza. 2008. "Modelado de la circulación marina y descargas hipotéticas en la Bahía del Callao, Perú." *IMARPE Informe* 35, no. 3: 181–92.

Crosby, Alfred W. 1973. *The Columbian Exchange: Biological and Cultural Conse-quences of 1492*. Westport, Conn.: Greenwood Press.

Cruikshank, Julie. 2007. *Do Glaciers Listen? Local Knowledge, Colonial Encounters, and Social Imagination*. Vancouver: University of British Columbia Press.

Crutzen, Paul J., and Eugene F. Stoermer. 2000. "The Anthropocene." *IGBP Newsletter* 41:17–18.

Csirke, J., A. Alegre, J. Argüelles, R. Guevara-Carrasco, L. Mariátegui, M. Segura, R. Tafúr, and C. Yamashiro. 2015. "Main Biological and Fishery Aspects of the Jumbo Squid in the Peruvian Humboldt Current System." Paper presented at the 3rd Meeting of the Scientific Committee, South Pacific Regional Fisheries Man-agement Organization, Port Vila, Vanuatu, September 23 to October 3.

Cushman, Gregory T. 2004a. "Choosing between Centers of Action: Instrument Buoys, El Niño, and Scientific Internationalism in the Pacific, 1957–1982." In *The Machine in Neptune's Garden: Historical Perspectives on Technology and the Marine Environment*, edited by James Fleming and Roger Launius, 133–82. Saga-more Beach, Mass.: Science History Publications.

Cushman, Gregory T. 2004b. "Enclave Vision: Foreign Networks in Peru and the Internationalization of El Niño Research during the 1920s." *Proceedings of the International Commission on History of Meteorology* 1, no. 1: 65–74.

Cushman, Gregory T. 2013. *Guano and the Opening of the Pacific World: A Global Ecological History*. Cambridge: Cambridge University Press.

de la Cadena, Marisol. 2000. *Indigenous Mestizos: The Politics of Race and Culture in Cuzco, Peru, 1919–1991*. Durham: Duke University Press.

de la Cadena, Marisol. 2015a. *Earth Beings: Ecologies of Practice across Andean Worlds*. Durham: Duke University Press.

de la Cadena, Marisol. 2015b. "Uncommoning Nature." *e-flux* 65. https://www.e-flux .com/journal/65/336365/uncommoning-nature/.

de la Rosa, Luis Miguel. 2010. *Huellas en el mar*. Lima: Editorial Elefant.

De la Torre, Gabriel E., Refat Jahan Rakib, Carlos Ivan Pizarro-Ortega, Diana Caro-lina Dioses-Salinas. 2021. "Occurrence of Personal Protective Equipment (PPE) Associated with the COVID-19 Pandemic along the Coast of Lima, Peru." *Science of the Total Environment* 774:145774.

Deloughrey, Elizabeth. 2017. "Submarine Futures of the Anthropocene." *Comparative Literature* 69, no. 1: 32–44.

Dietz, Henry. 1998. *Urban Poverty, Political Participation, and the State: Lima, 1970–1990*. Pittsburgh: University of Pittsburgh Press.

d'Orbigny, Alcide Dessalines. 1835. *Voyage dans l'Amerique méridionale: Le Brésil, la république orientale de l'Uruguay, la République argentine, la Patagonie, la répub-lique du Chili, la république de Bolivia, la république du Pérou, exécuté pendant les anées 1826–1833*. Paris: Chez Pitois-Levrault et C.

d'Orbigny, Alcide Dessalines. 1845. *Mollusques vivants et fossils: Ou description de toutes les epèces de coquilles et de mollusques, classes suivant leur distribution géologique et géographique*. Vol. 1. Paris: Imprimierie d'A. Sirou.

Doubleday, Zoë A., Thomas A. Prowse, Alexander Arkhipkin, Graham J. Pierce, Jayson Semmens, Michael Steer, Stephen C. Leporati, Sílvia Lourenço, Antoni Quetglas, Warwick Sauer, and Bronwyn M. Gillanders. 2016. "Global Proliferation of Cephalopods." *Current Biology* 26:R387–R407.

Douglas, Mary. 1966. *Purity and Danger*. New York: Routledge.

Driant, Jean Claude. 1991. *Las barriadas de Lima: Historia e interpretación*. Lima: Instituto Francés de Estudios Andinos.

Dym, Jordana, and Karl Offen. 2011. *Mapping Latin America: A Cartographic Reader*. Chicago: University of Chicago Press.

ENFEN (Comité Multisectoral Encargado del Estudio Nacional del Fenómeno El Niño). 2017a. "Comunicado official ENFEN No. 1" (January 16).

ENFEN. 2017b. "Comunicado official ENFEN No. 2" (January 24).

ENFEN. 2017c. "Comunicado official ENFEN No. 3" (February 2).

ENFEN. 2017d. "Comunicado official ENFEN No. 4" (February 15).

ENFEN. 2017e. "Comunicado official ENFEN No. 5" (March 2).

ENFEN. 2017f. "Comunicado official ENFEN No. 6" (March 16).

ENFEN. 2017g. "Informe técnico extraordinario No. 001–2017, El Niño Costero" (July 2017).

El Comercio. 1980. "Política no debe interferer en proyectco 'Costa Verde' afirmó el arquitecto Ernesto Aramburú." September 28, 1980.

El Comercio. 1992a. "Empresas japonesas y coreanas se benefican unilateralmente con explotación de la pota." October 23, 1992.

El Comercio. 1992b. "Pesquería no cuenta con los recursos para explotar la pota." October 24, 1992.

El Comercio. 2014. "Playa Carpayo del Callao es la más contaminada de Sudamérica." December 1, 2014.

El Comercio. 2016a. "Estas son las playas más contaminadas del Perú." January 18, 2016.

El Comercio. 2016b. "Costa Verde: 20 años con heridos y muertos por caída de rocas." January 20, 2016.

El Comercio. 2016c. "Analí Gómez se quejó de racism por falta de auspiciadores." February 6, 2016.

El Comercio. 2017a. "Daños por desbordes y huaicos son similares a El Niño de 1998?" February 3, 2017.

El Comercio. 2017b. "Madurez frente a El Niño." March 3, 2017.

El Comercio. 2017c. "No culpen a la Lluvia." March 21, 2017.

El Comercio. 2017d. "El Niño Terrible." March 22, 2017.

El Comercio. 2017e. "El Niño costero generó mayor presencia de peces en mar Peruano." May 2, 2017.

El Comercio. 2017f. "Pablo de la Flor: 'El desastre desnudó lo peor del Perú.'" May 14, 2017.

El Comercio. 2018. "Protestan por construcción de nuevo malecón en la Costa Verde." August 4, 2018.

El Comercio. 2019a. "Cómo el oceano puede convertirse en un enemigo letal para los humanos." September 25, 2019.

El Comercio. 2019b. "Las zonas costeras de Lima con mayor riesgo ante el incremento del nivel del mar." November 2, 2019.

El Comercio. 2022a. "Derrame de petróleo: Marina de Guerra abre proceso para determiner causas y responsabilidades del suceso." January 20, 2022.

El Comercio. 2022b. "Indecopi presenta demanda judicial contra Repsol por 4,500 millones de dólares." May 13, 2022.

Ezquerra-Brauer, Josafat Marina, and Santiago P. Aubourg. 2019. "Recent Trends for the Employment of Jumbo Squid (*Dosidicus gigas*) By-products as a Source of Bioactive Compounds with Nutritional, Functional, and Preservative Applications: A Review." *International Journal of Food Science and Technology* 54:987–98.

Faier, Lieba, and Lisa Rofel. 2014. "Ethnographies of Encounter." *Annual Review of Anthropology* 43:363–77.

Few, Martha, and Zeb Totorici. 2013. "Introduction: Writing Animal Histories." In *Centering Animals in Latin American History*, edited by Martha Few and Zeb Totorici, 1–27. Durham, N.C.: Duke University Press.

Fine, Gary Alan. 2007. *Authors of the Storm: Meteorologists and the Culture of Prediction*. Chicago: University of Chicago Press.

Finnegan, William. 2016. *Barbarian Days: A Surfing Life*. New York: Penguin Books.

Flores Galindo, Alberto. 1991. *La ciudad sumergida: Aristocracia y plebe en Lima, 1760–1830*. Lima: Editorial Horizonte.

Ford, Nick, and David Brown. 2006. *Surfing and Social Theory: Experience, Embodiment, and Narrative of the Dream Glide*. New York: Routledge.

Fortun, Kim. 2014. "From Latour to Late Industrialism." *HAU: Journal of Ethnographic Theory* 4, no. 1: 309–29.

Fraser, Barbara. 2018. "Peru Plans Oil Clean Up." *Nature* 562:18–19.

Frisancho, Jorge. 2022. "Daño capital." *La Mula*. January 26, 2022.

Gal, Susan. 2015. "Politics of Translation." *Annual Review of Anthropology* 44:225–40.

Gal, Susan, and Judith Irvine. 2000. "Language Ideology and Linguistic Differentiation." In *Regimes of Language: Ideologies, Politics and Identities*, edited by Paul V. Kroskrity, 35–83. Santa Fe: SAR Pres.

Gallegos, Juana. 2017. "Reconstrucción balance en rojo." *La República*. December 31, 2017.

Gallegos, Juliana. 2022. "Yuri Hooker: 'Un daño al ambiente no se puede reparar ni con todo el dinero del mundo.'" *La República*. February 20, 2022.

Gandolfo, Daniella. 2009. *The City at Its Limits: Taboo, Transgression, and Urban Renewal in Lima*. Chicago: University of Chicago Press.

Gandolfo, Daniella. 2014. "Illegality: Deviation." *Cultural Anthropology*. https://culanth.org/fieldsights/580-illegality-deviation.

Ganoza, Francisco, Juan Rubio, Octavio Morón, and Margarita Girón. 1997. "Investigaciones sobre el calamari gigante o pota en primavera 1996 en el área de Puerto Pizarro a Paita." *IMARPE Informe Progresivo* 65:23–53.

García, María Elena. 2021. *Gastropolitics and the Specter of Race: Stories of Capital, Culture, and Coloniality in Peru*. Berkeley: University of California Press.

Gelfenbaum, Guy. 2005. "Coastal Currents." In *Encyclopedia of Coastal Science*, edited by Maurice L. Schwartz, 259–60. Dordrecht, the Netherlands: Springer.

George, Rose. 2013. *Ninety Percent of Everything: Inside Shipping, the Invisible Industry that Puts Clothes on Your Back, Gas in Your Car, and Food on Your Plate*. New York: Metropolitan Books.

Gershon, Ilana. 2019. "Porous Social Orders." *American Ethnologist* 46, no. 4: 404–16.

Gestión. 2016. "SNI: Extraer 400 mil toneladas anuales adicionales de pota puede depredar dicha especie." September 25, 2016.

Gestión. 2017a. "Bruno Giuffra: 'Niño Costero' no tendrá un impacto en la temporada de pesca." March 9, 2017.

Gestión. 2017b. "Niño Costero afecta al 80% de la producción peruana de conchas de abanico." March 29, 2017.

Gestión. 2018. "SNP plantea asignación de cuotas individuales en pesca artesanal." September 4, 2018.

Gestión. 2019. "Nivel del mar podría subir más de un metro en 2100 por el calentamiento climático." September 25, 2019.

Ghosh, Amitav. 2016. *The Great Derangement: Climate Change and the Unthinkable*. Chicago: University of Chicago Press.

Gillis, John R. 2012. *The Human Shore: Seacoasts in History*. Chicago: University of Chicago Press.

Gillis, John R. 2013. "The Blue Humanities." *Humanities* 34, no. 3. https://www.neh.gov/humanities/2013/mayjune/feature/the-blue-humanities.

Gillis, John R. 2014. "Not Continents in Miniature: Islands as Ecotones." *Island Studies Journal* 9, no. 1: 155–66.

Glantz, Michael H. 2001. *Currents of Change: Impacts of El Niño and La Niña on Climate and Society*. Cambridge: Cambridge University Press.

Godfrey-Smith, Peter. 2016. *Other Minds: The Octopus, The Sea, and the Deep Origins of Consciousness*. New York: Farrar, Strauss and Giroux.

Graeter, Stefanie. 2020. "Infrastructural Incorporations: Toxic Storage, Corporate Indemnity, and Ethical Deferral in Peru's Neoextractive Era." *American Anthropologist* 122, no. 1: 21–36.

Greene, Shane. 2016. *Punk and Revolution: 7 More Interpretations of Peruvian Reality*. Durham: Duke University Press.

Grove, Richard, and George Adamson. 2018. *El Niño in World History*. London: Palgrave Macmillan.

Guilyardi, Eric. 2015. "Challenges with ENSO in Today's Climate Models." NOAA ENSO (blog). April 24, 2015. https://www.climate.gov/news-features/blogs/enso/challenges-enso-today's-climate-models.

Gustafson, Bret. 2020. *Bolivia in the Age of Gas*. Durham: Duke University Press.

Haddad, Sebastian. 2018. "La revanche de la negra." *La Tercera*. November 5, 2018. https://www.latercera.com/el-deportivo/noticia/la-revancha-la-negra/387378/.

Han, Clara. 2018. "Precarity, Precariousness, and Vulnerability." *Annual Review of Anthropology* 47:331–43.

Haraway, Donna J. 1988. "Situated Knowledges: The Science Question in Feminism as a Site of Discourse on the Privilege of Partial Perspective." *Feminist Studies* 14, no. 3: 575–99.

Haraway, Donna J. 1989. *Primate Visions: Gender, Race, and Nature in the World of Modern Science.* New York: Routledge.

Haraway, Donna J. 2008. *When Species Meet.* Minneapolis: University of Minnesota Press.

Haraway, Donna J. 2015. "Anthropocene, Capitalocene, Plantationocene, Chthulucene: Making Kin." *Environmental Humanities* 6, no. 1: 159–65.

Haraway, Donna J. 2016. *Staying with the Trouble: Making Kin in the Chthulucene.* Durham: Duke University Press.

Hardin, Garrett. 1968. "The Tragedy of the Commons." *Science* 162, no. 3859: 1243–48.

Harvey, Penelope. 2014. "Infrastructures of the Frontier in Latin America." *Journal of Latin American and Caribbean Anthropology* 19, no. 2: 280–83.

Harvey, Penny, and Hannah Knox. 2015. *Roads: An Anthropology of Infrastructure and Expertise.* Ithaca, N.Y.: Cornell University Press.

Hastrup, Kristen. 2013. "Anthropological Contributions to the Study of Climate: Past, Present, and Future." *Wiley Interdisciplinary Reviews: Climate Change* 4, no. 4: 269–81.

Helmreich, Stefan. 2011. "Nature/Culture/Seawater." *American Anthropologist* 113, no. 1: 132–44.

Helmreich, Stefan, and Caroline A. Jones. 2018. "Science/Art/Culture Through an Oceanic Lens." *Annual Review of Anthropology* 47:97–115.

Hessler, Stefanie, ed. 2018. *Tidalectics: Imagining an Oceanic Worldview through Art and Science.* London: TBA21-Academy.

Hetherington, Kregg. 2019. "Introduction: Keywords of the Anthropocene." In *Infrastructure, Environment, and Life in the Anthropocene*, edited by Kregg Hetherington, 1–13. Durham, N.C.: Duke University Press.

Hetherington, Kregg, and Jeremy M. Campbell. 2014. "Nature, Infrastructure, and the State: Rethinking Development in Latin America." *Journal of Latin American and Caribbean Anthropology* 19, no. 2: 191–94.

Higgins, James. 2005. *Lima: A Cultural History.* New York: Oxford University Press.

Hornby, Lucy. 2017. "A Bigger Catch: China's Fishing Fleet Hunts New Ocean Targets." *Financial Times.* March 27, 2017.

Hough-Snee, Dexter Zavalza. 2015. "'You Have the Right to Surf!': Riding Waves of Modernity, Decolonization, and National Identity in Peru." In *Sports and Nationalism in Latino/a America*, edited by Héctor Fernández L'Hoeste, Robert McKee Irwin, and Juan Poblete, 201–23. New York: Palgrave.

Hough-Snee, Dexter Zavalza, and Alexander Sotelo Eastman. 2017. "Introduction." In *The Critical Surf Studies Reader*, edited by Dexter Zavalza Hough-Snee and Alexander Sotelo Eastman, 1–28. Durham, N.C.: Duke University Press.

Hoving, H. J., W. F. Gilly, U. Markaida, K. J. Benoit-Bird, Z. W. Brown, P. Daniel, J. C. Field, L. Parassenti, B. Liu, and B. Campos. 2013. "Extreme Plasticity in Life-

History Strategy Allows a Migratory Predator (Jumbo Squid) to Cope with a Changing Climate." *Global Change Biology* 19:2089–103.

Hughes, David McDermott. 2013. "Climate Change and the Victim Slot: From Oil to Innocence." *American Anthropologist* 115, no. 4: 570–81.

Hughes, David McDermott. 2021. *Who Owns the Wind? Climate Crisis and the Hope of Renewable Energy*. London: Verso.

Hulme, Mike. 2010. "Cosmopolitan Climates." *Theory, Culture, and Society* 27, nos. 2–3: 267–76.

Hulme, Mike. 2015. "Better Weather? The Cultivation of the Sky." *Cultural Anthropology* 30, no. 2: 236–44.

Ibañez, Christian M., Roger D. Sepúlveda, Patricio Ulloa, Friedemann Key, and M. Cecilia Pardo-Gandarillas. 2015. "The Biology and Ecology of the Jumbo Squid *Dosidicus gigas* (Cephalopoda) in Chilean Waters: A Review." *Latin American Journal of Aquatic Research* 43, no. 3: 402–14.

Igoe, Jim. 2017. *The Nature of Spectacle: On Images, Money, and Conserving Capital*. Tucson: University of Arizona Press.

Ingersoll, Karin Amimoto. 2016. *Waves of Knowing: A Seascape Epistemology*. Durham: Duke University Press.

Ingold, Tim. 2002. *The Perception of the Environment: Essays on Livelihood, Dwelling and Skill*. New York: Routledge.

Ingold, Tim. 2013. "Anthropology beyond Humanity." *Suomen Antropologi: Journal of the Finnish Anthropological Society* 38, no. 3: 5–23.

Instituto del Mar del Perú (IMARPE). 2018. "Situación del calamar gigante durante el 2017 y perspectivas de pesca para el 2018." *Informe*. https://cdn.www.gob.pe/uploads/document/file/2065465/Informe-correspondiente-Oficio-199-2021-IMARPE-PCD.pdf.

Instituto Nacional de Estadística e Informática (INEI). 2016. *Planos estratificados de Lima Metropolitana a nivel de Manzana*. https://www.inei.gob.pe/media/MenuRecursivo/publicaciones_digitales/Est/Lib1403/index.html.

Intergovernmental Panel on Climate Change (IPCC). 2021. *Climate Change 2021: The Physical Science Basis. Contribution of Working Group I to the Sixth Assessment Report of the Intergovernmental Panel on Climate Change*. Edited by V. Masson-Delmotte et al. Cambridge: Cambridge University Press.

Jasanoff, Sheila, ed. 2004. *States of Knowledge: The Co-production of Science and Social Order*. Cambridge, Mass.: Harvard University Press.

Jasanoff, Sheila. 2005. *Designs on Nature: Science and Democracy in Europe and the United States*. Princeton: Princeton University Press.

Jasanoff, Sheila. 2013. "A World of Experts: Science and Global Environmental Constitutionalism." *Environmental Affairs Law Review* 40, no. 2: 439–52.

Jereb, P., and C. F. E. Roper, eds. 2010. *Cephalopods of the World: An Annotated and Illustrated Catalogue of the Cephalopod Species Known to Date*. Vol. 2, *Myopsid and Oegopsid Squids*. Rome: FAO.

Karstensen, Johannes, and Osvaldo Ulloa. 2019. "Peru-Chile Current System" In *Encyclopedia of Ocean Sciences*. 3rd ed. Edited by J. Kirk Cochran,

Henry Bokuniewicz, and Patricia Yager, 385–92. London: Elsevier Science & Technology.

Kirksey, Eben. 2015. *Emergent Ecologies*. Durham: Duke University Press.

Kirksey, S. Eben, and Stefan Helmreich. 2010. "The Emergence of Multispecies Ethnography." *Cultural Anthropology* 25, no. 4: 545–76.

Kohn, Eduardo. 2013. *How Forests Think: Toward an Anthropology beyond the Human*. Berkeley: University of California Press.

Kövecses, Zoltán. 2010. *Metaphor: A Practical Introduction*. Oxford: Oxford University Press.

Kruger, Lotta Clara, Sophia Kochalski, Arturo Aguirre-Velarde, Ivonne Vivar, and Matthias Wolf. 2018. "Coping with Abrupt Environmental Change: The Impact of the Coastal El Niño 2017 on Artisanal Fisheries and Mariculture in North Peru." *ICES Journal of Marine Science*. doi:10.1093/icesjms/fsy171.

Laderman, Scott. 2014. *Empire in Waves: A Political History of Surfing*. Berkeley: University of California Press.

Laderman, Scott. 2017. "A World Apart: Pleasure, Rebellion, and the Politics of Surf Tourism." In *The Critical Surf Studies Reader*, edited by Dexter Zavalza Hough-Snee and Alexander Sotelo Eastman, 47–61. Durham, N.C.: Duke University Press.

Lakoff, George, and Mark Johnson. 1980. *Metaphors We Live By*. Chicago: University of Chicago Press.

La Mula. 2022a. "Capitán del buque acusa a Repsol de cometer irregularidades durante derrame de petróleo." January 26, 2022.

La Mula. 2022b. "Derrame de Repsol: Pescadores y sus familias siguen haciendo ollas communes ante abandono del Estado." February 13, 2022.

La República. 2014. "Surfistas exigen no construir tercer carril en Costa Verde." December 22, 2014.

La República. 2015. "Inician obra para devolver el paso peatonal y una ciclovía en la Costa Verde." October 13, 2015.

La República. 2017a. "Not El Niño, But It Seems Like It," February 3, 2017.

La República. 2017b. "Gobierno no declarará estado de emergencia nacional." March 14, 2017.

La República. 2017c. "El Niño Costero." March 14, 2017.

La República. 2017d. "PPK in Huaycoloro: 'Todavía no es necessario declarer emergencia nacional.'" March 16, 2017.

La República. 2017e. "Caballa, barrilete y bonito entran con menores precios a los mercados." March 21, 2017.

La República. 2017f. "Kuczynski: 'Se vienen días impredecibles para el país.'" March 22, 2017.

La República. 2017g. "Piura: Población exige ayuda y presencia de sus autoridades." March 29, 2017.

La República. 2017h. "PPK: 'La reconstrucción inmediata costar 3 mi millones de dolares.'" April 7, 2017.

La República. 2017i. "Pobladores de Huarmey bloquean la Panamericana Norte." September 21, 2017.

La República. 2017j. "Chosica: dirigentes vecinales convocan a una asamblea para coordinar próxima marcha." September 26, 2017.

La República. 2018a. "Formalizan a pescadores de capturas de pota y perico." June 30, 2018.

La República. 2018b. "Ley que regula plásticos de un solo uso ya es realidad." December 18, 2018.

La República. 2020. "Estudio pronostica que el nivel del mar podría subir hasta 40 centímetros por el deshielo." September 17, 2020.

Larkin, Brian. 2013. "The Politics and Poetics of Infrastructure." *Annual Review of Anthropology* 42:327–43.

Latour, Bruno. 1987. *Science in Action: How to Follow Scientists and Engineers through Society.* Cambridge, Mass.: Harvard University Press.

Latour, Bruno. 1999. *Pandora's Hope: Essays on the Reality of Science Studies.* Cambridge, Mass.: Harvard University Press.

Lawler, Kristin. 2011. *The American Surfer: Radical Culture and Capitalism.* New York: Routledge.

Lenoir, Jonathan, Romain Bertrand, Lise Comte, Luana Bourgeaud, Tarek Hattab, Jérôme Murienne, Gaël Grenouillet. 2020. "Species Better Track Climate Warming in the Oceans Than on Land." *Nature Ecology & Evolution* 4:1044–59.

León, Jesica. 2015. "El 30% del terreno de los alcantilados de la Costa Verde presenta un estado crítico." *La República.* February 4, 2015.

León, Ricardo. 2022. "Derrame de Petróleo en Ventanilla: 'No había oleaje ni vientos.'" *El Comercio.* January 22, 2022.

Levinson, Marc. 2006. *The Box: How the Shipping Container Made the World Smaller and the World Economy Bigger.* Princeton: Princeton University Press.

Ley, Lukas. 2021. *Building on Borrowed Time: Rising Seas and Failing Infrastructure in Semarang.* Minneapolis: University of Minnesota Press.

L'Hereux, Michelle. 2014. "What is the El Niño-Southern Oscillation (ENSO) in a Nutshell?" NOAA ENSO (blog). May 5, 2014. https://www.climate.gov/news -features/blogs/enso/what-el-niño–southern-oscillation-enso-nutshell.

Li, Gang, Bilin Liu, Luoliang Xu, and Xinjun Chen. 2019. *Annual Report of China to the 2019 SPRFMO Science Committee, Part II: the Squid Jigging Fishery.* Technical report. South Pacific Regional Fisheries Management Organization. https://www .sprfmo.int/assets/2020-SC8/SC8-Doc20-Rev1-China-Annual-report-to-SC8 -Squid.pdf.

Longo, Stefano B., Rebecca Clausen, and Brett Clark. 2015. *The Tragedy of the Commodity: Oceans, Fisheries, and Aquaculture.* New Brunswick, N.J.: Rutgers University Press.

Losada, I. J., B. G. Reguero, F. J. Méndez, S. Castanedo, A. J. Abascal, and R. Mínguez. 2013. "Long-Term Changes in Sea-Level Components in Latin America and the Caribbean." *Global and Planetary Change* 104:34–50.

Magrin, G. O., J. A. Marengo, J.-P. Boulanger, M. S. Buckeridge, E. Castellanos, G. Poveda, F. R. Scarano, and S. Vicuña. 2014. "Central and South America." In

Climate Change 2014: Impacts, Adaptation, and Vulnerability. Part B: Regional Aspects. Contribution of Working Group II to the Fifth Assessment Report of the Intergovernmental Panel on Climate Change. Edited by V. R. Barros et al., 1499–1566. Cambridge: Cambridge University Press.

Malm, Andreas, and Shora Esmailian. 2012. "Ways In and Out of Vulnerability to Climate Change: Abandoning the Mubarak Project in the Northern Nile Delta, Egypt." *Antipode* 45, no. 2: 474–92.

Mariátegui, Luis, Gladis Castillo, Carlos Ruiz, Carlos Pais, Braulio Diaz, and Oscar Valladares. 1998. "Pesquería artisanal del calamari gigante (*Dosidicus gigas*) en el litoral norte, octubre a diciembre 1997." *IMARPE Informe Progresivo* 77:27–48.

Mariátegui, Luis, Octavio Morón, Roberto Vargas, and Betsy Buitrón. 1997. "Prospección pesquera costera del recurso calamar gigante o pota, *Dosidicus gigas*." *IMARPE Informe Progresivo* 70:29–45.

Mariátegui, Luis, Pablo Rojas, and Miluska Soto Ladrón. 2000. "Prospecciones sinópticas de la pesquería artisanal del calamar gigante (*Dosidicus gigas*) en el norte del Perú durante 1999." *IMARPE Informe Progresivo* 114:3–16.

Mariátegui, Luis, and Anatolio Taipe. 1996. "Distribución y abundancia relative del calamari gigante (*Dosidicus gigas*) en el Perú." *Informe Progresivo del IMARPE* 34:3–27.

Martello, Marybeth, and Sheila Jasanoff. 2004. "Introduction: Globalization and Environmental Governance." In *Earthly Politics: Local and Global in Environmental Governance*, edited by Sheila Jasanoff and Marybeth Martello, 1–29. Cambridge: MIT Press.

Masco, Joseph. 2010. "Bad Weather: On Plantetary Crisis." *Social Studies of Science* 40, no. 1: 7–40.

Mathews, Andrew S. 2014. "Scandals, Audits, and Fictions: Linking Climate Change to Mexican Forests." *Social Studies of Science* 44, no. 1: 82–108.

Matos Mar, José. 1984. *Desborde popular y crisis del estado.* Lima: Instituto de Estudios Peruanos.

Mauro, Chris. 2005. "The Surfer Interview with Sofia Mulanovich." *Surfer.* March 2005.

Mayo, Adriana. 2018. "Isla de plástico amenaza la vida marina frente a las costas de Perú y Chile." *La República.* June 28, 2018.

McCall Howard, Penny. 2017. *Environment, Labour, and Capitalism at Sea: "Working the Ground" in Scotland.* Manchester: Manchester University Press.

McClure, Max. 2015. "Jumbo Squid, *Dosidicus gigas*: Chile, Peru. Seafood Watch Report." https://www.seafoodwatch.org/recommendation/squid/jumbo-squid-1919.

McCormack, Fiona. 2017. *Private Oceans: The Enclosure and Marketization of the Seas.* London: Pluto.

McPhaden, Michael J. 1993. "TOGA-TAO and the 1991–93 El Niño-Southern Oscillation Event." *Oceanography* 6, no. 2: 36–44.

Melville, Elinor G. K. 1994. *A Plague of Sheep: Environmental Consequences of the Conquest of Mexico.* Cambridge: Cambridge University Press.

Mendoza, Raúl. 2015. "Historia de una costa Perdida." *La República*. May 9, 2015.

Mendoza Riofrió, Marcela. 2017. "Qué lecciones nos dejó el reciente Fenómeno del Niño costero?" *El Comercio*. May 9, 2017.

Mentz, Steve. 2009. "Toward a Blue Cultural Studies: The Sea, Maritime Culture, and Early Modern English Literature." *Literature Compass* 6, no. 5: 997–1013.

Millar, Kathleen M. 2018. *Reclaiming the Discarded: Life and Labor on Rio's Garbage Dump*. Durham: Duke University Press.

Ministerio de Producción. 2021. *Anuario Estadístico: Pesquero y Acuícola*. https://ogeiee.produce.gob.pe/index.php/en/shortcode/oee-documentos-publicaciones/publicaciones-anuales/item/1001-anuario-estadistico0-pesquero-y-acuicola-2020.

Miranda, Oscar. 2019. "El Mensaje de Greta." *La República*. September 29, 2019.

Mitchell, Timothy. 2002. *Rule of Experts: Egypt, Techno-politics, Modernity*. Berkeley: University of California Press.

Montgomery, Sy. 2015. *The Soul of an Octopus: A Surprising Exploration into the Wonder of Consciousness*. New York: Atria.

Moore, Jason. 2015. *Capitalism in the Web of Life: Ecology and the Accumulation of Capital*. New York: Verso.

Moore, Jason. 2016. "Anthropocene or Capitalocene? Nature, History, and the Crisis of Capitalism." In *Anthropocene or Capitalocene? Nature, History, and the Crisis of Capitalism*, edited by Jason Moore, 1–11. Oakland, Calif.: PM Press.

Moore, Jason, and Raj Patel. 2017. *A History of the World in Seven Cheap Things: A Guide to Capitalism, Nature, and the Future of the Planet*. Berkeley: University of California Press.

Nadasdy, Paul. 2007. "The Gift in the Animal: The Ontology of Hunting and Human-Animal Sociality." *American Ethnologist* 34, no. 1: 25–43.

National Oceanic and Atmospheric Administration (NOAA). 2021. "Why Does the Ocean Have Waves?" February 26, 2021. https://oceanservice.noaa.gov/facts/wavesinocean.html.

Oceana Perú, Dirección de Pesquerías. 2022. *Informe: Estimación del valor en playa de la pesca costera artesanal de Ancón y Chancay; Contribución para un programa de compensacion socioeconómica*. https://peru.oceana.org/informes/estimacion-del-valor-en-playa-de-la-pesca-costera-artesanal-de-ancon-y-chancay/.

Ojani, Chakad. 2021. "The (Ontological) Politics of Fog Capture in Lima, Peru." *Anthropology Today* 37, no. 1: 13–15.

Oliver-Smith, Anthony. 1986. *The Martyred City: Death and Rebirth in the Andes*. Albuquerque: University of New Mexico Press.

O'Reilly, Jessica, Cindy Isenhour, Pamela McElwee, and Ben Orlove. 2020. "Climate Change: Expanding Anthropological Possibilities." *Annual Review of Anthropology* 49:13–29.

Orlove, Ben, Renzio Taddei, Guillermo Podestá, and Kenneth Broad. 2011. "Environmental Citizenship in Latin America: Climate, Intermediate Organizations, and Political Subjects." *Latin American Research Review* 46:116–40.

Orsini, Davide. 2020. "Signs of Risk: Materiality, History, and Meaning in Cold War Controversies over Nuclear Contamination." *Comparative Studies in Society and History* 62, no. 3: 520–50.

Ortiz Tejada, Enrique. 2022. "Derrame de culpas y buenas intenciones: ¿Qué hacer ahora?" *La Mula.* January 25, 2022.

Pálsson, Gísli, and E. Paul Durrenberger. 1990. "Systems of Production and Social Discourse: The Skipper Effect Revisited." *American Anthropologist* 92, no. 1: 130–41.

Panfichi, Aldo. 1995. "La urbanización de Lima, 1535–1900." In *Mundos Interiores: Lima 1850–1950,* edited by Aldo Panfichi and Felipe Portocarrero, 15–42. Lima: Universidad del Pacífico.

Paredes, Carlos E., and Santiago de la Puente. 2014. *Situación actual de la pesquería de la pota (*Dosidicus gigas*) en el Perú y recomendaciones para su mejora.* Informe final: Proyecto Mediano Breve CIES PM-T1:1–110. http://www.cies.org.pe/es/investigaciones/medio-ambiente-recursos-naturales-y-energia/situacion-actual-de-la-pesqueria-de-la.

Parker, D. S. 1998. *The Idea of the Middle Class: White Collar Workers and Peruvian Society, 1900–1950.* College Park: Penn State University Press.

Peterson, Nicole, and Kenneth Broad. 2008. "Climate and Weather Discourse in Anthropology: From Determinism to Uncertain Futures." In *Anthropology and Climate Change: From Encounters to Actions,* edited by Susan Crate and Mark Nuttall, 70–86. Walnut Creek, Calif.: Left Coast Press.

Pezet, Federico A. 1896. "La contracorriente 'El Niño' en la costa norte del Perú." *Boletín de la Sociedad Geográfica de Lima* 5:457.

Pfeffer G. 1884. "Die Cephalopoden des Hamburger Naturhistorischen Museums." *Abhandlungen aus dem Gebiete der Naturwissenschaften, Hamburg* 8, no. 1: 1–30.

Pomar, Felipe. 1988. "Surfing in 1,000 BC." *Surfer* 29:4.

Poole, Deborah. 1997. *Vision, Race, and Modernity: A Visual Economy of the Andean Image World.* Princeton, N.J.: Princeton University Press.

Pörtner, H. O., D. C. Roberts, V. Masson-Delmotte, P. Zhai, M. Tignor, E. Poloczanska, K. Mintenbeck, A. Alegría, M. Nicolai, A. Okem, et al., eds. 2019. *IPCC Special Report on the Ocean and Cryosphere in a Changing Climate.* IPCC. https://www.ipcc.ch/srocc/.

Presidencia de la República del Perú. 2020. "Presidente Vizcarra anunció ampliación del Estado de Emergencia Nacional y aislamiento social obligatorio hasta el 12 de abril." March 26, 2020. https://www.gob.pe/institucion/presidencia/noticias/111519-presidente-vizcarra-anuncio-ampliacion-del-estado-de-emergencia-nacional-y-aislamiento-social-obligatorio-hasta-el-12-de-abril.

Prialé, Miguel. 2017. "Invierte: Pe para le reconstrucción." *El Comercio,* April 19, 2017.

Publimetro. 2018. "El mar de Lima y Callao es el más contaminado del Perú por basura Marina." June 24, 2018.

Pulwarty, Roger S., Kenneth Broad, and Timothy Finan. 2004. "El Niño Events, Forecasts and Decision-Making." In *Mapping Vulnerability: Disasters, Development and People.* Edited by Greg Bankoff, Georg Ferks, and Dorothea Hilhorst, 83–98. New York: Taylor and Francis.

Ramírez, Ivan J., and Fernando Briones. 2017. "Understanding the El Niño Costero of 2017: The Definition Problem and Challenges of Climate Forecasting and Disaster Responses." *International Journal of Disaster Risk Science* 8:489–92.

Reguero, Borja G., Iñigo J. Losada, Pedro Díaz-Simal, Fernando J. Méndez, and Michael W. Beck. 2015. "Effects of Climate Change on Exposure to Coastal Flooding in Latin America and the Caribbean." *PLoS One* 10, no. 7: e0133409. doi:10 .1371/journal.pone.0133409.

Reno, Joshua. 2015. "Waste and Waste Management." *Annual Review of Anthropology* 44:557–42.

Reuters. 2022. "'Smells Like Death': Peru Oil Spill Clear-Up Drags on as Fishermen Count Cost." January 21, 2022.

Roitman, Janet. 2014. *Anti-Crisis*. Durham, N.C.: Duke University Press.

Ross, Corey. 2017. *Ecology and Power in the Age of Empire: Europe and the Transformation of the Tropical World*. Oxford: Oxford University Press.

Rubio, Juan R., and Carlos C. Salazar. 1992. "Prospección pesquera del calamari gigante (*Dosidicus gigas*) a bordo del buque japones 'Shinko Maru 2.'" *IMARPE Informe* 103:3–32.

Ryan, Benjamin. 2021. "Managing the Majestic Jumbo Flying Squid: Warming Waters Attributed to Climate Change Help Fill People's Pockets and Dinner Plates." *New York Times*. June 4, 2021.

Salazar Albarca, Mishell. 2019. *El reto de Analí Gomez: La campeona de surf que surcó las olas de la discriminación*. Lima: La Universidad Peruana de Ciencias Aplicadas.

Sarachik, Edward, and Mark A. Cane. 2010. *The El Niño-Southern Oscillation Phenomenon*. Cambridge: Cambridge University Press.

Sayre, Nathan F. 2017. *The Politics of Scale: A History of Rangeland Science*. Chicago: University of Chicago Press.

Schenker, Michael. 1973. "Saving a Dying Sea—The London Convention on Ocean Dumping." *Cornell International Law Journal* 7, no. 1: 32–48.

Schneider, C. O. 1930. "Notas sobre la jibia chilena (*Ommastrephes gigas*, Hupé)." *Boletin de la Sociedad de Biología de Concepción* 3–4: 117–24.

Scott, James C. 1998. *Seeing Like a State: How Certain Schemes to Improve the Human Condition Have Failed*. New Haven, Conn.: Yale University Press.

Segura, Alonso. 2017. "Los desafíos por delante." *El Comercio*. April 2, 2017.

Seibel, Brad A. 2015. "Environmental Physiology of the Jumbo Squid, *Dosidicus gigas* (d'Orbigny, 1835) (Cephalopoda: Ommastrephidae): Implications for Changing Climate." *American Malacological Bulletin* 33, no. 1: 161–73.

Seibel, Brad A. 2016. "Cephalopod Susceptibility to Asphyxiation via Ocean Incalescence, Deoxygenation, and Acidification." *Physiology* 31:418–29.

Seibel, Brad A., and Rui Rosa. 2008. "Synergistic Effects of Climate-Related Variables Suggest Future Physiological Impairment in a Top Ocean Predator." *PNAS* 105, no. 52: 20776–80.

Seibel, Brad A., Jillian L. Schneider, Stein Kaartverdt, Karen F. Wishner, and Kendra L. Daly. 2016. "Hypoxia Tolerance and Metabolic Suppression in Oxygen Minimum

Zone Euphausiids: Implications for Ocean Deoxygenization and Biogeochemical Cycles." *Integrative and Comparative Biology* 56, no. 4: 510–23.

Seshia Galvin, Shaila. 2018. "Interspecies Relations and Agrarian Worlds." *Annual Review of Anthropology* 47:233–49.

Silva Santisteban, Rocío. 2019. "Greta y la indiferencia." *La República.* September 24, 2019.

Sodikoff, Genese Marie, ed. 2012. *The Anthropology of Extinction: Essays on Culture and Species Death.* Bloomington: Indiana University Press.

Staaf, Danna. 2017. *Squid Empire: The Rise and Fall of the Cephalopods.* Lebanon. N.H.: ForeEdge.

Staaf, Danna J., Louis D. Zeidberg, and William F. Gilly. 2011. "Effects of Temperature on Embryonic Development of the Humboldt Squid *Dosidicus gigas.*" *Marine Ecology Progress Series* 441:165–75.

Star, Susan Leigh. 1999. "The Ethnography of Infrastructure." *American Behavioral Scientist* 43:377–91.

Star, Susan Leigh, and James R. Griesemer. 1989. "Institutional Ecology, 'Translations' and Boundary Objects: Amateurs and Professionals in Berkeley's Museum of Vertebrate Zoology, 1907–39." *Social Studies of Science* 19, no. 3: 387–420.

Steenstrup, Japetus. 1857. "Oplysninger om en ny Art Blaeksprutter, Dosidicus Eschrichtii." *Oversigt over det Ongelige Danske Videnskabernes Selskabs Forhandlinger,* 1857: 1–14.

Steinberg, Phillip E. 2001. *The Social Construction of the Ocean.* Cambridge: Cambridge University Press.

Steinberg, Philip. 2009. "Sovereignty, Territory, and the Mapping of Mobility: A View from the Outside." *Annals of the Association of American Geographers* 99, no. 3: 467–95.

Steinberg, Philip, and Kimberley Peters. 2015. "Wet Ontologies, Fluid Spaces: Giving Depth to Volume through Oceanic Thinking." *Environment and Planning D: Society and Space* 33: 247–64.

Stensrud, Astrid B. 2021. *Watershed Politics and Climate Change in Peru.* London: Pluto Press.

Strathern, Marilyn. 2004. *Partial Connections.* Walnut Creek, Calif.: AltaMira Press.

Strauss, Sarah, and Ben Orlove. 2003. "Up in the Air: The Anthropology of Weather and Climate." In *Weather, Climate, Culture,* edited by Sarah Strauss and Ben Orlove, 3–16. Oxford: Berg.

Summers, Hannah. 2018. "Great Pacific Garbage Patch $20m Cleanup Fails to Collect Plastic." *Guardian.* December 20, 2018.

Swyngedouw, Erik. 2004. "Globalisation or 'Glocalization'? Networks, Territories, and Rescaling." *Cambridge Review of International Affairs* 17, no. 1: 25–48.

Szersynski, Bronislaw. 2010. "Reading and Writing the Weather: Climate Technics and the Moment of Responsibility." *Theory, Culture & Society* 2–3:9–30.

Taj, Mitra. 2022a. "Who Is Responsible for the 27-Mile Oil Spill in Peru?" *New York Times,* February 3, 2022.

Taj, Mitra. 2022b. "Imágenes revelan corrosión en tubos que se desprendieron en derrame de Repsol." *Ojo Publico*. February 13, 2022.

Takahashi, K., K. Mosquera, J. Aparco, Y. Ramos, J. Fajardo, and I. Montes. 2014. "Evaluación del posible impacto de la variabilidad y cambio climático en el nivel del mar en la costa de Lima." *Investigación en Variabilidad y Cambio Climático, Instituto Geofísico del Perú*. http://met.igp.gob.pe/proyectos/manglares/estudio_nivel_mar_IGP.pdf.

Takahashi, Ken, and Alejandra G. Martínez. 2017. "The Very Strong Coastal El Niño in 1925 in the Far-Eastern Pacific." *Climate Dynamics*. https://doi.org/10.1007/s00382-017-3702-1.

Takahashi, Ken, Kobi Mosquera, and Jorge Reupo. 2014. "El Índice Costero El Niño (ICEN): Historia y actualización." *Boletín Técnico: Generación de Modelos Climáticos para el Pronóstico de la Ocurrencia del Fenómeno El Niño* 1, no. 2: 8–9.

Tegell, Simeon. 2022. "How Peru Laid the Groundwork for an Oil Spill Disaster." *Foreign Policy*. February 15, 2022.

Tejada De la Cruz, Rosa Ximena. 2018. "Sectores costeros más vulnerables entre Lurín y Pucusana ante un posible aumento del nivel del mar como consecuencia del cambio climático: Adaptación y aplicación del índice de vulnerabilidad costera de Gornitz." *Espacio y Desarrollo* 31:61–87.

Telesca, Jennifer E. 2020. *Red Gold: The Managed Extinction of the Giant Bluefin Tuna*. Minneapolis: University of Minnesota Press.

Teves, N., G. Laos, S. Carrasco, C. S. Roman, L. Pizarro, G. Cardenas, and A. Romero. 1996. "Sea-Level Rise along the Lima Coastal Zone, Perú, Because of Global Warming: Environmental Impacts and Mitigation Measures." In *Adapting to Climate Change: An International Perspective*, edited by J. B. Smith et al., 283–98. Springer: New York.

Torres, Alfredo. 2017. "País de huaicos y terremotos." *El Comercio*. March 16.

Tsing, Anna Lowenhaupt. 2000. "The Global Situation." *Cultural Anthropology* 15, no. 3: 327–60.

Tsing, Anna Lowenhaupt. 2013. "Sorting out Commodities: How Capitalist Value Is Made through Gifts." *HAU: Journal of Ethnographic Theory* 3, no. 1: 21–43.

Tsing, Anna Lowenhaupt. 2015. *The Mushroom at the End of the World: On the Possibility of Life in Capitalist Ruins*. Princeton, N.J.: Princeton University Press.

Tsing, Anna Lowenhaupt. 2017. "The Buck, the Bull, and the Dream of the Stag: Some Unexpected Weeds of the Anthropocene." *Suomen Antropologi* 42, no. 1: 3–21.

Tsing, Anna Lowenhaupt, Andrew S. Mathews, and Nils Bubandt. 2019. "Patchy Anthropocene: Landscape Structure, Multispecies History, and the Retooling of Anthropology." *Current Anthropology* 60, no. S20: S186–97.

Ueber, Edward, and Alex MacCall. 2005. "The Rise and Fall of the California Sardine Empire." In *Climate Variability, Climate Change, and Fisheries*, edited by Michael H. Glantz, 31–48. Cambridge: Cambridge University Press.

Ugaz, José. 2017. "Reconstruir." *El Comercio*. April 3, 2017.

United Nations. 2017. "Factsheet: Marine Pollution." The Ocean Conference. oceanconference.un.org.

Vásquez-Léon, Marcela. 2009. "Hispanic Farmers and Farmworkers: Social Networks, Institutional Exclusion, and Climate Vulnerability in Southeastern Arizona." *American Anthropologist* 111, no. 3: 289–301.

Vaughn, Sarah E. 2017. "Disappearing Mangroves: The Epistemic Politics of Climate Adaptation in Guyana." *Cultural Anthropology* 32, no. 2: 242–68.

Venkateswaran, K., K. MacClune, and M. F. Enriquez. 2017. "Learning from El Niño Costero 2017: Opportunities for Building Resilience in Peru." ISET International and the Zurich Flood Resilience Alliance. http://floodresilience.net/resources/collection/perc.

Viatori, Maximilian. 2019. "Uncertain Risks: Salmon Science, Harm, and Ignorance in Canada." *American Anthropologist* 121, no. 2: 325–37.

Viatori, Maximilian, and Héctor Bombiella. 2019. *Coastal Lives: Nature, Capital, and the Struggle for Artisanal Fisheries in Peru.* Tucson: University of Arizona Press.

Vidal, José. 2014. "El tsunami de asfalto que arrasa la playa Redondo." *La República.* December 20, 2014.

Villalba, Karina. 2015. "Analí Gómez: 'Mi vida es el surf." *El Comercio.* December 26, 2015.

Walker, Charles F. 2008. *Shaky Colonialism: The 1746 Earthquake-Tsunami in Lima, Peru, and Its Long Aftermath.* Durham: Duke University Press.

Walker, Isaiah Helekunihi. 2008. "Hui Nalu, Beachboys, and the Surfing Boarder-Lands of Hawai'i." *Contemporary Pacific* 20, no. 1: 89–113.

Walker, Isaiah Helekunihi. 2011. *Waves of Resistance: Surfing and History in Twentieth Century Hawai'i.* Honolulu: University of Hawai'i Press.

Warshaw, Matt. 2010. *The History of Surfing.* San Francisco: Chronicle Books.

Weismantel, Mary. 2001. *Cholas and Pishtacos: Stories of Race and Sex in the Andes.* Chicago: University of Chicago Press.

West, Paige. 2016. *Dispossession and the Environment: Rhetoric and Inequality in Papua, New Guinea.* New York: Columbia University Press.

Weston, Kath. 2017. *Animate Planet: Making Visceral Sense of Living in a High-Tech Ecologically Damaged World.* Durham, N.C.: Duke University Press.

Westwick, Peter, and Peter Neushul. 2013. *The World in a Curl: An Unconventional History of Surfing.* New York: Crown.

Wilhelm, Ottmar, G. 1930. "Las mortandades de jibias (*Omamastrephes gigas*) en la Bahía de Talcahuano." *Boletín de la Sociedad de Biología de Concepción* 3–4: 23–28.

Wilhelm, Ottmar, G. 1954. "Algunas observaciones acerca de las mortandades de jibias (*Dosidicus gigas* d'Orb.) en el litoral de Concepción." *Revista de Biologia Marina* 4: 196–201.

William, Gilly, Unai Markaida, C. H. Baxter, and Barbara A. Block. 2006. "Vertical and Horizontal Migrations by Squid *Dosidicus gigas* Revealed by Electronic Tagging." *Marine Ecology Progress Series* 324:1–17.

Williams, Nigel. 2007. "Humboldt Expansion." *Current Biology* 17, no. 16: R620–21.

Williams, Wendy. 2010. *Kraken: The Curious, Exciting, and Slightly Disturbing Science of Squid.* New York: Abrams Image.

Wintersteen, Kristin A. 2021. *The Fishmeal Revolution: The Industrialization of the Humboldt Current Ecosystem*. Berkeley: University of California Press.

Wood, David. 2009. "On the Crest of a Wave: Surfing and Literature in Peru." *Sport in History* 29, no. 2: 226–42.

Wood, David. 2012. "Representing Peru: Seeing the Female Sporting Body." *Journal of Latin American Cultural Studies* 21, no. 3: 417–36.

Woody, Todd. 2019. "The Sea Is Running Out of Fish, Despite Nations' Pledges to Stop It." National Geographic. October 8, 2019. https://www.nationalgeographic .com/science/article/sea-running-out-of-fish-despite-nations-pledges-to-stop.

World Health Organization (WHO). 2017. "Guidelines for Drinking-Water Quality: Fourth Edition Incorporating the First Addendum." http://www.who.int/ publications/guidelines/en/.

World Wildlife Fund (WWF). 2018. "Towards Sustainable Fisheries: Peruvian Government Commits to the Formalization of One of the Largest Fisheries in the World." http://www.wwf.org.pe/en/?uNewsID=330856, July 11, 2018.

Yamashiro, Carmen, Wilbert Marín Soto, and Juan Argüelles Torres. 2016. "El recurso calamar gigante en la costa peruana y El Niño." *Boletín Trimestral Oceanográfico* 2, no. 1: 17–20.

Young, Talia, Emma C Fuller, Mikaela M Provost, Kaycee E Coleman, Kevin St. Martin, Bonnie J McCay, and Malin L Pinsky. 2019. "Adaptation Strategies of Coastal Fishing Communities as Species Shift Poleward." *ICES Journal of Marine Science* 76, no. 1: 93–103.

Yusoff, Kathryn. 2019. *A Billion Black Anthropocenes or None*. Minneapolis: University of Minnesota Press.

Zee, Jerry C. 2020. "Machine Sky: Social and Terrestrial Engineering in a Chinese Weather System." *American Anthropologist* 122, no. 1: 9–20.

Zeiderman, Austin. 2016. *Endangered City: The Politics of Security and Risk in Bogotá*. Durham, N.C.: Duke University Press.

INDEX

acidification, 8, 16, 19, 24, 73, 134
Alfaro, Arturo, 69, 77, 81, 88–89
anchoveta: effects of El Niño on, 106, 128,
    146, 189n17; jumbo squid and, 133, 139, 146
anchoveta fishery: boom-bust cycles of,
    128, 138, 139, 152–53, 163–64, 189n17; El
    Niño effects on, 106, 128, 146, 189n17;
    regulation of, 129, 138, 148, 150. *See
    also* fishmeal
Ancón, 45, 167–68, 170, 172
Andrade, Alberto, 47
Anthropocene, 16, 182n9
antiplastic campaigns, 77–79, 81
Aramburú Menchaca, Ernesto, 43–44, 45
Asociación para la Conservación de las
    Playas y Olas del Peru, 57
Autoridad del Proyecto Costa Verde
    (APCV), 46–49, 60–61

bacteria, 83, 85–87, 88, 94–97, 185n21
Barandiarán, Gonzalo, 38, 41, 57
Barranco, 3, 34, 46, 48, 63, 101
beaches: access to, 31–35, 32, 33, 61–64;
    cleanliness of, 21, 46, 83–89; cleanup

efforts, 66–69, 68, 76–77, 78, 93–94;
    construction and maintenance of, 8,
    43, 44, 47–49, 56–57, 60–61; effects
    of oil spills on, 167, 168; effects of sea
    level rise on, 10–11; as elite sanctuary,
    37, 42–43, 44–45, 80
Bejarano Ybarra, Gerardo Alberto, 51
Benites, Carlos, 139, 143
biologists, 21, 129–66, 167–68, 182n9
boats, wooden, 5–7, 7, 127–28, 138, 141,
    157, 158
breakwaters, 40, 43, 45, 75
bridges, pedestrian, 8, 31, 34, 43, 47–49,
    61–64, 103
Briones, Fernando, 110, 112

Cabo Blanco, 57
Callao, 3, 8, 20–21, 75, 102, 103, 158, 168.
    See also Playa Carpayo
capitalism: climate change and, 15, 24,
    25–26, 182n9; fossil fuels and, 175–77;
    oceans and, 18–19, 71–73, 81; plastic
    and, 76, 81; as world ecology, 131–32,
    135, 165–66. *See also* commodification

carbon dioxide (CO_2): effects of increased emissions, 9, 10, 19, 134, 176; oceans as a sink for, 19, 135, 166. *See also* acidification; sea levels; warming

Castañeda, Luis, 59–60

Castillo, Pedro, 168

cephalopods, 190n1. *See also* squid, Atlantic shortfin; squid, jumbo

Chamorro Díaz, Evangelina (*huaico* survivor), 103

Chancay, 170, 172

Chicama, 40, 52

Chillón River, 74, 102

China, 155–56

Chinese fishers, 129, 131, 149, 155–56

cholo/as, 46, 80

Chorrillos, 3, 46, 56–57, 66–69. *See also* dock, fishing (Chorrillos); Playa Agua Dulce

Chosica, 102–3, 119

cities, coastal, 9, 18, 26, 35, 71, 182n11. *See also* development; Lima

civil war, 46, 51, 70

class: elite discourses of (*see* elites); racial and spatial aspects of, 14–15, 26, 27, 36–37, 44–45

cliffs, 31, 47–49, 56–57, 60–64, 65, 183n4

climate, 104–5. *See also* weather

climate change: capitalism and, 15, 19, 24, 25–26, 182n9; understandings of, 11–17, 104–6; vulnerability to, 7, 10–11, 13, 15, 17, 20, 105–6, 113–14, 118, 125, 182n7, 182n11 (*see also* vulnerability)

Club Waikiki, 32, 34, 45, 50, 52, 62, 64

clubs, 32, 34, 45, 50. *See also* Club Waikiki; Lima Yacht Club

coastlines, 18–19, 20, 25, 56, 60–61, 65, 74–75

colonialism, 18–19, 42, 51, 182n9, 184n9, 186n5

El Comercio: on Costa Verde project, 44; on El Niño Costero, 112–14, 120; on garbage and waste problems, 69; on

IPCC report, 9–10; on jumbo squid fishery, 141; on oil spill, 168, 170; on protests, 64; on surfing, 39, 53

Comisión Permanente del Pacifíco Sur, 88–89

Comité de Pesca y Acuicultura de la Sociedad Nacional de Industrias (SNI), 152

Comité Multisectorial Encargado del Estudio Nacional del Fenómeno El Niño (ENFEN), 110–12

commodification, 29, 130, 132, 136, 140, 142–43, 165

Concepción, Chile, 137

Conservamos por Naturaleza, 55–56, 78. *See also* Sociedad Peruana de Derecho Ambiental

consumption, green, 77–78, 98–99

Costa Verde, 21, 23, 26–27, 31–37, 43–44, 45–49. *See also* individual beaches

Costa Verde de Todos, 64

COVID-19 pandemic, 170, 185n31

crisis (conceptual framework), 104, 106, 114–20, 124–26, 188n12

cryosphere, 8–9

currents, 2, 72–75, 184n6

development, coastal: beach alterations caused by, 56–57; competing priorities, 26–27, 34–37, 42–43, 49–65, 80; legal restrictions on, 58; media coverage of, 22, 44; planning and maintenance, 47–49. *See also* Costa Verde; infrastructure

development, urban, 36–37, 46–47, 69–70, 74–75, 103, 113, 116–17

Dirección de Hidrografía y Navegación (DHN), 41

Dirección General de Salud Ambiental e Inocuidad Alimentaria (DIGESA), 83, 85–87

disaster (conceptual framework), 103–6, 113–20, 122, 124–26, 174, 188n12 dock, fishing (Chorrillos), 3, 22; author's visits to, 5–7, 66–69, 89–97, 100–101, 121–24, 127–28; economic position of, 121; elite view of, 82–83, 87–88, 95–96; fishing association of, 67, 157, 159, 160; gendered work patterns and, 162–63; management and maintenance of, 95–96, 157, 160, 161; as refuge, 90–91; unloading jumbo squid at, 127, 156, 158–64, *162*

Dogny, Carlos, 50

drought, 28, 182n12, 188n9

elites: attitudes toward migrants, 44–49, 62–64, 70, 74, 80–89, 117–18; recreational services provided to (*see also* clubs; development; surfing); social geographies of, 44–45, 79–80; summer migrations of, 44–45, 63–64, 80; understandings of, 14–15, 25–26, 44–49, 79–89, 95–96, 116–18

El Niño: concept of, 28, 107, 108, 186n5; meteorological zones of, 2, 108–10, 187n8; monitoring and forecasting, 108–10, 188n9. *See also* La Niña

El Niño Costero (2017): artisanal fishers and, 106, 120–25, 189n18; author's experience of, 21, 100–101, 121; environmental effects of, 21, 92, 100–101, *102*, 102–3, 106; failure to predict, 103–12; media coverage of, 22, 112–14, 189n17; response to, 113–20; understanding, 103–6, 108, 112–26, 189n17

El Niño events: 1925 El Niño, 110; 1997-98 El Niño, 188n14; 2015-2016 super El Niño, 109; 2017 coastal El Niño (*see* El Niño Costero (2017)); forecasting, 107, 109–13, 125; frameworks for understanding, 28, 103–6, 113–20, 125–26; vulnerabilities to, 28, 113, 120–25

El Niño-Southern Oscillation (ENSO), 107, 109, 186n4, 187n7, 187n8, 188n9

Empresa Municipal Administradora de Peaje de Lima (EMAPE), 47, 59, 62–63

environmentalism, 12–17, 24–28, 74–81, 98–99, 166

erasure, 11, 13–14, 17, 175, 177

erosion, 8, 21, *23*, 33–34, 36, 45, 59

expressway: construction and maintenance of, 43, 44, 47–48; elitism of, 31, 62; expansion of, 34–37, 44, 49–50, 57–60, 62; vulnerability of, 8, 21, *23*, 36, 37, 48

Federación Deportiva Nacional de Tabla (FENTA), 55

fish: anchoveta (*see* anchoveta); *ayanque* (Peruvian weakfish), 122; *bonito*, 128, 163; *caballa* (chub mackerel), 120; *coco* (Peruvian banded croaker), 122; commodification and extraction of (*see* fisheries; fishmeal); *corvina* (corvina drum), 92; El Niño effects on, 100–101, *101*, 120–24; hake, 133, 149; jack mackerel, 133; *lisa* (striped mullet), 90, 91, 92, 120, 121–22; *lorna* (drum), 90, 91, 92, 122; *marao ojón* (Agujon needlefish), 100, *101*; movement of, 91–92; *pejerrey* (Peruvian silverside), 90, 123; *perico* (mahimahi), 128, 151; spawning grounds of, 93; water conditions and, 90, 91, 92; water temperature and, 90, 91, 100–101, *101*, 120–24

fish cleaners: Josefina, 124; Luisa, 163

fisheries: anchoveta (*see* anchoveta fishery); artisanal fishers' knowledge of, 6, 21, 89–97; effects of El Niño events on, 128, 189n17, 189n18; effects of oil spills on, 168, 170–73; effects of sewage contamination on, 94–95; jumbo squid (*see* jumbo squid fishery); management of, 28–29, 132–33, 141, 148, 150–51, 153–54; mapping, 142–46; market prices and, 101, 106, 120–23, 141, 158–59, 162, 164, 172; overfishing (*see*

overfishing); parallels with rangelands, 190n4; as simplification, 132–33, 135
fishers, artisanal: alternative work of, 124, 127, 156–64, *162*, 171; anchoveta fishery and, 129, 138; César, 90, 92, 93–94; desire for autonomy and dignity, 121, 157–58, 172–73; Domingo, 91; ecological knowledge of, 6, 21, 28, 89–97; effects of 2017 El Niño Costero on, 106, 120–25, 189n18; effects of 2022 oil spill on, 167–77; effects of COVID-19 pandemic on, 170; elite attitudes regarding, 14, 88–89, 96, 97–99; Enrique, 5, 7, 100–101, 122, 159–62; Felipe Trillo Piedra, 171; gendered work of, 162–63; high-seas fishing by, 158; jumbo squid fishery and, 127, 129, 141, 148–56, 158–64, *162*; local focus of, 92–94, 95, 96, 97–99, 157; Lorenzo, 66–67; Luis, 57–58, 66–68, 90–92, 94, 95, 121–22; Marcos, 122–23, 124; numbers of, 121; organization of, 157; precarity of, 7, 21, 106, 120–25, 127–28, 157–59, 161–64; regulation of, 127–28, 129, 138, 141, 150–52, 165; Roberto Zamora, 173; Walter de la Cruz, 168; wooden boats of, 5–7, *7*, 127–28, 138, 141, 157, 158. *See also* dock, fishing (Chorrillos)
fishers, industrial, 29, 92, 93, 106, 138, 150, 152–53, 165
fishers, non-Peruvian, 129, 131, 140–42, 146, 149, 155–56, 191n11, 191n17. *See also* Chinese fishers; Japanese fishers
fishing: at night, 90, 122, 128; regulation of, 127–29, 138, 141–42, 148, 149–55, 165, 191n11; as way of life, 93. *See also* overfishing
fishmeal, 138, 147, 150, 164–65
fixity, 17–19
flash floods. *See huaicos* (flash floods)
flooding, 8–11, 20–21, 102–3, 111, 113, 117–19, 182n12. *See also huaicos* (flash floods)

forecasting, 112–13, 186n6, 188n11
fossil fuels, 18–19, 73, 175–77. *See also* oil spills; plastics
frontiers, 142–46, 191n13
Fujimori, Alberto, 188n15
Fujimori, Keiko, 115
Fujimori, Kenji, 188n15

garbage. *See* waste
garbage patches, 72–74, 185n30
glaciers, 8, 182n11
government officials: development and (*see* development); fisheries regulation by (*see* fisheries); knowledge frameworks of, 25–26, 28, 60–61, 64–65, 81–89, 95–99, 104, 106, 124–25, 173–75; regulation of pollution and waste by (*see* sewage; waste); response to disasters, 103, 113–15, 118–20, 188n12; response to oil spills, 167–70
Great Pacific Garbage Patch, 185n30. *See also* garbage patches
Gutiérrez Weselby, Pablo, 56–57
gyres, 72–74. *See also* currents

Hawai'i, 42, 50
heat waves, 28, 121, 182n12
Hough-Snee, Dexter Zavalza, 50–51, 54
huaicos (flash floods), 102–3, 111, 116–17, 119, 121–22, 182n12
Huarmey, 119
Huaycoloro River, 103, 119
Hunga Tonga-Hunga Ha'apai (volcano), 169

Indice Costero El Niño (ICEN), 110, 111–12
Indigenous people, 79, 80, 182n8; Andean, 37, 44–45, 70, 80–81 (*see also* migrants); as surfers, 42, 54, 183n6. *See also* Native Hawai'ians
"informality": of artisanal fishers, 127, 150–52, 154; of urban development, 11, 15, 20, 49, 74, 82, 103–4, 117–18

infrastructure: inequalities of, 26–27, 42–43, 117–20; instability of, 8, 18–19, 25, 103, 176, 189n18; nature as, 42–43; protests regarding, 26, 34–37, 49–50, 57–60, 64. *See also* bridges; expressway; sanitation; stairways; walkways
instability, 17–19, 38, 42, 48, 65, 104–5, 153, 175–76. *See also* precarity
Instituto del Mar del Perú (IMARPE), 138–46, 147–48, 153
Instituto Geofísico del Perú, 89
Instituto Nacional de Defensa Civil (INDECI), 112–13
Instituto Nacional de Defensa de la Competencia y de la Protección de la Propiedad Intelectual (INDECOPI), 170
Instituto Peruano de Deporte (IPD), 55
Intergovernmental Panel on Climate Change (IPCC), 8–9, 12–13, 181n2
International Coastal Cleanup, 76–77
International Maritime Organization, 71
Intertropical Convergence Zone, 109

Japanese fishers, 191n11, 191n17
Japanese government, 129, 140–41
Japanese Marine Fishery Resources Research Center (JAMARC), 140
jigging, 128, 139, 140
Joint Environment Unit (JEU), 168
jumbo squid. *See* squid, jumbo
jumbo squid fishery: access to, 129, 141–42, 149–56; artisanal fishers and, 129, 141–42, 148–49, 150–52; development of, 22, 128–29, 130, 131, 139–42; foreign participation in, 141–42, 149, 155–56, 165; productivity of, 141–42; regulation of, 141–42, 150–56, 165, 191n17; tenuous nature of, 25, 28–29, 131. *See also* squid, jumbo

Kahanamoku, Duke, 183n5
knowledge: author's positionality, 23–24; gendered aspects of, 24; hierarchies of,

11–17, 23, 182n8; scales of, 12–17, 173–75; semiotics of, 13–14; translations of, 12–17, 184n10
Kuczynski, Pedro Pablo, 103, 114–16, 188n15

La Chira, 3, 46, 94
La Herradura, 56–57
landslides. *See huaicos* (flash floods)
La Niña, 28, 109, 146, 147–48, 186n4, 188n9
langosta (lobster), 100
La Pampilla, 32, 32–33, 33, 40, 40, 52, 56, 59–60
La Pampilla refinery, 167, 168, 192n1
licensing, 141, 149–52, 165, 191n11
Life Out of Plastic (LOOP), 77–78
Lima: beaches of (*see* beaches; Playa Agua Dulce; Playa Carpayo; Playa Makaha); as coastal city, 9–11, 102; coastline of (*see* Costa Verde); development of (*see* development); districts of (*see* Barranco; Chorrillos; Magdalena Del Mar; Miraflores; San Isidro; San Miguel; Villa El Salvador); history of, 20, 44–45; infrastructure of (*see* infrastructure); population of, 9, 46, 70 (*see also* elites; migrants); social geographies of, 20–21, 44–45, 79–80; vulnerabilities of, 10–11, 20–21, 182n11, 182n12 (*see also* flooding; *huaicos*; sea levels; seismic activity)
Lima Yacht Club, 45, 64, 66, 80, 82–83
lisa (striped mullet), 90, 91, 92, 120, 121–22
London Convention, 71
London Protocol, 71
lorna (drum), 90, 91, 92, 122
Lurín River, 74

Magdalena del Mar, 3, 46
Makaha. *See* Playa Makaha
Manuel, Juan, 107–9
maps, 142–46, 191n13

marao ojón (Agujon needlefish), 100, *101*
Mare Doricum (tanker ship), 168, 169–70
Mariluz, Omar, 169
Marine Stewardship Council, 151
Marta (APCV employee), 60–61
Martello, Marybeth, 12
masks, disposable, 185n31
maximum sustainable yield, 153–54
measurements, 30
media: on climate change, 9–10; on
    coastal development, 22, 44; on El
    Niño events, 22, 112–14, 120; on
    garbage and waste problems, 22, 69,
    84–88; on impoverished populations,
    69, 84–88; on jumbo squid fishery,
    141; on oil spills, 168, 169, 170, 175; on
    protests, 64; on sea level rise, 9–10; on
    surfing, 39, 53
men, 24, 33, 34, 50–54, 162–63
meteorologists, 103, 104, 105–6, 107–9,
    112–13
migrants: elite attitudes regarding, 44–49,
    62–64, 70, 74, 80–89, 117–18; social
    geographies of, 20–21, 36–37, 45, 62–
    64, 119–20
Ministerio de la Producción (Produce),
    150–52, 158
Ministry of Fisheries, 141–42
Miraflores, *3*, 31, 44–45, 46, 56, 60, 79,
    80, 101

National Oceanic and Atmospheric
    Administration (NOAA), 38, 108–9,
    110, 187n7
National Surfing Federation, 55–56
Native Hawaiʻians, 42, 184n9
natural gas. *See* fossil fuels
navy, Peruvian, 34, 41, 55, 59, 76, 89
nets, 5–7, *7*, 72
non-governmental organizations (NGOs),
    13. *See also* specific NGOs

Oceana Perú, 167–68, 172
Ocean Conservancy, 69, 76–77

oceans: alternative understandings of,
    90–97, 177–78; as carbon sinks, 19,
    135, 166; colonial impacts on, 18–19;
    complexity of, 26, 132–33; as dump-
    ing grounds, 19, 71–72, 73, 175 (*see
    also* garbage patches); fluidity and
    instability of, 17–19, 24, 25, 38–43, 65
    (*see also* waves); personal relationships
    with, 90–91, 93–94 (*see also* fishers,
    artisanal; surfers); representation in
    maps, 142–46; social nature of, 24–25;
    temperature of (*see* temperature); as
    "wild," 24–25, 41–42, 78
Office for the Coordination of Humanitar-
    ian Affairs (OCHA), 168
oil spills, 29, 167–77
Ortiz Tejada, Enrique, 175
overfishing, 16, 25, 28–29, 92–93, 128, 138,
    153, 165

Pacific Ocean, 2, *3*, 6; climate change and
    (*see* climate change); currents (*see* cur-
    rents); view of, *6*; weather systems (*see*
    El Niño-Southern Oscillation (ENSO);
    weather). *See also* coastlines; oceans
Paita, 152
Palacín Gutiérrez, Julián, 170
parking, 31–36, *33*, 49–50, 58–59, 61–62,
    66–67, 160
parks, 31, 34, 37, 43, 47, 62–64
Peru: civil war, 46, 51, 70; demographic
    shifts in (*see* migrants); government
    of, 47, 81, 103, 114–16, 167–70, 188n15
    (*see also* specific agencies); navy of, 34,
    41, 55, 59, 76, 89; vulnerabilities of (*see*
    drought; flooding; *huaicos*; sea levels;
    seismic activity). *See also* Lima
Peru Current, 2, 72, 74–75, 184n7
Peru International Surfing Champion-
    ships, 50–51
pituco/as, 46, 84
Piura, 119
plastic waste, *68*; awareness of, 16, 24, 27,
    76–77; cleaning up beaches, 21, 66–69,

68, 76–77, 78; COVID pandemic and, 185n31; as global and local concern, 27–28, 69–70, 71–72, 76; microplastics, 73, 185n30; regulation of, 76–77; understandings of, 16, 27–28, 69–70, 76–78, 80–81. *See also* waste

plastics, 76, 77–79, 185n31

Playa Agua Dulce, *3*; elite perceptions of, 84–85; freshwater spring of, 67, 84–85; pollution of, 66–69, 75, 87–88; public use of, 82–83, 84–85, 87, 88. *See also* Chorrillos

Playa Carpayo, *3*, 66–69, 75. *See also* Callao

Playa Cavero, 168

Playa Makaha, *3*, 8, 22, 34, 52, 56, 57–58

Playa Pescadores, 83–85, 88

point breaks. *See* surf breaks

Point Nemo, *3*, 72–73

pollution. *See* sewage; waste

Pomar, Felipe, 54, 183n6

port cities, 18–19, 20

pota (jumbo squid). *See* squid, jumbo

poverty. *See* precarity; vulnerability

precarity: of artisanal fishers, 7, 21, 106, 120–25, 127–28, 157–59, 161–64. *See also* vulnerability

Produce. *See* Ministerio de la Producción (Produce)

protests, 26, 34–37, 49–50, 57–60, 64, 119, 151–52

pseudonyms, use of, 29–30

Pucusana, 45, 100, 158, 159

pueblos jóvenes (young towns), 20–21, 76–77

Punta Hermosa, 52, 84

Punta Roquitas, *3*, 31–32, 52, 55, 56, 61–62

quotas (for fishery catches), 141–42, 148, 149–55, 165

race: class and spatial aspects of, 14–15, 26, 27, 36–37, 44–45; elite discourses of (*see* elites); in surfing, 52–55

rains, torrential, 28, 102–3, 108–9, 111, 188n18. *See also* flooding

rangelands, 132, 190n4

reconstruction (after disasters), 103, 113–15, 118–20, 188n12

recycling, 77, 81

Redondo, 56, 59, 64

Repsol, 167–77, 192n4

Rímac River, 20, 45, 74, 79, 102–3

Riveros, Juan Carlos, 167–68

rivers: as conduits for waste, 71–72, 74–75, 80, 92, 137, 175; development along, 45, 113, 117–18; effects on ocean waters, 71–72, 74–75, 92, 122–23, 137, 184n6; flooding, 102–3, 113, 115, 119, 122–23

Rompientes de Miraflores, 55

salinity, water, 72, 144–45, 184n6, 189n18

San Isidro, *3*, 46, 62–63, 80

sanitation, 46, 74–75, 87–88. *See also* sewage

San Juan de Lurigancho, 84

San Miguel, *3*, 46

Santa Rosa, 170

sardine, 133, 138

Save the Waves Coalition, 35

scales, 12–17, 27–28, 72, 97, 104–6, 132–35, 173–77, 180n1

scientists: biologists, 21, 129–66, 167–68, 182n9; capitalism and, 132; meteorologists, 103–9, 112–13

sea levels, 8–11, 14–16, 19–21, 65, 182n7, 182n12, 187n7

seismic activity, 48, 89, 114, 116–17, 188n13. *See also* tsunamis

Servicio Nacional de Meteorología e Hidrología del Perú (SENAMHI), 107–8

sewage: bacterial pathogens in, 94–95, 185n21; infrastructure for, 46, 71–72, 74–75, 80, 85, 86, 92; linked to social contamination, 82, 84–85, 86–87. *See also* sanitation

shantytowns, 36, 117

shellfish, 100, 123

shipping, 18–20, 73, 144

sidewalks, 8, 21, 23, 31–34, 33, 54, 64

Sociedad Nacional de Pesquería (SNP), 150, 152, 154

Sociedad Peruana de Derecho Ambiental (SPDA), 55–56, 78, 173

South Korean government, 140–41

South Pacific Gyre, 72–73

South Pacific Regional Fisheries Management Organization (SPRFMO), 155–56, 165

squid, 155, 191n8, 191n11

squid, jumbo: abundance of, 136–37, 139–40, 142, 146, 147–49, 153; adaptability of, 29, 129–30; biology and behaviors of, 133–37, 139, 147–48, 191n9; catching, 128, 139, 148; commodification of, 130, 140, 143, 148, 164–65; effects of climate change on, 134–35, 165; mass die-offs of, 137; meat and meal of, 140, 164–65; ranges of, 2, 142–46; unloading catches of, 21, 127, 156, 158–64, 162. See also jumbo squid fishery

stairways, 8, 31, 44, 45, 47–49, 61–64

summer hours, 45

surf breaks: as coastal infrastructure, 34–37, 40, 43; conditions at, 31–32; protection of, 53–60; types of, 39–40, 41

surfers: Analí Gómez, 39, 52–53, 54–55; beaches used by, 31–34, 32, 33, 40 (see also beaches; surf breaks); competitive, 50–54; demographics of, 43, 51–54; knowledge of, 39–43, 54–55; Mario, 61–62; protests by, 34–37; Raúl, 56, 62, 63; Sofia Mulanovich, 52–53

surfing: competitions, 50–54; elitism of, 37, 42–43, 46, 50–54; infrastructure of, 21, 27, 31–37, 32, 33, 40, 43, 60–61, 64–65 (see also surf breaks); origins of, 42–43, 54, 183n5, 183n6, 184n9; racism of, 53; schools and instructors, 34, 51, 52, 54, 56, 57–58; sexism of, 50–54

surfing instructors: José, 57–58; Luis, 57–58, 66–68, 90–92, 94, 95, 121–22; Roberto, 54

technology: as driver of solutions, 15–17, 98–99, 105, 132, 142, 174. See also infrastructure

teleconnections, 108–10, 188n9

temperature, oceanic: effects on squid, 134–35, 137, 140, 153; effects on weather, 16, 38, 72, 186n7, 186n8; El Niño cycles and, 28, 100–102, 108–11, 129, 188n9, 189n17, 189n18; La Niña cycles and, 109; mapping, 144–45; reading, 6, 89, 91–92; seasonal, 31, 94

time, capturing in maps, 144–45

tourism, 14, 35, 67–68, 121, 171; surfing-focused, 35, 51, 52, 57–58

traffic, 8, 46, 62, 80, 103, 107

translation, 12–17, 75–76, 86–87, 96–99, 177, 184n10

transportation, public, 62, 64

Tropical Atmosphere Ocean (TAO) array, 187n7

Tropical Ocean Global Atmosphere (TOGA) program, 187n7

tsunamis, 20, 62, 89. See also waves

UN Environment Program (UNEP), 168

urban planners, 22, 48–49, 103–4. See also development

Valderrama, Patricio, 117–18

Valdivieso, Violeta, 139, 143

Van Den Wall Bake, Tine, 169

vendors, 93, 121, 162–63; Ana, 93, 163; Angélica Sánchez Valderrama, 171–72; Mercedes, 123–24

Ventanilla, 168

Vida, 76–77

Villa El Salvador, 10

Villarán, Susana, 49, 58–59

Vizcarra, Martín, 81, 115, 188n15

vulnerability: blaming vulnerable populations, 15, 27–28, 69–70; to climate change, 7, 10–11, 13, 15, 17, 20, 105–6, 113–14, 118, 125, 182n7, 182n11; debate over concept, 181n6 walkways, pedestrian: erosion of, 8, 36, 65, 69; as part of coastal infrastructure, 32–33, *33*, 35–36, 43–44, 47, 59–60, 96. *See also* sidewalks

warming. *See* climate change; El Niño; water temperature

waste: competing narratives of, 75–76, 79; garbage patches, 72–74; management of, 19, 71–72, 73, 85, 96–98, 170; narratives regarding, 45, 75–76, 79, 82, 84–85, 87–89, 93–99; ocean as dumping ground for, 19, 71–72, 73; as "out of place," 27–28, 70, 75; sources of, 27, 69, 71–76, 79, 85; unequal impacts of, 16, 20, 22, 27, 88–89. *See also* plastic waste; sewage

water color, 91–92

water quality, 83, 85–86, 96–97, 144–45. *See also* bacteria

water temperature: effects on sea life populations, 34, 90, 91, 100–101, *101*, 120–24, 146; effects on surfing, 31; mapping, 144–45

waves: alterations to, 49–50, 57–60; global weather systems and, 38–39; high, 8, 59, 169; perception of, 41–42; protection of, 55–56; surf breaks' effects on, 39–40 (*see also* surf breaks); surfers' knowledge of, 39–43; types of, 38

weather: concept of, 104; low-pressure systems, 38–39, 41; severe, 9, 16, 19, 20, 26 (*see also* El Niño events). *See also* forecasts

weediness, 129–30

wharf. *See* dock, fishing (Chorrillos)

wind, 38–39, 72, 109, 161, 184n6, 187n7. *See also* weather

women, 50, 52–53, 54–55, 77–78, 163

World Wildlife Fund, 152

Yacht Club. *See* Lima Yacht Club

ABOUT THE AUTHOR

Maximilian Viatori is a professor of anthropology in the Department of World Languages and Cultures at Iowa State University. He has conducted ethnographic and archival research on social inequalities, neoliberalism, and political ecology in Ecuador and Peru since 2001. He is the co-author of *Coastal Lives: Nature, Capital, and the Struggle for Artisanal Fisheries in Peru* and author of *One State, Many Nations: Indigenous Rights Struggles in Ecuador*.